KU-481-511

# LIFE CYCLES IN ENGLAND
# 1560–1720

*L ife Cycles in England* equips and encourages students of social history at
all levels to engage with source materials. The theme of the book is the
human life cycle, and in the first section each chapter deals with a different part of this cycle, from birth through childhood and youth to marriage,
old age and death. *Life Cycles in England* features

- an outline of the life cycle of men and women in England, roughly between
  1560 and 1720;
- a collection of extracts from a broad range of texts written in the
  period, together with an accompanying commentary;
- a collection of photographs of images and artefacts from the period.

These features combine to provide the student with a lively and accessible
introduction to the discipline of social history and a rich resource of material for continuing study.

**Mary Abbott** is Principal Lecturer in History at Anglia Polytechnic
University, and author of *Family Ties* (1993).

# LIFE CYCLES IN ENGLAND 1560–1720

## 1560–1720

*Cradle to Grave*

**Mary Abbott**

London and New York

First published 1996
by Routledge
11 New Fetter Lane, London EC4P 4EE

Simultaneously published in the USA and Canada
by Routledge
29 West 35th Street, New York, NY 10001

*Routledge is an International Thomson Publishing company*

© 1996 Mary Abbott

Designed and Typeset in Palatino by
🖅 Tek Art, Croydon, Surrey

Printed and bound in Great Britain by
Biddles Ltd, Guildford and King's Lynn

All rights reserved. No part of this book may be reprinted or
reproduced or utilized in any form or by any electronic,
mechanical, or other means, now known or hereafter
invented, including photocopying and recording, or in any
information storage or retrieval system, without permission in
writing from the publishers.

British Library Cataloguing in Publication Data
A catalogue record for this book is available from the British Library

Library of Congress Cataloging in Publication Data
Abbott, Mary
Life cycles in England 1560–1720: cradle to grave / Mary Abbott. p. cm.
1. England – Social life and customs — 17th century.
2. England – Social life and customs — 16th century.
3. England – Social life and customs — 18th century.
4. Life cycles, Human. I. Title. DA380.A23 1996
942. 06–dc20   95–37392

ISBN 0–415–10842–X (hbk)
0–415–10843–8 (pbk)

# CONTENTS

# INTRODUCTION

This is a book in three parts. It was conceived as a portable archive. The idea was that, faced by empty shelves in the library and too broke to buy a book to prepare for the week's seminar, the student who had a copy of *Life Cycles in England 1560–1720* would never be reduced to the single received authority of the conventional key text. The portfolio of images and the dossier of extracts, although selected and introduced by the author, would offer alternative perspectives.

The first section of the book plots the human career in England, roughly between 1560 and 1720, from birth to old age. It opens with a chapter, Worlds of Difference, designed to put the life stories in context. The chapter which follows, 'Live to Die', examines what I would argue is one of the most notable differences between their world and ours, the manner and the meaning of death. The plan of this section of the book is straightforward: there are chapters on the first stages of life from conception to weaning, on childhood, youth, love and marriage, householding and old age. If you feel that death should come at the end of the book, feel free to read this chapter last. The material is drawn primarily from the personal testimonies of letters, diaries and memoirs. Chapters end with a list of suggestions for further reading.

The second section is a collection of extracts from texts written between 1560 and 1720, the great majority transcribed in the Rare Books Room in Cambridge University Library. This is a dossier of public material, much of it published during the period in question. This section is not designed to be read from beginning to end. The dossier and the portfolio of photographs are your pocket library or museum, the quarry which you are expected to 'mine' for evidence.

If you are not used to reading material written three or four hundred years ago, you may find some of the texts hard going at first. Language is a living medium; the meanings of words alter across time. I have given definitions for those I suspect will prove puzzling or problematic but there may be others which I have not identified. Context may help but a big dictionary is a better solution: the multi-volume *Oxford English Dictionary* is the best. Persevere and you will enjoy the fascination of exploring a world very different from our own – but one in which people wrote and spoke in a language we can understand. We can share the jokes they told each other and eavesdrop on the trials for witchcraft and murder which riveted the attention of seventeenth-century readers and hearers.

The order in which the texts appear is to some extent arbitrary. Many of them provide evidence on a range of topics. To take one example: the account of the trial of two Suffolk women on charges of witchcraft (pp. 201–9). A trial is a debate about the reliability of evidence and the ways in which that evidence should be stacked up: the historian, like the judge and jury, is concerned with evidence and interpretation. The evidence and argument, presented as a verbatim account taken down by a member of the audience at this public spectacle, is clearly relevant to the broad theme of difference between the ways we perceive the world we inhabit and the ways in which our predecessors interpreted their experiences. Incidentally, it also provides information (how accurate? how typical?) about various aspects of everyday life. What was the nature of the important business which led Dorothy Durent to leave her baby son in the care of a neighbour she suspected of being a witch? Or were her suspicions of Amy Duny only retrospectively significant? Did childminders normally use the breast to pacify fractious infants? Did people often try to trap mice with tongs and dispose of them on the fire or was this a particular response to mice which were believed to be the familiars of a witch?

The third section is a collection of photographs of images and artefacts made in England between 1560 and 1720. They are not included simply to decorate and delight: they are documents to be 'read'. (I was interested to discover that Nicolas Poussin, the French painter, born in 1594, talked about viewers reading his pictures.) And they are a reminder that the study of history is not an activity confined to the classroom and the library – an observant student can find material not only in museums and art galleries but in churches and on the 'heritage trail'.

### FURTHER READING

The following books should be readily available in the library you use. To complement *Life Cycles in England 1560–1720*, your best buy would be Houlbrooke's *Family Life*.

## General studies

Houlbrooke, Ralph (1984) *The English Family, 1450–1716*, London
—— (1988) *English Family Life, 1576-1700: An Anthology from Diaries*, London
Laslett, Peter (1979) *The World We Have Lost*, London
Sharpe, James (1987) *Early Modern England, A Social History, 1550–1760*, London
Wrightson, Keith (1982) *English Society, 1580–1680*, London

# Diaries and memoirs

The diary of Samuel Pepys and the memoirs of Celia Fiennes and Richard Gough provide lively and idiosyncratic commentaries on their lives and times.

Fiennes, Celia (n.d.) *The Illustrated Journeys of Celia Fiennes*, Christopher Morris (ed.) London

Gough, Richard (1981) *Human Nature Displayed in the History of Myddle*, with an Introduction and Notes by David Hey (ed.), London

Pepys, Samuel (1982) *The Illustrated Pepys*, extracts from the diary selected by Robert Latham (ed.), London

——(1985) *The Shorter Pepys*, selected by Robert Latham (ed.) from the diary of Samuel Pepys, London.

——(1995) *The Diary of Samuel Pepys*, R. C. Latham and W. Matthews (eds), 11 volumes including Companion and Index, London.

# PART ONE

# Life cycles in England
# 1560–1720

# Contents

# CHAPTER 1

# Worlds of difference

For most of us, it will be the attempt to see the world through the eye sockets of our predecessors that requires the greatest effort of imagination.

Three or four hundred years ago it was held that the will of God determined that man should have dominion over all living things and justified the subordination of women. Man's unlimited jurisdiction over the creatures of the world was in stark contrast with his impotence in the face of sickness and the elemental forces: winds, flood, fire. This powerlessness was a source of anxieties which were magnified by the widespread belief that those who suffered were targets either of human malice or divine disapprobation. Since earthly existence was understood as a brief prelude to eternity, serious-minded men, women and even young children were exercised about their destination in the afterlife. Many feared hellfire.

This chapter is designed to highlight key aspects of difference and similarity between the early modern habitat and our own. These themes will be developed and illustrated in later chapters and in the dossier of documents.

The technological disadvantage suffered by our predecessors in Tudor and Stuart England is probably the easiest difference to appreciate. Many of us have the experience of living – temporarily – without gas, electricity or running water. Although it is inappropriate to draw close parallels between seventeenth-century England and developing countries today, we have all seen films of regions in which walking is still the normal way of getting from one place to another and much of the water, food and fuel consumed has to be carried on the heads or shoulders of human beings or slung across the backs of pack animals. We are aware, if only at second hand, of material deprivation and of the killing power of hunger and epidemic disease. It may be harder to envisage a world without telephones, sound recordings, film, radio or television, a world in which only a minority of adults possessed the skills of reading and writing, a world in which watches and mirrors were novelties.

## THE SOCIAL ORDER

William Harrison (born 1534), the Rector of Radwinter, not far from Saffron Walden in Essex, published his *Description of England* in 1577. In his view,

We in England divide our people commonly into four sorts, as gentlemen, citizens or burgesses, yeomen and artificers [skilled craftsmen] and labourers. Of gentlemen, the first and chief (next the King) be princes, dukes, marquises, earls, viscounts and barons and these be called gentlemen of the greater sort, or (as our common usage of speech is) lords and noblemen; and next unto them be knights, esquires and, last of all, they that are simply called gentlemen.

'Gentlemen of the greater sort' had hereditary titles and were summoned to the House of Lords. Bishops were also 'called Lords and [held] the same room in the Parliament House'. In Harrison's England, the critical social boundary separated gentlemen from the rest – the plebeians – but mere gentlemen (gentlemen who were not peers, knights or esquires) proved harder to define than their superiors. Harrison argued that those who were able and willing 'to bear the port, charge and countenance' or, to put it in language which might be used today, to maintain the appearance, dignity, responsibilities and expenses associated with the rank of gentleman were recognised as such. Harrison specifically included those with an academic background like his own – he was a Master of Arts of the University of Oxford.

Yeomen, though not gentlemen, were men of substance and 'commonly' kept 'good houses'. Most were farmers, but a good many of them had interests in other industrial or commercial enterprises, as millers or innkeepers, for instance.

The majority of people in England belonged to Harrison's large and miscellaneous 'fourth and last sort': the smaller farmers, the poorer craftsmen and wage earners. Although he lumps them together, the 'last sort' was not by any means a homogeneous group. Most English towns and villages were small-scale face-to-face societies; people had a very shrewd idea of their neighbours' worth: money, connections and personal repute all played a part in the equation. Some of the 'fourth . . . sort' played a significant part in their local community, as Harrison acknowledged: it was from among their ranks that many of the officers who ran the parishes were recruited. Others were regarded as parasites or threats to law and order. Coping with the problems presented by the poor and destitute of their neighbourhood was a standing item on the agenda of the churchwardens, constables and overseers of the poor. Harrison devoted a later chapter in his *Description* to this topic. Poverty was, he rightly observed, an issue of European dimensions:

There is no commonwealth at this day in Europe wherein there is not great store of poor people, and those necessarily to be relieved by the wealthier sort, which otherwise would starve and come to utter confusion. With us the poor is commonly divided into three sorts, so that some are poor by impotency, as the fatherless child, the aged, blind and lame, and the diseased person that is judged to be incurable; the second are poor by casualty [accident] as the wounded soldier, the decayed householder, and the sick person visited with grievous and painful diseases; the third consisteth of the thriftless poor, as the rioter that hath consumed all, the vagabond that will abide nowhere but runneth up and down from place to place (as it were seeking work and finding none), and finally the rogue and strumpet, which . . . run to and fro over all the realm . . . .

For the first two sorts, that is to say the poor by impotency and the poor by casualty, which are the true poor indeed and for whom the Word [of God] doth bind us to make some daily provision, there is order taken throughout every parish in the land that weekly collection shall be made for their help and sustentation, to the end that they should not scatter abroad and, by begging here and there, annoy both town and country. Authority is also given unto the justices . . . to see . . . that these two sorts are sufficiently provided for . . . . But if they refuse to be supported by this benefit . . . and will rather endeavour . . . to maintain their idle trades, then they are adjudged to be parcel of the third sort and so . . . are often corrected with sharp execution and whip of justice abroad.

Harrison's politically conscious contemporaries would have recognised this as a reference to a recent piece of legislation, 'An act for the punishment of vagabonds and the relief of the poor and impotent [powerless]'. These principles were enshrined in the definitive version of the Poor Law which was enacted in 1601 and remained on the statute book until 1834.

To a late twentieth-century reader, the absence of women from Harrison's analysis is a striking omission. But contemporaries would have found nothing amiss. It was assumed that men would head households, manage businesses and participate in public affairs; women who appeared in these roles generally did so as stand-ins for their fathers, their brothers, their husbands or their sons.

In the seventeenth century the currency of rank was devalued. More peers were created. In 1611, in the reign of James I, the first baronets were appointed. Their heirs inherited the title 'Sir' but, unlike holders of superior titles, baronets did not have a seat in the Upper House of Parliament. Courtesy titles like 'Esquire' and 'Mr' were used more freely. The debasement of titles did not erode social distinctions: knowing your place, deferring to your superiors, indoors as well as in the wider community, were obligations drummed in infancy. Day by day, your gender, the food you ate, the clothes you wore, the company you kept proclaimed your status in the social pecking order.

As Harrison's analysis suggests, wealth, power and status were concentrated in the hands of a tiny minority of gentlemen landowners. Theirs was not a closed caste. The fortunes accumulated by government servants, successful lawyers, merchants and farmers invested in the purchase of lands – and appropriate accessories – could secure their descendants' admission to the aristocracy. The linear descendants of William Cecil (born 1520) still occupy the prodigious houses which his sons built – Burleigh, which dominates the town of Stamford, and Hatfield in Hertfordshire.

Refined and wealthy townspeople, who shared the landowners' culture, also qualified as gentlemen and -women. Independent farmers and craftsmen headed the plebeian majority of the population. Samuel Pepys, born a plebeian in 1633, made his fortune as an official of the Navy Board: his increasing wealth and style of living were signalled in the way he was addressed. Had he taken up his father's trade and become a not-very-successful tailor, like his younger brother Tom, he would have stayed plain 'Sam Pepys'. As a graduate of the University of Cambridge he was promoted to 'Mr Pepys'. As a rising servant of the Crown, to his delight, flattering correspondents addressed him as 'Samuel Pepys Esq.', a style formally the preserve of the younger sons of peers and their eldest sons and the eldest sons of knights and their eldest sons.

Some elements of a plebeian inheritance were harder to shed than eating habits and dress codes. Isaac Newton, a posthumous child born on the Feast of the Nativity in 1642, was, according to the popular superstitions of his day, doubly destined for success. The son of an illiterate Lincolnshire farmer, he worked his way through Trinity College, Cambridge. By the time that he was knighted by Queen Anne in 1705 he was Master of the Mint and President of the Royal Society, in his sixties, forty years away from the daily task of fetching and carrying, emptying chamber pots for his fellow undergraduates. What disturbed him was his birth – his mother was carrying him when she married – and his humble descent. Plebeian women quite frequently went pregnant to the altar; among gentlewomen prenuptial pregnancy was exceptional. When the first Earl of Sandwich and his clerk Samuel Pepys were discussing the current 'story about how the Duke of York got my Lord Chancellor's daughter with child' in October 1660, the Earl repeated 'one of his father's many old sayings . . . that he that doth get a wench with child and marries her afterward' was as ill-advised as the man who 'should shit in his hat and then clap it on his head'. In attempts to present his family in the best light, Newton made at least four versions of the pedigree which was required of new knights by the College of Heralds. In the copy now in Jerusalem he backdated his parents' marriage to 1639.

Harrison's 'fourth and last sort' – the labourers – were rarely literate; by no means all farmers and craftsmen could read and write. Female literacy was low. Other codes were used to convey information. Pub signs are common today: in the past all sorts of tradesmen hung out signs to indicate the services they offered. Writing masters commonly traded under the *Hand and Pen* – as Richard Gething did in Fetter Lane in 1616, Christopher Smeaton in the Strand in 1685, Eleazar Wigan on Great Tower Hill in 1696 and John Rayner in St Paul's Churchyard in 1709. In the 1690s you would have found Henry Walton, locksmith at the sign of the *Brass Lock and Key* in St Martin's Lane; Ralph Sterop and John Yarwell at the *Archimedes and Three Pair of Golden Spectacles* in Ludgate Street could have supplied you with reading glasses and telescopes. (All these examples come from London.) The county maps which Robert Plot included in the *Natural Histories* of Oxfordshire and Staffordshire which he published in the reign of Charles II have heraldic borders with a key to enable readers to identify the houses of the gentry. A coat of arms was a gentleman's badge and would have been well known to everyone in his neighbourhood, readers or not.

However, some familiarity with the meanings of Latin words was a prerequisite for understanding most serious books and, for academic work, a command of Latin was essential. Nevertheless readers, and hearers, who had no Latin, had access to a rich literary store. The chapbooks, cheap and crudely printed, illustrated with bold woodcut pictures and decorations, were widely read and heard: they came in two varieties – the 'godly' and the 'merry', which contained advice to the lovelorn, jokes, love stories and tales of dering-do, horoscopes and guides to palmistry.

The English version of the Bible was, of course, the best known text of all, the book most commonly mentioned in inventories. It was a treasury of stories and poetry, a masterpiece of translation begun by William Tyndale in the reign of Henry VIII and revised by a committee of scholars under James I. The story of the Prodigal Son was as familiar as the tale of Dick Whittington. Biblical phrases were echoed in the spoken and written language of readers and hearers. The Bible, of course, was considerably more than an ordinary book since it gave, partly in clear and partly in cipher, access to the mind of God, existing outside time. It could be consulted not merely as a general guide to theology and personal conduct but also as a source of specific divinely inspired advice on the right response to particular circumstances. Oaths were sworn on it – kissing 'the book' endorsed a promise. The habit of using the family Bible to record the dates of birth and names of children is further evidence for its special status. The Bible was also a political text. Used to justify inequalities of rank and gender by the establishment, it was also, as Tudor regimes recognised, a potentially subversive text. It was easy for the disaffected to represent the tiny army of righteous men who march through the books of the Old Testament, and indeed the New, finding grace in the eyes of the Lord, as heroes of dissent.

John Bunyan, whose *Pilgrim's Progress*, published in 1678, was a steady seller for well over a hundred years, second only to the English Bible in popularity, was the son of a man who mended pots and pans. He had very little schooling – the Bible provided him with his higher education. The careers of Samuel Pepys and Isaac Newton, however, illustrate the value of a formal university education to the ambitious plebeian youth.

At all social levels women were disadvantaged by comparison with their male counterparts; in the middle and upper ranks of society they had much more restricted access to formal education. The great raconteur John Aubrey (born 1626) preserved a story about the revenge which a group of Thomas Goffe's university educated friends took on his stingy wife, which underlines the linguistic gulf between graduate men and their female kin. (Mrs Goffe is an interesting example of a clergy widow who married her husbands' successor.)

One time some of his Oxford friends made a visit to him. She looked upon them with an ill eye, as if they had come to eat her out of house and home (as they say). She provided a dish of milk and some eggs for supper, and no more. They perceived her niggardliness and that her husband was inwardly troubled at it (she wearing the breeches), so they resolved to be merry at supper, and talk all in Latin, and laughed exceedingly. She was so vexed at their speaking Latin, that she could not hold, but fell out a-weeping and rose from the table. The next day Mr Goffe ordered a better dinner for them, and sent for some wine.

## THE CREATED ORDER

This sketch of the social order omits the crucial other-worldly dimension of the environment as it was understood by the generations of men, women and children who were born between the 1560s and the 1720s. The Christian churches, whatever else they disagreed about, taught that the heavens and earth had been created and populated by God. In a theologically divided world this conviction was a common denominator which united the official Anglican Church, Protestants who dissented from it and Roman Catholics who were, for long stretches of time, treated by the English government as agents of hostile foreign powers. The biblical account of Creation was accepted as literal truth. Calculating the dates of the beginning and end of the world were projects to which the most eminent intellectuals of the period devoted their energies. Archbishop Ussher of Armagh (born 1581) used his immense learning to identify 4004 BC as the year of Creation. John Napier (born 1550), the Scot whose *Wonderful Logarithms* relieved mathematicians of much laborious calculation, computed that 'the days of God's judgement appear[ed] to fall betwixt the years of Christ 1688 and 1700'. It was widely believed that the Day of Judgement was imminent.

According to the Book of Genesis, the first Book of the Old Testament, plants were the lowest form of life on earth, then, above them, came 'the fish of the sea', 'the fowl of the air', 'the beasts of the earth' and, finally, at the apex of earthly creation, man. The Old Testament story of Creation supplied the framework for scientific analysis of the environment. When Robert Plot (born 1640), who was to become Secretary of the Royal Society and Editor of its Journal, Curator of the Ashmolean Museum and Professor of Chemistry in the University of Oxford, set out to write the *Natural History of Oxfordshire*, he began with inanimate creation, the county's soil and stone, and worked up to plants, the living things 'that hold the lowest place'. 'Having done with the vegetative', he proceeded to the animals, tackling first 'all manner of brutes' which were 'void of reason' and then 'man, whom God created male and female and them only in his image, and a little lower than the angels'. Men and women were, like angels, spiritual, intellectual beings but they also shared the fleshly, carnal appetites of the beasts. The first item in the dossier (p. 153) tells the story of Adam and Eve, their defiance of God's commands and their consequent expulsion from the Garden of Eden. Long after the Fall God offered the possibility of redemption to mankind through the incarnation and sacrificial death of Jesus which gave humanity a second chance, if not to restore the earthly paradise, at least to hope for heaven.

Wilfulness was a characteristic inherited by Adam and Eve's descendants: all mainstream churches fostered a sense of sin and set out to inculcate a habit of deference. It was the duty of those who exercised authority – magistrates, clergymen, masters, husbands, parents – to teach their charges to know their places, obey their superiors and fear God. The seductive power Eve had exercised over Adam justified the need to keep women in check and explained the pangs and perils of childbirth they endure: 'in sorrow thou shalt bring forth children and . . . thy husband . . . shall rule over thee'. And, since it was Eve's persuasive tongue which led Adam astray, The Good Woman, on the sign sometimes used by innkeepers and other tradesmen, had no head.

Although they were cast out of Eden, Adam's descendants held sway over earthly creation. After the Flood, God affirmed the authority of Noah and his descendants:

> The fear of you and the dread of you shall be upon every beast of the earth and upon every fowl of the air, upon all that moveth upon the earth, and upon all the fishes of the sea, into your hands they are delivered. Every living thing that moveth shall be meat for thee, even as the green herb have I given you all things.

In man's absence, the earth would have been 'without aim or purpose'.

The dividends of this dominion were not, of course, evenly distributed. In keeping with the belief that man shared his intellect with the angels, his body with the irrational brutes, privilege was signified by exemption from dirty, heavy, undignified work, labour which numbed the mind and brought sweat to the brow. Writers contemptuous of the labouring poor, of vagrants, of the Irish, of the inhabitants of the Cape of Good Hope, routinely compared them to animals: 'brutish' and 'beastly' are their most overworked adjectives. At the bottom of the human hierarchy man and apes were believed to interbreed. In August 1661 Samuel Pepys (born 1633) saw a 'great baboon' captured in West Africa. It was 'so like a man in most things that (though they say there is a species of them) yet I cannot believe but that it is a monster got of a man and a she-baboon'. In view of current debates about primates' ability to learn human language, it may be worth recording that Pepys believed that the creature could understand 'much English' and 'might be taught to speak or make signs'.

The pains of childbirth – 'labour' or 'travail' – another word which describes physical work – were a price paid by women for 'grandmother Eve's' insubordination. (Incidentally, to know that 'travail' and 'travel' were originally identical in meaning helps us to realise how arduous life was for the labouring poor who tramped the rough roads of Tudor and Stuart England.) There was, however, a paradoxical nobility associated with exertion in the hunting field: hunting was a prerogative of the landowner; horse, hound and hawk were among the nobleman's distinctive properties. Equally, it was the King's pleasure to sweat upon the tennis court. Indeed Charles II, an amateur of science, had himself weighed before and after a match to ascertain how many pounds he had lost while playing.

Rank decided the quantity and quality of food to which an individual was entitled. Within a household which included people of different ranks, bread was a ready test of status. Henry Best, a rustic gentleman who farmed in Yorkshire in the middle of the seventeenth century, used 'best wheat' for the pies he ate and a mixture of grain for the 'folks'' pie crusts and the bread he ate himself. Gentlemen more pretentious than Best would have had wheaten bread on their table every day. 'For the folks' puddings' he used 'barley but never . . . any rye for puddings because it maketh them run about the platters. In harvest time they have wheat puddings'. (The safe gathering in of harvest secured grain for puddings, pies, bread, pottages and ale or beer for the year to come. It was the best paid work of the year in cash and kind.)

Grain was the staple food of the majority; fresh-butchered meat was a rare item in the diet of most ordinary people. When Charles II, a fugitive after his defeat at the Battle of Worcester in September 1651, was asked by his plebeian protectors, the Pendrills, what he would like for his Sunday dinner, he answered, 'Mutton'. Buying mutton, they responded, would focus undesirable attention on the household – they had not had mutton in the house since their eldest child's christening party. A stolen lamb provided the King with suitable food. The Pendrills and their friends were people of some substance in their community, there were many worse-off families and, as William Harrison had observed seventy-odd years earlier, 'among the poorer sort, they generally dine and sup when they may'. Even within privileged communities, among the Fellows of New College, Oxford, for example, status was marked at table. On Christmas Day the Officers of the College had a rabbit each for supper, Senior Fellows half a rabbit each and the Juniors 'a rabbit between three'.

Exotic items normally made their first appearance in the diet of the elite. Sugar, a rarity in the Middle Ages, was to be found in the pantries of quite modest housewives by the middle of the seventeenth century – as the list of Isaac Newton's teenage transgressions, reproduced later in this chapter, makes clear. In the middle of the seventeenth century tea and coffee were still novelties. By the beginning of the eighteenth, tea drinking had become such a well-established ritual in polite female society that, when Alexander Pope wanted to point to the contrast between the majesty of the Crown and the essential ordinariness of the woman who wore it, he used the teapot:

> And thou, great Anna, whom three realms obey,
> Does sometimes counsel take and sometimes tay.

Dress signified the wearer's standing. Indeed, from 1337 to 1604, dress was formally regulated by sumptuary laws. An Act of Parliament of 1533 explained the object of the legislation. It was devised to achieve 'the necessary repressing', of the

> inordinate excess daily more and more used in the sumptuous and costly array and apparel customarily worn in this realm, whereof hath ensued and daily do chance such sundry high and notable inconveniences as be to the great, manifest and notorious detriment of the common weal, the subversion of good and politic order in knowledge and distinction of people according to their estates, pre-eminence, dignities and degrees, and to the utter impoverishment and undoing of many inexpert and light persons inclined to pride, Mother of all vices. . . .

In the sixteenth century sumptuary laws seem to have been most frequently enforced in London and at the Universities of Oxford and Cambridge, which still operate their own peculiar dress codes. The accused were generally those who had fallen foul of authority for some other reason: in 1576 a Fellow of King's College, Cambridge, who was in dispute with the Provost, was penalised for wearing 'under his gown a cut taffeta doublet . . . and a great pair of galligastion hose'. 'Galligastion', or as the adjective was more commonly rendered 'galligaskin', meant *à la grecque*, baggy hose like a Greek's, in other words. This was clearly an outrageous costume – one to turn heads in Petty Cury. We have very little detailed evidence of what ordinary people normally wore or how they looked.

Portraits, painted or sculpted, which provide us with images of men, women and children of the ruling classes, some sombre and stately, others rich and gaudy in their dress, almost invariably show them as they or their friends wished them to appear. Samuel Pepys has left an account of the making of a portrait, for which he sat in the spring of 1666. It underlines both the artificiality of the exercise and the authority of the client:

> [17 March] This day I begun to sit, and he will make me, I think, a very fine picture . . . I sit to have it full of shadows, and do almost break my neck looking over my shoulder to make the posture . . . .

> [30 March] Thence home and eat one mouthful, and so to Hales's and there sat till almost quite dark working upon my gown, which I hired to be drawn in – an Indian gown.

> [13 April] I am for his putting out the landscape . . . and so it shall be put out – and made a plain sky, like my wife's picture [which Hales had finished in March], which will be very noble.

Some portraits carried coded messages. To the modern eye, Mark Gheeaerts' painting of Sir Thomas Lee, made in 1594, when Lee was 43, is among the most striking and unexpected of Elizabethan icons. Lee is shown heavily armed, gun and sword at his waist, spear in his right hand, helmet tucked under his left arm, but semi-clothed. His shirt, flowery with embroidery, with a filigree of fine lace at his throat and cuffs, is open-necked and girded up to leave his thighs bare. The more sophisticated Elizabethans would have recognised this as a representation of an Irish knight, bare-legged for the bogs. Gheeaerts' image encapsulated Lee's rank, wealth and cultivation, as well as his employment, although he is more properly a knight in Ireland than an Irish knight. When he posed for his portrait he had been soldiering there for the better part of twenty years and had put his reflections on the Irish troubles of his own day down on paper under the title *A Brief Declaration of the Government of Ireland . . . Discovering the Discontentments of the Irishry and the causes moving those expected Troubles, and showing means how to establish quietness in that kingdom honourably, to Your Majesty's* [Queen Elizabeth's] *profit, without any increase of charge.* It would be rash to assume that Gheeaerts depicted Lee in his authentic campaigning kit. That was not his object.

Portraits which are not intended to convey such a complex set of ideas nevertheless generally depict their subjects in clothes carefully chosen to display their rank, wealth and taste. The survival of the embroidered linen jacket worn by Margaret Layton (born 1579), the wife of a Yorkshire landowner, when she sat for her portrait some time between 1610 and 1620 suggests that this was not an everyday garment designed to be worn out or passed on. Both the jacket and the portrait can now be seen in the Victoria and Albert Museum in London.

We have occasional glimpses of what people of high rank and wealth wore when comfort was of greater importance than style. For instance, Sarah Churchill, Duchess of Marlborough, recalled that when she

> was within three months of my reckoning [the date when her baby would be born], I could never endure to wear any bodice at all; but wore a warm waistcoat wrapped about me like a man's and tied my petticoats on top of it. And from that time never went abroad but with a long black scarf to hide me, I was so prodigiously big.

But, at her least formal, Sarah Churchill was not dressed like a pregnant plebeian – the superior quality of the fabric, cut and stitching of her garments were apparent to the eye and to the touch.

The contrast between the most utilitarian clothing of the privileged and the garments worn by plebeians is vividly conveyed in the narratives of Charles II's flight after his defeat in the Battle of Worcester. The King found sanctuary with sympathetic country men who disguised him in their own clothes. Probably of necessity, it was a collaborative effort. Richard Pendrill provided the coat, breeches and doublet, the hat was the miller's, Edward Martin supplied the shirt and William Creswell the shoes. These were respectable men, men of a rank from which churchwardens and other parish officers were drawn. The description of the King's appearance comes from eye witnesses but, since it was published and very likely written in the 1680s, it should be read as an account of the general impression a respectable neighbour in his working clothes might have made on the mind's eye of a country landowner and his domestic chaplain rather than a precise inventory of the King's costume in the late summer of 1651. The clothes were made of native products: wool and flax (the raw material from which linen was made), coarse spun, and leather. (Leather was the best available defence against wind and water – buckets were made of leather; smiths who worked with hot metal wore leather aprons.)

> He had on his head a long white steeple-crowned hat without any other lining than grease, both sides of the brim so doubled with handling that they looked like two spouts; a leather doublet full of holes and half black with grease above the sleeves, collar and waist; an old green . . . coat, threadbare and patched in most places; with a pair of breeches of the same cloth, and in the same condition, the flaps hanging loose to the middle of his legs; hose and shoes of different parishes; the hose were grey stirrups, much darned and clouted [patched], especially about the knees, under which he had a pair of flannel riding stockings of his own with the tops cut off. His shoes had been cobbled with leather patches both on the soles and the seams and the upper leathers [and] so cut and slashed to adapt them to his feet that they could no longer defend him either from water or dirt.

The shoes, although 'stuffed . . . with white paper . . . had extremely inflamed and galled his feet'. The linen shirt 'coarse' and 'patched', 'by its roughness extremely incommoded him and hindered his rest'.

This description of the plebeians' patched and darned garments is a reminder that we are visiting a society in which worn items were rarely discarded – they were mended and made good. As these doggerel lines which circulated in the sixteenth century explain:

> Then when this bottle it doth grow old
> And will good liquor no longer hold
> Out of its side you may take a clout
> [Which] Will mend your shoes when they are out.
> Else take it and hang it on a pin
> It will serve to put many an odd trifle in.

Among the curiosities in the Ashmolean Museum is a pair of shoes said to have belonged to John Bigg, the Dynton Hermit, who died in Buckinghamshire in 1696 – they can best be described as patchwork.

Inventories, the records of goods and chattels made after their owners' deaths, bear out the impression that the novelties of one generation became commonplace in those that followed. Although statistical data are not available, the number of those who could afford comfortable bedding and padded or cushioned seating clearly increased between 1560 and 1720.

During this period domestic clocks and pocket watches became familiar, though not common. John Aubrey's story about Thomas Allen (1542–1632) suggests how extraordinary a mechanical timepiece might seem on first acquaintance. (It helps to know that Allen was 'the best astrologer of his time' and that 'in those dark times', before Aubrey was born, 'astrologer, magician and conjuror were accounted the same things'.)

One time, being at Holme Lacy in Herefordshire, at Mr John Scudamore's . . . he happened to leave his watch in the chamber window. (Watches were then rarities.) The maids came in to make the bed, and hearing a thing in a case cry *Tick, Tick, Tick,* presently concluded that was his Devil, and took it by the string with the tongs, and threw it out of the window into the moat (to drown the Devil). It so happened that the string hung on a sprig of elder that grew out of the moat, and this confirmed to them 'twas the Devil. And so the good old gentleman got his watch again.

Looking glasses also became more common in the seventeenth century, with the result that more men and women had a reasonably accurate image of their appearance. Most of these glasses were pocket or hand mirrors: among the 'very frivolous expenses' and 'unnecessary charges' with which Lady Clayton, the Warden's wife, allegedly burdened Merton College was, as the local raconteur Anthony Wood sourly described it, 'a very large looking glass for her to see her ugly face and body to the middle and perhaps lower, which was bought in Hilary Term [between Christmas and Easter] 1670'.

For all ranks of society, sanitary arrangements remained primitive. Historians working in England have tended to avoid discussion of stale sweat, urine and faeces but there is ample evidence that, before the introduction of modern plumbing, English people of all ranks had constant pungent reminders of the less pleasing aspects of the physical nature of mankind. Anthony Wood (born 1632) commented on the 'very nasty and beastly' habits of the courtiers who left 'their excrements in every corner, in chimneys, studies, coal houses, cellars' when they departed after a sojourn in Oxford as refugees from the plague of 1665. Where servants were employed, it was, of course, usually their job to empty the chamber pots and commodes (the contemporary term was close stool) used by their employers; this was among the tasks routinely performed by poor students working their way through university.

The emptying of the chamber pot was not the end of the nuisance: the slops had to be disposed of. At New College, Oxford, the problem of dealing with human waste was resolved for long periods at a stretch by the Long Room, a range of first-floor latrines built over a huge cesspit. This arrangement Robert Plot described as

the house of easement commonly called 'the long house'. . . a stupendous piece of building, it being so large and deep that it has never been emptied since the foundation of the College, which was above three hundred years since, nor is it ever like to want it.

Plot was wrong. The college records indicate that the cesspit had been emptied in 1485; episcopal visitors who reported on the state of the college in 1567 thought that it was ready to be emptied again. (Their injunctions also contained the instruction that urine should not be thrown out of upper windows.)

Celia Fiennes, a gentlewoman of landowning stock, travelled for the sake of her health and to satisfy her curiosity about her native land – at a time when young men of her rank were embarking on the Grand continental Tour. Her careful description of a water closet, which she inspected at the very beginning of the eighteenth century in the apartment of Queen Anne's consort Prince George, indicates that it was an unfamiliar article. She saw 'a little place with a seat of easement of marble with sluices of water to wash all down'. Celia Fiennes was an aristocrat.

In spite of the Bible's undoubted priority as the text for these times, perhaps the most graphic summation of the differences between our world and the world as it was four hundred years ago is provided by Sir John Harington's *The Metamorphosis of Ajax*, published in 1596. Although it was written in the vulgar tongue, the vast majority of English men and all but a handful of women, readers or listeners, would have made sense of only two of the words: 'the' and 'of'. There were no dictionaries to consult. Metamorphosis has a Greek root; Ajax is a leading character in the story of the Trojan War. But this is not a book about the transformation of the notoriously sulky Ajax into a sweet-natured man. Harington is playing with words; the title is more aptly printed *The Metamorphosis of A Jax* – a jakes was a privy – since it is, in fact, a manifesto for the water closet Harington had designed. Among the verses he included in his wide-ranging promotion is the two-line injunction

To keep your houses sweet, cleanse privy vaults,
To keep your souls as sweet, mend privy faults.

Neither Harington nor his readers would have seen anything incongruous in this parallel between well-scoured privies and purged consciences: it was not defecation but orgasm that was held to be incompatible with spiritual reflection. *The Metamorphosis of Ajax* is thus a salutary reminder of the physical conditions of life; of social and cultural divisions separating the genders and the ranks of the English population; and of the need to monitor the health of one's soul because, at any moment, death might bring the final reckoning.

## FORCES BEYOND CONTROL

In the view of its inhabitants, the created world was a hazardous environment. Health was a focus of anxiety. Neither professional nor homely remedies were effective against the old scourge of smallpox nor the new and virulent form of syphilis – 'the pox' – which invaded Europe in the 1490s. The poet and playwright William Davenant (born 1606) survived syphilis; his verses acknowledging the contribution which his physician made to his recovery are first-hand testimony to the harshness of the standard medical treatment – doses of the 'Devil Mercury'. Although he recovered – and outlived his physician, Dr Cadman, and indeed married his widow –

Davenant lost part of his nose. A jingle went the rounds of literary London linking his facial disfigurement with the apostrophe he had adopted in pursuit of a more aristocratic style (his father had been an innkeeper in Oxford and one of his sisters kept the family business going until she died):

> This Will, intending D'Avenant to grace
> Has made a notch in's name like that in's face

Sick jokes are not an invention of the twentieth century.

Intervention in the natural process of childbirth endangered mother and baby: uncomplicated births were the safest. Lack of knowledge of female anatomy was an additional hazard. With neither effective anaesthetics nor an understanding of the causes of post-operative infection, surgery was a desperate resort. Samuel Pepys like other survivors of an operation to remove a kidney stone caused his old tormentor to be cased in precious metal as a memento.

Three or four hundred years ago people depended on fire, wind and water for heat, light and power. Watermills were used to process iron, lead, leather, paper, tin, for sawing wood, grinding grain, crushing cider apples. Wind power was important for drainage works as well as for milling. But wind and water were both unreliable and menacing servants. Robert Plot described

> the storm of wind that happened one night in February Anno Domini 1662, which though general, (at least all over England) yet was remarkable at Oxford.

– he was an eye witness -

> In the morning there was some batement of its fury, it was yet so violent that it laved water out of the river Cherwell, and cast it quite over the bridge at Magdalen College, above the surface of the river near twenty foot high, which passage, with advantage of holding the college walls, I had then the curiosity to go to see myself, which otherwise, perhaps, I should have as hardly credited as some other persons may now do.
> [In] the second tempest of thunder and lightning of the 10th of May 1666 ... two scholars of Wadham College, alone in a boat, and new thrust off shore to come homewards, being struck off the head of the boat into the water, one of them stark dead, and the other one stuck fast in the mud like a post, with his feet downward, and for the present so disturbed in his senses, that he neither knew how he came out of the boat, nor could remember either thunder or lightning that did effect it.

Calm and contrary winds also caused problems. In 1636 it took one crew intent on crossing the Atlantic the months of June, July and August to sail from Gravesend to the Isle of Wight.

There was a general, justified, terror of fire. It haunted the householder, as Samuel Pepys' diaries make clear. On 15 May 1661, he came 'home and found all my joiners' work now done but only a small job or two, which

R.T.C. LIBRARY, LETTERKENNY
942
.06

did please me very well' – they were building a new staircase – but he went 'to bed – being in a great fear of fire because of the shavings which lay up and down the house and cellar'. Five weeks later Pepys 'whipped' his incorrigibly defiant footboy Wayneman Birch for lying and other acts of disobedience 'till he did confess that he did drink the whey, which he denied, and pulled [plucked] a pink [dianthus], and above all did lay the candlestick upon the ground, which he denied this quarter of this year'. That night Pepys went to bed with his 'arm very weary'. Others of his servants were inclined to carelessness. On 2 March 1665, evidently a chilly morning, Pepys got up before his maids and found them 'with their clothes on, lying with their bedding on the ground close by the fireside – and a candle burning all night'. He was 'vexed'.

Drought increased the probability of fire and made it harder to deal with. Pepys, whose eyewitness description of the Great Fire of London in 1666 is one of the great set masterpieces of his diary, attributed its ferocity to the combination of 'the wind mighty high and driving ... and everything after so long a drought proving combustible, even the very stone of churches'. As the fire raged out of control, the Lord Mayor, Sir Thomas Bludworth, watched impotent, 'crying like a fainting woman, "Lord, what can I do? I am spent. People will not obey me. I have been pulling down houses. But the fire overtakes us faster than we can do it"'.

Among English towns, London was in a league of its own, a conurbation of international significance – by 1700 it had a population of 575,000 out of an estimated national total of under 6 million. A metropolitan firestorm was, as we shall see, rare enough to invite monumental commemoration. William Stout's account of the conflagration at Lancaster on 21 February 1698 could, by contrast, be matched in villages and towns all over England. Notice the implied solution: rebuilding in fire-resistant materials.

> The fire ... burned down in Lancaster above twenty dwelling houses. It began about nine in the morning ... in the north-west corner of the house belonging to John Johnson's children where their mother then dwelt, by her daughter Anne Tinkler, aged about fifteen years, carrying out ashes to that corner not well quenched. The thatch being not two yards above it, a spark got to it and was not discovered until it got to the roof. And there was a strong east wind and a dry season, it spread in an instant, and in half and hour to the farthest where it was stopped by stone and slated buildings. It was so quick and violent that people had not time to get out their most necessary and valuable goods. All that was burnt was on the north side of the street, except one house, and the main industry was to keep it on that side. There were two stone and slated houses which were burnt round, yet escaped.

As happened quite frequently, a national appeal was organised 'but the charge of collecting was so great that not one fourth part of the value did not come to the sufferers'. In Stout's day the double negative was used to add emphasis.

Fortunately, England was not much subject to earthquakes.

4 0014594

## EXPLANATIONS

From its outbreak, the Great Fire of London was blamed on Roman Catholic saboteurs. In 1681, at a time when popular feelings against Catholics ran high, the official monument erected to celebrate London's rise from its ashes was inscribed: 'This pillar was set up in perpetual remembrance of that most dreadful burning of this Protestant city begun and carried out by the treachery and malice of the papists'.

Conspiracies could involve supernatural accomplices. It was widely believed that some individuals, generally women, could summon up malignant powers to help or harm their neighbours: witchcraft was a capital crime. Reginald Scot, who died in 1599, wrote an early exposé, the *Discoverie of Witchcraft*, questioning whether it was plausible that the women of the sort commonly charged with witchcraft had access to any source of power beyond the rough side of their own tongues and their neighbours' gullibility. As he described them,

> They went about from house to house, and from door to door for a pot of milk, yeast, drink, pottage [soup] or some such relief, without which they could hardly live, neither obtaining for their service of their pains, not by their art, nor yet at the devil's hands (with whom they are said to make a perfect and visible bargain) either, beauty, money, promotion.

These women were condemned out of their own mouths: curses directed at uncharitable neighbours were cited at their trials as evidence for the prosecution.

Until the middle of the seventeenth century, sceptics were rare. In 1603 the physician Edward Jorden appeared as witness for defence in the case of a woman accused of afflicting a young girl with fits of choking. His medical explanation was successfully countered by four of his professional colleagues who diagnosed witchcraft and the defendant was sentenced to imprisonment and the pillory – a savage punishment which exposed the victim to stoning as well as being pelted with filth and decaying vegetable matter; targets were sometimes blinded. The following year Jorden was moved to publish *A Brief Discourse of a Disease called the Suffocation of the Mother*. Tactfully, he wrote not in Latin, the language of professional discourse, but in English, 'a vulgar tongue' and, at least formally, addressed those uneducated people 'who are apt to make everything a supernatural work, which they do not understand'. Cautiously, he

> did not deny that . . . there may be possessions by the Devil . . . but such examples being very rare nowadays, I would in the fear of God advise man to be very circumspect in pronouncing a possession: both because the impostures be many and the effects of natural diseases be strange to such as have not looked thoroughly into them.

The disease he diagnosed was 'called . . . in English "the mother", or "the suffocation of the mother", because most commonly it takes them with choking in the throat and it is an effect of the mother or womb'. It was caused, in his opinion, by 'the want of due and monthly evacuation [menstruation]' or by deprivation of sexual intercourse 'in such as have been accustomed or are apt thereunto'. Both conditions bred 'a congestion of humours about that part, which increasing or corrupting in the place', caused 'that disease'. The 'passive condition of womankind' made her particularly susceptible. In putting forward a natural explanation, Jorden nevertheless revealed himself as a man of his time.

Supernatural explanations of familiar phenomena remained part of the repertoire of sophisticated men throughout the seventeenth century. In 1686, a decade after the publication of his *Natural History of Oxfordshire*, Robert Plot brought out a similar work on the county of Stafford. Among other unexplained phenomena, he addressed

> the nature and efficient cause of those rings we find in the grass, which they commonly call fairy circles. Whether they be caused by lightning or are indeed the rendezvous of witches or the dancing places of those little pygmy spirits they call elves or fairies.

Plot devoted a good deal of print to the witches and the fairies before rehearsing natural explanations. One school of thought held that

> at least some of them be occasioned by the working of moldwarps [moles] ... perhaps by instinct of nature they may work in circles. Others have fetched their origins from the dung and urine of cattle fed in wintertime at the same pout of hay ... their heads meeting at the hay at the centre and their bodies representing as it were so many radii.

Plot's own preference was for the lightning theory. Lightning, he believed, carried 'a sort of shingles ... i.e. a disease that creeps on in the out parts, the middle growing well'.

Three or four hundred years ago magic and malice were among the more palatable explanations of distress. The Old Testament is studded with examples of God's readiness to punish the wilfully disobedient, a category which evidently included the overwhelming majority of mankind: only Noah and his family were spared extermination in the Flood and the devout were inclined to search their consciences for explanations of illness and other adversities which might be interpreted as a punishment from God. Living under the eye of God and feeling the smart of his hand (he was a punitive father) fostered the sense of guilt and the habit of introspection. In 1662, when he was 19 and an undergraduate at Trinity College, Cambridge, Isaac Newton compiled a shorthand account of the sins he had committed. The list is notable for its failure to discriminate between thinking and doing wrong and between what we could be inclined to define as little and grave offences. Young men like Newton, whose stepfather was a parson, were brought up to fear that what we might perceive as trivial misdemeanours of thought, word or deed were liable to bring the wrath of God down on the sinner's head.

**Before Whitsunday 1662**

1  Using the word 'God' openly
2  Eating an apple at Thy house
3  Making a feather [quill pen] while on Thy day
4  Denying that I made it
5  Making a mousetrap on Thy day
6  Contriving of the chimes on Thy day
7  Squirting water on Thy day
8  Making pies on Sunday night
9  Swimming in a kimnel on Thy day
10  Putting a pin in John Key's hat to pick [prick] him
11  Carelessly hearing and committing many sermons [to memory]
12  Refusing to go to the close [enclosure] at my mother's command
13  Threatening my [step]father and mother to burn them and the house over them
14  Wishing death and hoping it to some
15  Striking many
16  Having unclean thoughts, words and actions and dreams
17  Stealing cherry cobs from Edward Storer
18  Denying that I did so
19  Denying a crossbow to my mother and grandmother though I knew of it
20  Setting my heart on money, learning, pleasure more than Thee
21  A relapse
22  A relapse
23  A breaking of my covenant renewed in the Lord's Supper
24  Punching my sister
25  Robbing my mother's box of plums and sugar
26  Calling Dorothy Rose a jade
27  Gluttony in my sickness
28  Peevishness with my mother
29  With my sister
30  Falling out with the servants
31  Divers ommissions of all my duties
32  Idle discourse on Thy day and at other times
33  Not turning nearer to Thee for my affections
34  Not living according to my belief
35  Not loving Thee for Thyself
36  Not loving Thee for Thy goodness to us
37  Not desiring Thy ordinances
38  Not longing for Thee in [illegible]
39  Not fearing Thee so as not to offend Thee
40  Fearing man above Thee
41  Using unlawful means to bring us out of distresses
42  Caring for worldly things more than God

43 Not craving for a blessing from God on our honest endeavours
44 Missing chapel
45 Beating Arthur Storer
46 Peevishness at Master Clark's for a piece of bread and butter
47 Striving to cheat with a brass half crown
48 Twisting a cord on Sunday morning
49 Reading the history of the [illegible] Champions on Sunday

## Since Whitsunday 1662

1 Gluttony
2 Gluttony
3 Using Wilford's towel to spare my own
4 Negligence at the chapel
5 Sermons at St Mary's
6 Lying about a louse
7 Deceiving my chamberfellow of the knowledge of him that took him for a sot [a naturally stupid person or one habitually stupified by drink]
8 Neglecting to pray
9 Helping Pettit to make his water watch at 12 of the clock on Saturday night.

Unlike many of his contemporaries Newton did not, on this occasion at least, make an explicit link between the sin and the penalty.

## FURTHER READING

Cressy, David (1989) *Bonfires and Bells: National Memory and the Protestant Calendar in Elizabethan and Stuart England*, London

Houlbrooke, Ralph (1984) *The English Family, 1450–1700*, London

——(1988) *English Family Life, 1576–1716: An Anthology from Diaries*, Oxford

Hutton, Ronald (1994) *The Rise and Fall of Merry England: The Ritual Year, 1400–1700*, Oxford

Larner, Christina (1981) *Enemies of God: The Witch Hunt in Scotland*, Baltimore and London

Laslett, Peter (1979) *The World We Have Lost*, London

Sharpe, James (1987) *Early Modern England, A Social History, 1550–1760*, London

Thomas, Keith (1983) *Man and the Natural World: Changing Attitudes in England, 1500–1800*, London

Underdown, David (1991) *Fire From Heaven: The Life of an English Town in the Seventeenth Century*, London

Weatherill, Lorna (1988) *Consumer Behaviour and Material Culture in Britain, 1660–1760*, London

Wrightson, Keith (1982) *English Society, 1580–1680*, London

# CHAPTER 2

# 'Live to die'

## COUNTING DEATHS

Although, from 1538, parishes were required to keep a record of burials, there were no arrangements for counting up, breaking down or publishing the totals by age or sex or cause of death. In consequence, impression and anecdote characterise Tudor and early Stuart writers' statements about patterns of mortality. Location, age, rank and gender are all cited as significant factors. Always and everywhere the deaths of infants and young children, though often deeply felt, were commonplace. Richard Downe, who was buried in Devon in 1710, was among those whose road from cradle to grave was short. His epitaph is as economical as could be:

> In speechless silence my youthful day soon sped, I left my cradle and came here to bed.

Bad harvests and wars against foreign or domestic enemies pushed up the death rate – in particular among the poor (even in the worst of times the wealthy could get hold of food; remarkably few noblemen died on active service). Epidemics manifestly made more work for the gravedigger in some years than in others. Plague and rumours of plague caused particular alarm. In London the weekly Bills of Mortality acted as a barometer: 'the theatres were closed whenever the death rate reached thirty . . . . They were dark during virtually the whole of 1603, for more than half the year in 1604, 1606, 1610 and for nearly all of 1607 to 1609. Between July 1608 and November 1610, the theatres were shut for twenty-four months'. Official action and the natural reluctance of buyers and sellers to expose themselves to infection hit trade. The casually employed were put out of work and the cost of living soared as markets were shut down. The better off fled.

The captions which an anonymous printmaker used for four scenes recording the dislocation and destruction of human life caused by the last great visitation of the plague, which afflicted London in 1665, suggest the terror it inspired.

- Multitudes flying from London by water in boats and barges
- Flying by land
- Burying the dead with a bell before them. The Searchers [their role is described on p. 26]
- Carts full of dead to bury.

This poster, or broadsheet as it was called at the time, is preserved in the collection made by Samuel Pepys whose diary for the summer of 1665 plots the remorseless progress of the epidemic: fear and powerlessness are the dominant themes. At the end of April there were 'great fears of sickness . . . in the City'. But it was not until 7 June that, 'much against his will', Pepys saw 'two or three houses marked with a red cross' signalling infection 'upon the doors' in Drury Lane 'and Lord have mercy on us writ there – which was a sad sight to me being the first of that kind that to my remembrance I ever saw'. A couple of days later he came home to supper 'and there to my great trouble hear that the plague is come into the City but where should it begin but in my good friend and neighbour's Dr Burnett in Fenchurch Street'. (Dr Burnett himself was to die of the plague late in August.) Early in July Elizabeth Pepys and two of her maids moved out of London, down river to Woolwich, to lodge with one of her husband's colleagues. One servant, 'the little girl' Susan, stayed behind to keep house for her master. On 12 July, and every following first Wednesday of the month until the epidemic subsided, there was 'a solemn fast day for the plague growing upon us'. On the night of 25/26 July forty people died in Pepys' parish alone, the bell which tolled for the dead was 'alway going'. By day, the streets were ominously empty. Coming home after dark, Pepys was in 'great fear of meeting of dead corpses carrying to be buried'. In the week ending 7 September 6,988 died of the plague, 'a most dreadful number'. The middle of the month saw a drop in the number of deaths, nevertheless, close to home, the plague continued to rage. Pepys met 'dead corpses . . . carried to be buried . . . at noonday'; he saw a 'person sick of the sores carried close by' him 'in a hackney [hired] coach'. The Angel and Rose and Crown, two of his local drinking places, were shut up. 'Poor Payne', the waterman who rowed him to and from business meetings – in those days, when the Thames was a London highway, the waterman was the equivalent of the modern civil servant's official driver – 'poor Payne' had 'buried a child and was dying himself'. In one week Will Hewer, Pepys' clerk, and Tom Edwards, his boy, both 'lost their fathers, both in St Sepulchre's parish, of the plague'. In his entry for 15 October Pepys exclaimed:

> Lord how empty the streets are, and melancholy, so many poor sick people in the streets, full of sores, and so many sad stories overheard as I walk, everybody talking of this dead and that man sick . . . . And they tell me that in Westminster there is never a physician and but one apothecary left, all being dead

or fled. But October ended 'merrily' and by the last week in November things were getting back to normal:

> at my old oyster shop . . . bought two barrels of my fine woman of the shop, who is alive after all the plague – which is the first observation or enquiry we make at London concerning everybody we knew before it.

The earliest statistical analysis of deaths was published in 1662. No doubt 'how burials increased or decreased' in London had been 'a text to talk upon' since the first weekly Bills of Mortality for the city and its suburbs came out in Queen Elizabeth's reign but it was not until John Graunt (born 1620) brought out his *Observations* on the Bills that they were publicly dissected. A Londoner by birth and a haberdasher by trade, Graunt was a cautious and sceptical pioneer of statistical method or 'political arithmetic', as he and his fellow practitioners called it. Graunt began his *Observations* with a description of the way the Bills were compiled. Every week in every parish,

> when anyone dies, then either by the tolling or ringing of the bell or by bespeaking of a grave of the sexton, the same is known to the searchers. The searchers hereupon (who are ancient matrons sworn to their office) repair to the place where the dead corpse lies and, by the view of the same and other enquiries, they examine by what disease or casualty the corpse died. Hereupon they make their report to the Parish Clerk, and he every Tuesday night carries an account of all the burials and christenings happening that week

to the official responsible for making up the Bills which were then printed and published on Thursdays.

Burials, as Graunt pointed out, were a better index of deaths than christenings were of births. There was a body of 'religious opinion against the baptism of infants'; some clergymen had scruples about christening the children of godless parents; some parents grudged 'the little fee to be paid for the registry'.

Graunt's research confirmed the intermittent toll taken by 'epidemical and malignant disease': 'in some years or months there died ten times as many as others'. The corpse was not easily hidden but the cause of death was sometimes concealed to protect the interests or feelings of survivors. Graunt suspected 'that a fourth part more die of the plague than are set down'. He was convinced that deaths from syphilis were under-recorded: 'ulcers and sores' were usually given as the cause. 'From thence', he concluded, 'only hated persons and such whose very noses were eaten off were reported by the searchers to have died of this too frequent malady'. In spite of 'the vast numbers of beggars swarming up and down this city', few starved. Predictably, very many departed this life as babies and young children. Graunt estimated that '36 per centum' of Londoners 'died before six years old'. On the other hand, death in childbirth was much rarer than the constantly reiterated fears of pregnant women and their friends might have led his readers to suspect: 'not one woman in a hundred . . . dies in her labour'. Deaths by accident and misadventure were common but 'the number of those that have been drowned, killed by falls from scaffolds or by carts running over them' was of little interest to Graunt. Such deaths could not be forecast accurately and he aimed at 'science and certainty'.

Studies of English parishes undertaken in the last thirty years have confirmed the broad outlines of Graunt's study, including his conviction that the experience of the population of London differed in a number of ways from that of smaller towns and country parishes. Largely as a result of immigration, London's population expanded very rapidly from the middle of the sixteenth century and in 1700 it was three times what it had been a century before. Over the same period the national population had less than doubled. Poor incomers, predominantly young and male, unable to find employment in the countryside, settled in the new East End suburbs – Spitalfields, Whitechapel, Wapping, Limehouse, Poplar, Bethnal Green, Mile End – and across the river in Southwark. Then there were the more fortunate young unmarried men and women in their teens and twenties who had come to the capital to work and learn: servants, apprentices, law students; the litigants and MPs; the envoys, merchants and sailors from overseas. London's birth rate was depressed by the large number of single people and temporary residents; the death rate was pushed up by the over-crowding, poor sanitation and atmospheric pollution. The eminent physi-cian William Harvey, who carried out the post-mortem on Thomas Parr, 'the old, old, very old man', who died in 1635, identified the London air as the primary cause of his death. Brought to London as a curiosity of long-evity, Parr, who had 'inhaled' air 'of perfect purity' at home in Shropshire, was, in Harvey's view, a victim of atmospheric pollution – the 'immense concourse of men and animals', the 'filth and offal', lying 'scattered about, to say nothing of the smoke engendered by the general use of sulphurous coal as fuel' poisoned the air.

Some other districts were notoriously unhealthy. According to William Lambard, who put his description of Kent together in 1570, people had to be 'stark mad' to settle in Romney Marsh. In spite of its 'good and fertile soil', which provided such valuable grazing that it was worth shielding with laboriously constructed 'banks and walls from the rage of the sea', the marsh was virtually uninhabited: a modern calculation suggests that there were 44 acres to every man, woman or child. Lambard attributed this to 'an unwholesome air': malaria is the modern explanation.

## UNDERSTANDING DEATH

To Graunt's contemporaries, death was not a simple biological event. (For all his stress on 'science and certainty', nor was it to Graunt, a Catholic convert who accepted the Church's teaching that the soul survived the death of the body.) Tudor and Stuart explanations of the causes of death were far reaching and complex. The 'disease or casualty' by which a corpse died might be interpreted as an expression of the will of God, the mach-inations of a witch, the consequence of planetary influences – or blind chance. The traditional personification of Death as a skeletal 'he' playing 'catch' with living people of all ages and conditions was a reminder that Death was 'a great leveller', no respecter of power or wealth. The Dance of Death, or the *danse macabre,* as it is usually known, was a favourite theme of the artists who decorated English churches before the break with Rome. A 'rich-ly painted' picture of the Dance of Death, which had adorned the 'great cloister' on the north side of St Paul's Cathedral, was destroyed in 1549, a casualty of the government's policy of ridding churches of icons.

The grim humour of the Dance survived to be reproduced in later memorials. The brass to the Hertfordshire gamekeeper James Gray, who died in 1591 in his sixty-ninth year, shows him firing his gun at a stag while the skeleton representing Death plunges his spears into both man and beast. The image was a reminder that death could strike at any moment but at the same time it was a sly dig at the professional killer who had got his come-uppance. William Lawrence, an ecclesiastical administrator, died in 1621. According to the punning verse commemorating him,

> Shorthand he wrote. His flower in prime did fade
> And hasty death short hand of him hath made
> Well could he number and well measured land
> Thus doth he now the ground whereon you stand. . . .

Many people today will find the memorial to Thomas Tomkins of Llandinabo in Herefordshire, a small boy who was drowned in 1629, particularly hard to come to terms with. The brass shows young Thomas waist deep in a round pond reminiscent of a baptismal font, his hands joined in prayer; the Latin inscription links his three washings – first in the pure water of his baptism, in which he was born again as a Christian child, then in the muddy water which drowned him, and finally in the blood of Christ which cleansed him of the stains of sin.

Frequently, death was interpreted as the wages of sin. The parson Richard Leake (born 1568), who preached a series of sermons in Westmorland in the plague year of 1599, had no doubt about the cause of the epidemic but in making his point he usefully rehearses other explanations which were put forward at the time.

> It was not the infection of the air, distemperature in their bodies, much less the malicious or devilish practices of witches, or yet blind fortune, or any such-like imagined causes which were the breeders of these evils but the mass and multitude of our sins.

To his mind, the 'great and capital sins' which provoked God's retribution included 'gross popery and blind superstition . . . filthy drunkenness, abominable whoredoms, open profanation of the sabbath'.

Almost a century later, in a sermon preached in 1686, John Scott adopted a very similar position:

> Let us learn under all our calamities to acknowledge our sins to be the cause of them, to trace up our evils to their fountain head, which we shall find is in our own bosoms. From hence spring all those wasting wars, those sweeping plagues, those devouring fires that make such devastations in the world.

God, it was believed, exacted heavy penalties for what might today be perceived as the trivial misdemeanours of individual men and women. Ralph

Josselin (born 1617), parson of Earl's Colne in Essex, noted in his diary for 23 February 1648:

> Whereas I have given my mind to unseasonable playing at chess . . . . Whereas I have walked with much vanity in my thoughts . . . have served divers lusts too much in thoughts and in actions, whereas both body and soul should be the Lord's who hath called me to holiness, God hath taken away a son.

'Whereas I have given my mind to unseasonable playing at chess . . . God hath taken away a son'.

Very often, however, it was believed, God tempered justice with mercy.When her daughter was three months old, Lady Harrison was given up for dead. For 'two days and a night' she lay in a coma, 'to all outward appearance she was dead'. On her recovery, she told her husband that during her 'trance' she had experienced 'great quiet' and 'great happiness'. All that troubled her was 'the sense of leaving my girl'. 'Two clothed in white garments' granted her dearest wish – to 'live fifteen years to see my daughter a woman'. The sentence of death was suspended; the day she faced the final reckoning 'made just fifteen years from that time'.

The hand of God was also detected in 'the miraculous deliverance of Ann Greene, who being executed at Oxford December 14 1650, afterwards revived' – with some assistance from the Professor of Anatomy and his colleagues who had arrived on the scene expecting to dissect her corpse. Ann Greene, a single woman, had been condemned to hang for the murder of her bastard child. Robert Plot's description of the events leading up to her trial makes the charge of murder questionable.

> Through overworking herself with turning of malt [she] fell into travail [labour] about the fourth month of her time. But, being but a young wench and not knowing what the matter might be, repairs to the house of easement [privy] where, after some straining the child (scarce above a [hand]span long), of what sex not to be distinguished, fell from her unawares.

The foetus was later 'found on top of the ordure' (excrement).

According to the account 'written by a scholar in Oxford for the satisfaction of a friend', half an hour or so after she was hanged,

> when everyone thought she was dead, the body, being taken down and put into a coffin, was carried thence to a private house where some physicians had appointed to make a dissection. The coffin being opened, she was observed to breathe and, in breathing (the passage of her throat being straitened [constricted]) obscurely to ruttle. Which being perceived by a lusty fellow that stood by, he (thinking to do an act of charity by ridding her of the small relics of a painful life) stamped several times on her breast and stomach with all the force he could. Immediately after, in came Dr Petty of Brasenose College, our Anatomy Professor, and Mr Thomas Willis of Christ Church, at whose coming, which was about nine o'clock in the morning, she yet persisted to ruttle as before, laying all the while stretched out in a coffin in a cold room and season of the year.

They, perceiving some life in her . . . fell presently [at once] to act in order to her recovery. First, having caused her to be held up in the coffin, they wrenched open her teeth, which were fast set, and poured into her mouth some hot and cordial spirits, whereupon she ruttled more than before and seemed obscurely to cough; then they opened her hands (her fingers being stiffly bent) and ordered some to rub and chafe the extreme parts of her body.

Meanwhile the authorities, eager 'to cooperate with divine providence in saving her . . . were pleased to grant her a reprieve'.

The secular authorities did not automatically acquit those who survived hanging. 'Not long after' Ann Greene's remarkable escape 'viz. in the year 1658', again according to Plot,

Elizabeth the servant of Mrs Cope of Magdalen parish, Oxon, was indicted at the city sessions for killing her bastard child and putting it in the house of office [privy]; of which being convicted, she was condemned to die, and accordingly, was hanged at Green Ditch, the place appointed for the execution of the city malefactors, where she hung so long that one of the bystanders scrupled not to say, that if she were not dead, he would be hanged for her: hereupon being cut down (the gallows being very high) she fell with such violence on the ground that it would have been the death of many another person only to have had such a fall. Being thus cut down, she was put into a coffin and brought to the George Inn in Magdalen parish aforesaid which, when opened, they found perfect life in her, as in the former: whereupon breathing [opening] a vein and putting her to bed with another young wench by her side, she came quickly to herself, and might no question have lived as many years after, but having no friends to appear for her, she was barbarously dragged the night following by the order of one Mallory, then one of the bailiffs of the city, to Gloucester Green, and there drawn over one of the arms of the trees, and hanged a second time till she was dead.

Diaries and autobiographies reveal the conflict between the Christian duty to submit to God's authority and the human instinct to fight to preserve the lives of the near and dear. Elizabeth Walker (born 1623), the pious wife of an Essex clergyman, recognised that it was her duty to defer unquestioningly to God's will. Between 1651 and 1665, as her husband put it, 'God was pleased to give her strength to go her full time of eleven children; six sons and five daughters besides some untimely or abortive births'; three of the eleven were stillborn. Though racked with grief, she accepted the early deaths of every one of her children as God's 'just judgements' yet she saw no contradiction in her struggles to prolong her loved ones' lives. When her last surviving descendant, her darling grandson Johnny (born 1675), fell desperately ill at the age of 6, she sent to London for a doctor. This time 'God was pleased' to bless the endeavours of the physician and the grandmother-nurse and 'reverse the sentence' of death.

In the understandings of many, natural, religious and astrological interpretations co-existed. The physician Nicholas Culpeper (born 1616), whose diagnoses and prescriptions were informed by his belief in astrology, ascribed the symptoms of his terminal illness to the 'destructive tobacco' he 'too excessively took'. While hope of recovery remained, he used 'his most studious endeavours' to cure himself but, 'reduced ... to a very skeleton or anatomy', and 'seeing no remedy', he submitted himself to God's verdict that his time on earth was up. A fellow astrologer, John Gadbury, plotted the fatal conjunction of heavenly bodies which 'necessarily portended' Culpeper's death – the chart for his nativity, *'anno 1616. October 18, paulo post meridiem* [a little after midday]', revealed, he concluded, the probability that he would die 'of a consumption'.

Some godly women and men met death rejoicing. Susanna Bell, whose children were grown up by the time she died in 1672, set down her life story as a *Legacy to her Mourning Children*, 'not to tickle your ears but to better your hearts'. As the Introduction to her autobiography has it,

> Never did the espoused maid long more for the marriage day, nor the apprentice for his freedom, nor the captive for his ransom, nor the condemned man for his pardon, nor the traveller for his inn, nor the mariner for his haven, nor the sick man for his cure, nor the hungry man for his bread, nor the naked for clothes than she did long to be with Christ.

## THE NEED TO DIE WELL: NATURAL DEATHS

The Christian Church had always taught that death marked the transition from one life to another, from a material to a spiritual world. As the death of the body was a hereditary penalty justly exacted of the descendants of the first Adam, 'of the earth earthy', so eternal life was the gift of the second Adam, Jesus Christ, the Lord of heaven. It was not, however, an unconditional gift. Medieval Christians had a comforting understanding that the ordinary soul was consigned to purgatory until it was fit for heaven. After the break with Rome, the Church of England discarded purgatory along with other 'popish' beliefs. According to the new orthodoxy, set down by men who had learned their theology from John Calvin and his disciples, the destination of the soul was preordained but popular attention focused on conduct in life and, more particularly, in the hour of death. Sudden death, which caught its victim unawares, was feared.

It was widely believed that a child or adult who died well not only secured places in heaven but also set a good example to those present in the flesh, possibly also to later hearers and, indeed, in some cases, the readers of printed funeral sermons and manuals giving advice on the craft of dying. With the support of family and friends very young children made exemplary deaths. In January 1669 Elizabeth Walker's daughter Mary 'suddenly fell ill of a sore throat', she was 'six years and a quarter old'. Four days later she was dead. Here, in her mother's words, is a description of the last stages of her illness and its immediate aftermath:

A few hours before she died she desired to go to bed (out of which she had been taken by reason of the phlegm that troubled her) . . . where she fell asleep in Jesus, enfolded in the arms of everlasting mercies. She resigned up her soul with these and the like expressions: 'Lord let me come to thee' . . . and 'Lord Jesus receive my spirit'.

The words were not her own, they 'were given to her but she readily received then and oft repeated them though she could not speak without difficulty'. Mary died on Sunday, 23 January 1669. Her mother was grief-stricken but

That same Lord's Day in the afternoon my daughter Elizabeth (whom God gave me June 8 1658) to our great satisfaction and comfort suddenly broke out in a flood of tears and most pathetical vehement desires after God and his grace.

For their parents

This day was a tragi-comedy . . . bitterness turned into a surprising sweetness. The briny tears for the natural death of one very desirable child were swallowed up by the tears of gladness for the lively symptoms of the spiritual birth of another not less dear.

Delirium, which prevented the dying from uttering appropriate expressions of faith, spontaneously or with prompting, was a cause of anxiety to friends and families. The last survivor of Elizabeth Walker's eleven children died of a fever 'scarce eleven months from her marriage' and only sixteen days after giving birth to her son, Mrs Walker's dear grandson Johnny. 'The disease took her head' and 'deprived of her understanding' but 'God guarded her tongue [so] that she did not dishonour him' by raving.

Tom Pepys (born 1634), brother of the more famous Samuel, made a less commendable death in March 1664. On the 13th Samuel was summoned to his bedside. Tom was 'so ill as they feared he could not long live', 'deadly ill . . . and which is worse that his disease is the pox [syphilis]'. (The diagnosis was later withdrawn.) For form's sake, Pepys went to him. He found Tom 'in bed, talking idle'. Tom, a tailor, was an embarrassment. He had fathered a bastard child on his maidservant and he was in bad money trouble, 'whether he lives or dies, a ruined man' – it transpired that he owed £307. 'If he lives', Pepys wrote, 'he will not be able to show his head, which will be a very great shame to me'. It is notoriously difficult to calibrate the pounds, shillings and pence of the past against current costs and valuations. When compared with his elder brother's spending and saving for the year, Tom Pepys' debts may not appear excessive: in 1664 Samuel, a rising civil servant in the Navy Board, whose influence attracted many 'sweeteners', spent £420 and 'laid up' over £540. The wages Samuel Pepys paid his maids, £3 or £4 a year on top of their keep, may be a better yardstick of Tom's troubles.

Towards the end, Pepys

began to tell him something of his condition and asked him whither he thought he should go. He, in distracted manner, answered me – 'Why, whither should I go? There are but two ways. If I go the bad way, I must give God thanks for it. And if I go the other way, I must give God more thanks for it; and I hope I have not been so undutiful and unthankful in my life but I hope I shall go that way'. That was all the sense, good or bad, I could get out of him this day.

His soul's destination was in doubt and his last moments lacked dignity: 'continuing talking idle and his lips working even to his last, that his phlegm hindered his breathing, and at last his breath broke out, bringing forth a flood of phlegm and stuff out with it, and so he died'.

## THE NEED TO DIE WELL: CAPITAL PUNISHMENT

Almost without exception, the political upheavals which punctuated the history of England in the sixteenth and seventeenth centuries were accompanied by treason trials and executions. The full penalty for treachery, not usually inflicted on the well born or those with influential friends, was to be hanged, drawn and quartered: the traitor was taken down from the gibbet while he was still alive, castrated, disembowelled, dismembered and displayed. Beheading was not only more dignified and perhaps less painful but also, since the severed head was commonly sewn back on before burial, one which minimised mutilation and was therefore less offensive to those who believed in the resurrection of the body.

Charles I, to his adherents the 'blessed king and martyr', was the most notable political prisoner to die on the scaffold. The minute accounts of his end made by his attendants enable us to observe the preparations he made. Very shortly before his death on 30 January 1649 he bequeathed his Bible, books on theology and mathematics to his four children. His son and heir Charles was to receive in addition a detailed letter of spiritual comfort and advice. His dying declaration to his people Charles entrusted to Bishop Juxon who had attended him in his last hours; a clandestine press ensured that it went into almost immediate circulation. Facing execution in the open air in a bitter winter – the Thames had frozen over – Charles wore two shirts for fear he might be seen to shiver: 'I would have no imputation of fear', he explained.

Almost twelve years later on 13 October 1660 Lord Sandwich lay late in bed. His cousin and confidential clerk Samuel Pepys seized the opportunity to go 'to Charing Cross to see Major-General Harrison hanged, drawn and quartered'. 'Thus', as he observed, ' it was my chance to see the king beheaded at Whitehall [in 1649] and to see the first blood shed in revenge for the king at Charing Cross'. A week later, 'going through London and calling at Crowe's the upholsterer . . . I saw the limbs of some of our new traitors set up upon Aldersgate'. The next day, a Sunday, an acquaintance took him 'up to the top of his turret where there is Cooke's head set up for a traitor, and Harrison's on the other side of Westminster Hall. Here I could see them plainly, also a very fair prospect about London'. A fortnight or so afterwards Pepys bumped into 'Mr Christmas, my old schoolfellow. . . . He did remember that I was a great Roundhead when I was a boy, and I was much afeared that he would have remembered the words that I said the day that the king was beheaded (that were I to preach on him my text would be: "The memory of the wicked shall rot") but I found afterward that he did go away from school before that time'.

Dudley Ryder (born 1691), a law student and Hanoverian sympathiser, went to the House of Lords to see Lord Kenmure plead guilty to the charge of rebellion in support of the Jacobite invasion of 1715. ('There is nothing like a good assurance and impudence to get in at such places', he noted in his diary.) In due course Ryder described Kenmure's death. He went to Tower Hill and found a good place to view the spectacle.

> I never saw so large a collection of people in my life, and a vast circle was made by the horse guards round the scaffolds and a great many foot guards in the middle. At length Lord Derwentwater and Kenmure came in two hackney [hired] coaches from the Tower . . . .
>
> Kenmure came upon the scaffold and looked with all the courage and resolution of an old Roman. He walked about the stage with a great air of unconcernedness. The clergymen attended him upon the stage and prayed, he being a Protestant. When he was beheaded his body was put in a coffin. What he said, I have not yet heard. [He prayed for James 'III', the Stuart claimant.] There was no disturbance made at all . . . the mob were quiet as lambs, nor did there seem to be any face of sorrow among the multitude. . . .
>
> I was very well pleased to see that the king [George I] had resolution enough to execute these lords. I think he has given in this greater proof than ever of his fitness to govern this nation, and I am persuaded it will have a good effect at home . . . and abroad to raise his character in foreign nations.

In the evening, Ryder went to a coffee house where the execution was the chief topic of conversation.

Many crimes against life and property carried the death sentence, among them breaking and entering a premises with intent to steal. Those found guilty were expected to play a part in the theatre of the public execution. For many this meant dressing the part of a man of means, as one condemned victim of the gallows put it, 'No one shall say I was hanged in a dirty shirt and ragged coat'. Some opted out of the charade: M. Misson, a Frenchman, who visited England at the end of the seventeenth century, noted that while some of those condemned to hang took 'care to get . . . shaved and handsomely dressed, either in mourning or in the dress of a bridegroom . . . there are many that go slovenly'. The reality was sordid enough – as the proverb went, 'a man hanged will piss when he cannot whistle'. In London the condemned 'went west' in carts which took them from Newgate to Tyburn, riding backwards, with the rope about their necks, to the fatal tree. The executioner stops the cart under one of the crossbeams of the gibbet and fastens to that ill-favoured beam one end of the rope, while the other is round the wretch's neck. This done, he gives the horse a lash with his whip, away goes the cart, and then swing my gentlemen, swinging in the air. The hangman does not give himself the trouble to put them out of their pain but some of their friends and relations do it for them. They pull the dying person by the legs, and beat his breast to despatch him as soon as possible.

For the London crowd, a hanging meant a day out. Contact with the warm throttled neck of a hanged man was a therapy prescribed for victims of skin diseases. Tutors and students of anatomy found subjects for dissection hard to come by legitimately: bodies were snatched from the gallows at Tyburn to supply their wants. The prospect of being 'cut and torn and mangled after death', to use the words of Martin Gray, hanged in 1721, added to the distress of the condemned and their friends. Thus in eighteenth-century London many hangings ended in a fight over the corpse. Friends, workmates and family, who came from the four corners of England for the purpose, combined forces to prevent the seizure of the body.

Paul Lorrain (died 1719), the 'Ordinary' or Chaplain of Newgate at the beginning of the eighteenth century, developed a profitable trade in dying confessions marketed under the title *The Ordinary of Newgate, His Account of the Behaviour, Confession and Dying Words of the Malefactors who were executed at Tyburn*.

## PROVIDING FOR SURVIVORS

For those with adult responsibilities, the approach of death was the occasion for settling domestic as well as spiritual affairs. Wills, very frequently composed by those who believed they were dying, dealt with both issues. William Prior's will, made eighteen days before his burial in April 1615, is a neat illustration of the customary approach:

> In the name of God Amen. I, William Prior of King's Langley in the County of Hertford, yeoman, being sick in body but of perfect memory, thanks be to God, do make this my last will and testament the eleventh day of April Anno Domini 1615 in manner and form following:
>
> First, I give and bequeath my soul into the hands of God my maker, with full assurance of salvation through the merits of Jesus Christ, my Saviour and Redeemer, and my body to be buried in the churchyard of King's Langley aforesaid. And for my worldly goods I dispose of them after this manner . . . .

There follows a distribution of his modest household stuff to his son Nathaniel and his daughters Ellen and Priscilla; their brother Joshua being executor and residuary legatee. (Prior was a widower; his wife Mary was buried in January 1614.)

With the approach of death, old grievances were revisited, perhaps in the hope of shaming those named into honouring past promises. Thomas Holmes of Raynham in Essex, who made his will in 1571, left his daughter '£50 in her grandmother's hands, part of the £100 which I should have had at the marriage of my wife'.

Nuncupative wills – wills made in emergencies and based on the recollections of those who had gathered round the dying person (as opposed to wills dictated more formally by the testator with or without the assistance of a scribe) – quite frequently omit the pious preamble. Perhaps time was too short to extract the appropriate phrases even with assistance. Hugh Downes, another King's Langley man, buried three months after William Prior, 'made and declared' this 'last will and testament nuncupative' on 'the 17th of July 1615 in the presence of Mr Gregory Grove, Bridget Whitney, wife of Roger Whitney, and others'.

> The said Hugh Downes, being of perfect mind and memory, yet sick in body, and being asked how he would dispose of his goods if God should call him, he said, 'I will that my son Robert [christened 1599] shall have my clothes, a coffer and a platter. And that Sara [christened 1595] and Susan [her half-sister, christened 1607], my daughters, shall each of them have a coffer and a platter. And that Isabel [christened 1611], my daughter, shall have my cupboard in the hall. All which things except my apparel to be delivered after the decease of Susan, my wife.

Will makers often made provision for a child as yet unborn, as Thomas Hawkes, an Essex man, did in 1567, dividing his goods even-handedly between his two sons and his daughter on condition that, if his wife proved to be with child, the coming baby should have its equal share: that is 'a fourth part'. Hugh Downes failed to make this provision. His last child Mary 'daughter of Susanna Downes, widow' was christened in March 1616.

On her marriage, a woman's possessions, current and future, passed to her husband. This explains the many, to our minds, surprising bequests such as 'half the household stuff she brought to her marriage', left by Edward Harvey to his wife Joan in 1572, or 'a carpet of needlework of her own making' secured to Helen Hollingworth by her husband Reynold's will of 1573. Henry Fortescue, an Essex gentleman, put the matter very plainly in 1576:

> Forasmuch as my daughter Dorothy Nokes cannot enjoy quietly anything I should bequeath to her in certainty (being under . . . the yoke of matrimony, but that the same may be taken from her by her husband, of whom I have no good opinion), I request my wife to use her godly and good discretion to dispose of her benevolence hereafter as well towards the relief and comfort of my daughter as to every of her children.

Because of their legal situation, many mothers' bequests were confined to blessings and guidance. Mrs Joceline (born 1595), a bishop's granddaughter, convinced that she would die giving birth to her first child, laid down 'an eternal portion' of spiritual advice, a bequest more valuable – to her mind – than the land and treasure men of her rank sought 'to store up . . . for their unborn babes'. Mrs Evelyn died in September 1635 'about the thirty-seventh of her age and the twenty-second of her marriage'. Almost four weeks earlier she had summoned her children to her bedside, as her son John recalled:

> She expressed herself in a manner so heavenly, with instructions so pious and Christian as made us strangely sensible [conscious] of the extraordinary loss then imminent; after which, embracing every one of us in particular, she gave to each a ring with her blessing and dismissed us. Then, taking my father by the hand, she recommended us to his care . . . she was extremely zealous for the education of my younger brother. . . . There was not a servant in the house whom she did not expressly send for, advise and infinitely affect with her counsel and thus she continued . . . either instructing her relations or preparing herself

until 'on the 29 September' the crisis came in the form of a 'profound sweat'. 'After which, laying her hand upon every one of her children and [having] taken solemn leave of my father, with elevated heart and eyes, she quietly expired and resigned her soul to God'.

A handful of women committed their dying advice to paper. Two months before she died Elizabeth Walker sent 'the last large letter she ever wrote', a letter full of prudent, pious counsel', to her 'dear grandchild then at Felsted School'. She warned her 'dear Johnny' at length against the 'gawds and vanities of the world' which would divert him from God but she also nagged him about the importance of behaving himself like a grown-up gentleman:

> Dear Johnny – Do nothing that looks despicably childish, foolish, piddling with thy fingers, picking thy buttons, going with thy hands in thy pockets, or the like. . . . Keep thy hands and clothes clean – think of what I have sometimes said to thee: All cleanly people are not good but there are few good people but are cleanly.

> Dear Johnny. . . . Endeavour to speak plain, clear and true. Pronounce the last syllable distinctly and do not drown it. . . . Get no ill-affected tone in speech.

## THE CORPSE

The physical state of the corpse was a taken as evidence of the condition of the departed spirit. Adam Martindale contrasted the appearances of his godly mother and his flighty sister Jane who died close together in 1632:

> Whereas my mother who, notwithstanding her beauty, was very humble, lay with a clear and seemingly smiling countenance after she was dead, as if she

had been still alive, my sister, that was too proud of hers, became extremely ugly before she died, her face being sadly discoloured and so swelled that scarce any form of visage was discernible.

According to the gossip of the time, preserved for us by John Aubrey, Sir Kenelm Digby had married,

> much against his mother's consent, that celebrated beauty and courtesan, Mrs Venetia Stanley, whom Richard Earl of Dorset kept as his concubine, and had children by her, and settled on her an [extraordinarily lavish] annuity of £500 per annum . . . . Sir K. D. . . . would say that a handsome, lusty man, that was discreet, might make a virtuous wife out of a brothel house. This lady carried herself blamelessly.

Lady Digby (born 1600) died suddenly in May 1633. Immediately, her husband summoned Van Dyck, the leading portrait painter in England, to her bedside. Apart from 'rubbing her face' to bring 'a little seeming colour into her cheeks', Digby claimed that he had captured her appearance exactly, with nothing 'added or altered'. Van Dyck portrayed her as a sleeper, not a corpse subject to the flesh's decay. This portrait was Digby's constant companion. Van Dyck's picture of Lady Digby as *Prudence* provides us with clues to the symbolic meaning of *Venetia Stanley on her Deathbed*. *Prudence* is an emphatic testimony to her virtue. Above Lady Stanley's head hover baby angels, ready to crown her with a laurel wreath; her hands are occupied with the doves of chastity and the serpent of wisdom. With her foot she checks Cupid, the god of profane love while two-faced Deceit cowers at her side.

Traditionally, the nobility safeguarded their bodies against decomposition by employing the services of surgeons skilled in embalming – the condition of bodies exhumed after two hundred years suggests that the techniques were effective. However, a revulsion against disembowelling, an essential part of the procedure, led noblewomen, in particular, to instruct their executors that their bodies should be spared, in death, experiences which would, in life, have violated their modesty.

## FUNERALS

Today few people are familiar with the stench of corruption. Three or four hundred years ago the stink of bad meat, of bodies decomposing before burial or in vaults reopened to receive new corpses, the cadavers of felons left to rot on the gallows filled the nostrils of men, women and children. When Tom Pepys was buried at St Bride's Church in Fleet Street in 1664 the sexton, as a favour and for a small consideration, agreed to 'disturb other corpses that are not quite rotten', jostling them together to 'make room for him'. Not unnaturally (but mistakenly) John Weever (died 1672), the author of *Ancient Funeral Monuments*, believed that the word 'sepulchre' was derived from the Latin 'semipulchra', 'half beautiful', 'the external part . . . being gloriously beautified and adorned' but the tomb 'having nothing within but dreadful darkness, loathsome stink, and rottenness of bones'.

From the 1660s printed funeral invitations became common. The surviving examples display the familiar division between the specially printed invitation and those which came off the shelf and needed to have the particulars added in ink. The images which surround the text would strike many people today as in the poorest of taste. They are crude representations of the shape of things to come: the gravedigger's pick and shovel; the skeleton; the grinning skull and crossbones, more familiar from the pirates' flag; and, perhaps most distressing to the late twentieth-century viewer, the worms which feasted on cadavers. Three hundred years ago the horror was outweighed by the confidence that the soul of the godly had exchanged the, now stinking, carcass for 'an incorruptible, immortal, strong and perfect body'.

Whether or not they were embalmed, corpses were dressed for the grave. Some were loosely shrouded, others tightly bandaged in a winding sheet, very much as a new-born baby was swaddled. Indeed there is some evidence that strips of swaddling clothes were saved to tie grave clothes. The Cambridgeshire yeoman Richard Goodyear (died 1622) left his daughter Mary 'a christening sheet and a towel and all the other childbed linen which was her mother's but one sheet' for his burial; his will does not explain the thinking or emotions which lay behind his instruction, but the strength of the link between being born and dying is clear.

Unless they died at sea, perished accidentally or by design far from human habitation or were condemned to dissection on the anatomist's slab, to swing on a gibbet or ornament the city gate until the flesh rotted from their bones, it was assumed that the dead would be committed to the earth with the degree of ceremony which befitted their place in society. Of course, from time to time the customary practices went unobserved. When epidemics were at their fiercest, unnamed bodies were consigned to common graves with little ceremony. Sometimes the lax administration in the Church was to blame: at Copenhall in Staffordshire where the rector was an absentee, the parishioners reported in 1674 that they had 'no curate to visit the sick, baptise the infants or to visit the dying . . . so that many and several parishioners and other persons have within these few years last past been interred in the parish church without any Christian burial'.

Families with little property invested in goods which would add dignity to their funerals. Henry Darrant, an Essex man who farmed in a small way, died in 1573 and left his daughter Mary his 'bearing sheet with a black seam' and his granddaughter Elizabeth his 'other bearing sheet with a white seam'. Many churches owned coffins and other funeral goods for the use of parishioners who could not afford their own. Parishes met the cost of graves and grave clothes of those whose families lacked the means to pay for them. In London, workmates and neighbours set up 'box clubs' or friendly societies to give their members a 'decent funeral'.

Not only the manner but also the place of burial reflected the standing of the dead. When Tom Pepys died in 1664, his brother Samuel, mindful of his own reputation, 'altered' his 'resolution of burying him in the church-yard among my young brothers and sisters – who had died in childhood – and buried him in the church in the middle aisle as near as I can to my mother's pew'. This higher-status grave cost '20 shillings more'. The bereaved evidently took comfort from burying a loved one close to the fam-ily pew or to a relative's grave.

Funerals were occasions for hospitality, for feasting friends and for offer-ing largess to the poor. Strictly, 'the dead man's dole' or 'the banquet of charity', as it was sometimes known, had been outlawed by the state Church as a superstitious relic of medieval Catholicism but treating poor neigh-bours at funerals was an entrenched habit. Adam Martindale describes how the family brought his 'father home handsomely':

> all that came to the house to fetch his corpse thence (beggars not excepted) we entertained with good meat, piping hot, and strong ale in good plenty. Then at Prescot, when the corpse was interred and the souls of the auditors feasted with an excellent sermon . . . there was a rich dinner ready in the tavern for the kindred, and so many more as a great room would receive, with plenty of wine and strong drink, and for all the rest, tag and rag, sufficient store of such provisions as are usual at ordinary burials.

The account books of the Browne family of Troutbeck in Westmorland record their expenditure on funerals in 1702 and 1728. In 1702 beef, bacon, wheat bread and drink were drawn from the household stores; money was laid out on more bread, 'arvel' [funeral] cheese, meat, sugar and tobacco. 'The poor of our town and no one else' received a dole of 'sixpence a piece'. The funeral trade was an important source of income for local suppliers. William Stout, a Lancaster shopkeeper, noted that, in the 1690s,

> we sold much cheese for funerals in the country from thirty to one hundred pound weight, as the deceased was of ability [according to his rank], which was shived [cut] into two or three in the pound, and one [slice] with a penny manchet [a loaf of fine white bread] given to all the attendants [attenders]. And then it was customary in Lancaster at funerals to give one or two of the long Naples biscuits to each attending the funeral by which from twenty to near one hundred pounds was given, according to the deceased's ability. I think they were near to a shilling a pound.

The more sophisticated urban tastes were apparent in London in the 1660s: Pepys invited 120 guests to his brother's funeral and, gratifyingly, 'many more' came than he had bid; 'their service was six biscuits apiece and what they pleased of burnt claret'. In 1728 the Brownes offered their guests wine, cakes and four dozen Kendal 'wiggs' (sweet yeasted buns flavoured with caraway seeds, often eaten during Lent), as well as the more robust traditional fare.

## MEMORIALS

Those with the means left a more permanent mark. Their plans, as John Weever, the historian of funeral monuments, observed, were often made well in advance.

> It was usual in ancient times, and so it was in these days, for persons of especial rank and quality to make their own tombs and monuments in their lifetime; partly for that they might have a certain [secure] house to put their head in (as the old saying is) whensoever they should be taken away with death, out of this tenement, the world, and partly to please themselves in beholding of their dead countenance in marvel. But especially because thereby they thought to preserve their memories from oblivion.

His poor state of health persuaded Thomas Howard, second Earl of Arundel, to make his will in 1617. A chief preoccupation was to provide fit resting places for his kin and especially his father Philip, beheaded in Elizabeth Tudor's reign and recognised as a martyr saint by the Roman Catholic Church in 1970;

> My earnest desire is that my father may be removed out of the Tower to Arundel and have a decent tomb there with my mother. And likewise my grandmother of Norfolk from Framlingham thither and have a tomb likewise because she brought that Honour and place [Framlingham] to our house [family].

Howard's fear of imminent death proved exaggerated and a subsequent will, made a quarter of a century later, reaffirms this desire: 'if my grandmother of Norfolk's body could be found in St Clement's Church . . . it might be carried to Arundel . . . for I desire persons of my family being of so eminent virtues . . . might have record left worthy of them'.

The monument commissioned by Lady Coventry to commemorate her only son, who died at the age of 32 in 1687, cost the large sum of £322 10s. The terms she agreed with Grinling Gibbons combine a confident assertion of the dead man's now irrelevant worldly rank with a proper diffidence about the destination of his spirit. The dominant features of the monument were to be

> Three statues as big as the like, one, the principal whereof, to be the semblable [recognisable] and perfect figure of the said John, late Lord Coventry, in all his baron's robes, lying upon a tomb properly adorned, with his coronet tumbled at his feet, and his right hand stretched out to catch at a starry crown, presented towards him by the serene statue representing Faith and standing at the Head of the First Statue. And the Third Statue representing Hope, and standing at the Feet of the First Figure . . . on each side of the Tomb, a death's head with bones . . . . And the name of the said Grinlin [sic] Gibbons to be engraved in some convenient place as the artificer of the said monument.

Lord Coventry's starry crown was unfortunately mislaid when the church at Croome d'Abitot in Worcestershire was dismantled and reconstructed on another site when Croome Court, the family seat, was rebuilt in the eighteenth century.

A similar warning is more starkly conveyed in a crude but nearly life-sized skull, shoulders and ribcage which were cut into the walls of Norwich Cathedral with this inscription:

> All you that do this place pass bye
> Remember death for you must dye
> As you are now even so was I
> And as I am so shall you be
> Thomas Gooding here do staye
> Wayting for God's judgement daye.

Weever's definition of memorials embraced 'all religious foundations, all sumptuous and magnificent structures . . . as well as tombs and sepulchres'. 'Religious foundations' included schools and colleges. Thomas Bodley (born 1545), who gave his name to the University Library in Oxford, is perhaps the pre-eminent example of those who sought to perpetuate their names by educational endowments. Like many of his contemporaries whose principal bequests took this form, Bodley was childless. Thomas Bodley was not a man of exceptional wealth but he had, as he recorded in his autobiography, 'four kinds of aids' essential for success: 'knowledge, as well in the learned and modern tongues as in such other sorts of scholastical literature . . . some purse-ability . . . [and] very great store of honourable friends'. At the end of the sixteenth century the University Library at Oxford 'lay ruined and waste to the public use of students'. According to Anthony Wood, who produced his *History of the University of Oxford* in 1674, the University's original library had been dispersed in the early 1550s. Books thought to be contaminated with popish heresy were burned; others were sold off

> either to booksellers, or to glovers to press their gloves, or to tailors to make measures [patterns] or to bookbinders to cover books bound by them [more substantial bindings were normally chosen by the purchaser], and some also kept by the Reformers for their own use.

A series of letters, beginning in 1598 and running for almost fourteen years, unfolds Bodley's great scheme. Bodley's own 'portion' was 'too slender' to meet the whole cost of the project. When he had taken care of the 'mechanical works' – the shelves, desks and seats – he busied himself 'about gathering books'. As early as 1600 he had persuaded his friends and acquaintances to make over the best part of a thousand printed volumes; in 1610 the Stationers' Company agreed to give the library, since 1604 named in his honour, a copy of every book published by its members. Gifts of money and manuscripts poured in. Bodley's brother Laurence plundered the library of Exeter Cathedral, where he was a canon, of eighty-one manuscripts including one of its great treasures, the Leofric missal, which had been in the Cathedral since the middle of the eleventh century. 'Mr Paul Pindar, consul of the Company of English Merchants of Aleppo, a famous port in the Turk's dominions . . . procure[d] . . . some books in the Syriac, Arabic, Turkish and Persian tongues'. There were Chinese books too. Bodley put his mind to the admissions regulations: he hoped that not only graduates but 'any gentleman' who wanted to use its holdings 'for his furtherance in some study' would 'become a freeman of the library'. Bodley died in March 1613 – at his request, sixty-seven poor scholars, one for every year of his life, attended his corpse to its burial in Merton, his old college, in mourning he had paid for.

Samuel Pepys, a Cambridge graduate, who died the best part of a century after Bodley, was another childless man who set out to create a memorial library. Bodley perceived his work as the foundation of a dynamic institution; Pepys, as the extract from his will which is reproduced in the dossier makes clear, wanted the identity of his collection preserved.

The well off arranged for the distribution of small lasting tokens such as rings. The Essex gentlewoman Dame Frances Powlett, who made her will in 1599, left memorial rings of two different patterns. Her cousin Mistress Wilmott was to have 'a ring with a death's head on it'; her sister and her sister-in-law were to receive rings with 'Pray for me' engraved on them. This injunction was contrary to the official teaching of the Church of England and, since Dame Frances also left a 'little cross of gold with wood in it', a fragment associated with a saint or Christ himself, it would appear that she clung to the old ways of her youth. The death's head, or, as we would say, the skull and crossbones, remained a favourite image throughout the seventeenth century but a new and ultimately prevailing taste for rings and other items which preserved plaited locks of the loved one's hair developed.

In 1688 Charlotte Holgate wrote from London to inform her cousin Mary, who had settled on the Isle of Wight after her marriage to Sir John Oglander, of the rings she had commissioned to commemorate Lady Oglander's father, a London alderman: 'I thought rings would be better than lockets because you had nothing to put in the lockets, and without hair I thought they would not look well. The rings are of the same size and weight and they come just at your price'. Miss Holgate had selected appropriate mourning garments for her country cousins :

> I have sent you a striped lustring [glossy silk] petticoat. It will look good under your crepe, and I think it is cheap. I had it for three shillings and sixpence a yard. Capes for children are out of fashion. I sent you the finest that I could get. Mourning shoes for children they do make with wooden heels. When you wear your gown there is a roll for your head. Boys of William's age [he was born in 1680] do not use to wear bodices, a coat is enough. I hope you like your petticoat. You may wear it with a fringe or without.

Thus did metropolitan taste penetrate the provinces.

The poor left their mark in the memory of family and community but rarely achieved the immortality conferred on those whose names and reputations were carved in stone or published in print. Richard Gough, who wrote his *History of Myddle* in Shropshire at the beginning of the eighteenth century, stands proxy for the raconteurs whose good stories kept the names of obscure men and women on the lips of later generations.

## THE CONSEQUENCES FOR SURVIVORS

The consequences of death were not straightforward. In towns and villages the epidemics which reduced poor families to destitution also opened up opportunities for those capable of stepping into dead men's shoes. The victims of epidemics yielded their places in the local economy to young adults who had yet to establish themselves. The death of one inmate opened the door of the almshouse to another stricken with poverty, age and infirmity. The havoc and opportunities created by deaths within a community were replicated in the family.

Within the smaller community of the family, the significance of a death was determined by the circumstances and feelings of survivors.

The death of a spouse might be perceived by the survivor as a release or as a devastating blow. Rachel Wriothesley recovered rapidly from the loss of her first husband Lord Vaughan, who died of the plague in 1667. The execution for treason of her second husband Lord Russell in 1683 was a parting of a different order:

> my heart mourns too sadly, I fear, and can't be comforted because I have not that dear companion and sharer of my joys and sorrows. I want him to talk with, to walk with, to eat and sleep with; all these things are irksome to me now; the day unwelcome and the night so too . . . . When I see my children before me, I remember the pleasure he took in them and my heart shrinks.

For the remainder of her life, 26 June, 13 July and 21 July, the anniversaries of his arrest, trial and execution were sacred days.

The story, told by an early biography, about Lady Russell's economy with the fact of the death of her younger daughter in 1711 illustrates the importance of stoicism:

> Her younger daughter, the Duchess of Rutland, having been the mother of nine children died in childbed.
>
> Of her death Lady Russell has left us no particulars, we only know that as her eldest daughter, the Duchess of Devonshire, was at that time lying in, Lady Russell had the resolution to conceal from her her sister's death . . . and to prevent her from hearing it suddenly, avoided the too particular enquiries of the Duchess of Devonshire by saying that she had that day seen her sister 'out of bed', when in fact she had seen her in her coffin.
>
> Yet this daughter she dearly loved . . . .

Among property-holding families, death had major financial implications. Cynics claimed that the outward mourning of many an inheriting adult was a mask assumed to hide his inner glee. From the perspective of the family's fortunes, there were few objective reasons to regret the death of James Cecil, fourth Earl of Salisbury (born 1666) in 1694. 'Enormously fat' and 'notably imprudent', he 'lacked the instinct for self-preservation'. Having come into an already depleted inheritance – the fortune gained by the first earl in the service of Queen Elizabeth and King James I had been eroded by the building of Hatfield and subsequent mismanagement – the fourth earl misread his prospective father-in-law's intentions and so forfeited half the estates settled on his bride. He declared himself a Catholic just as the Catholic King James II vacated the throne to be succeeded by his Protestant son-in-law and daughter. He was subject, in consequence, to penal taxation. In Lawrence Stone's words: 'He spent the next few years in and out of the Tower of London on suspicion of conspiracy until he finally died in 1694 to the universal relief of all who knew him'.

His death made an important contribution to the recovery of the Cecil family's fortunes. 'The fact that the fifth earl was only three years old when his father died meant that there was a long period of minority . . . when income could be kept to a very low level indeed'. Aristocratic widows were a drain on the heir's resources – in the early 1590s the Earl of Rutland was paying large allowances to the widows of his three predecessors: Bridget, whose husband had died in 1563; Isabel, whose husband had died in 1587; and Elizabeth, whose husband had died in 1588.

The property and persons of orphaned children, and especially children left in the care of step-parents, were widely perceived to be at risk. Robert Thurston, a small farmer in Essex, who made his will in 1571, evidently did not trust his wife to take proper care of her step-children or his property. Her continued occupation of his house – for a fixed period of four years – was conditional on her 'entering into bonds' with his executors to keep his sons John and James 'to school till they have sufficiently learned to read and write the English tongue perfectly and also keep my houses in good repair'. It is striking that a high proportion of the labouring men who were literate and self-conscious enough to write accounts of their lives seem to have been boys whose training for better things had been cut short by their fathers' deaths. Single women were seen as particularly vulnerable by their male relatives: John Fuller took steps to provide his 'poor sister Joan Fuller' with a suitable roof over her head for the rest of his life. Ralph Upney, who farmed in a small way at Dagenham in Essex, had taken his Aunt Alice into his house; she had not come empty-handed. During his life time she and his wife had 'agreed together' that if they were to fall out after his death Alice was to get back the money he owed her and a capital sum besides.

And whatever its particular impact on survivors, every death brought home to those left behind that their days were numbered. The fourteen gold rings that Thomas Dalton of Bury St Edmunds left by his will of 1672 were aptly inscribed with the injunction: 'Prepare to follow TD'.

## FURTHER READING

Beier, Lucinda (1987) *Sufferers and Healers: The Experience of Illness in Seventeenth-century England*, London

Houlbrooke, Ralph (ed.) (1989) *Death, Ritual and Bereavement*, London

Litten, Julian (1992) *The English Way of Death: The Common Funeral since 1450*, London

Llewellyn, Nigel (1991) *The Art of Death: Visual Culture in the English Death Ritual c. 1500–c. 1800*, London

# CHAPTER 3

# Conception, birth, infancy

## A MEANS OF CHEATING DEATH

In this uncertain world raising a child offered a means of cheating death 'by prolonging life into future ages and generations'. A son was the ideal channel through which land, a title, a trade, a faith, a family or a given name could be transmitted. Daughters, though legally and practically much less effective, made their contribution: the parson Ralph Josselin recorded the birth of 'a daughter intended for a Jane' in November 1645; in 1585 Henry Greaves, tenant of a very small holding in Cambridgeshire, left his property to his wife 'and after her death to my child, be it man or woman, if it please God she be with any'. For many getting a son was an agonisingly slow business. It took James II the best part of thirty years and fifteen pregnancies by his two wives to achieve a son and heir. The marriage of his elder daughter, later Queen Mary (born 1662), and her husband William of Orange was childless. The seventeen pregnancies endured by his younger daughter, later Queen Anne (born 1665), failed to yield a child who survived her. In such a climate infertility was a cause of misery and resentment. First marriages which were successful in spite of childlessness were noteworthy.

As Chapter 6 makes clear, few women entered their childbearing years before their middle twenties. The exceptions were the daughters of landowners and the richer merchants and professional men who tended to find (or be found) husbands when they were several years younger. Many first babies were conceived by the older plebeian brides during courtship but the overwhelming majority of births took place within marriage. Bastard bearing, and indeed extramarital sex, was an offence. So strong was the presumption that an unmarried mother would resort to infanticide 'to avoid shame and to escape punishment' that an Act passed in 1624 determined that, if her child was found dead, she should be executed for its murder unless she could produce proof that it was stillborn. For a variety of reasons, therefore, the sexually active population included some people who were desperate to conceive and others equally concerned to avoid pregnancy.

## AIDS TO CONCEPTION

An entry in Samuel Pepys' diary for 26 July 1664 allows us to eavesdrop on the 'opinions and advice' given to a young man eight years married and still without children by a group of perhaps slightly tipsy London women at a christening party. He noted ten of their suggestions:

> 1. Do not hug my wife too hard nor too much. 2. Eat no late suppers. 3. Drink juice of sage. 4. Tent [red wine] and toast. 5. Wear cool holland [linen] drawers. 6. Keep stomach warm and back cool. 7. Upon my query whether it was best to do it at night or morn, they answered me neither one nor other, but when we have a mind to it. 8. Wife not to go too straightlaced. Myself to drink mum [strong spiced ale] and sugar . . . . The 3rd, 4th, 6th, 7th and 10th they all did seriously declare and lay much stress upon them, as rules to be observed indeed, and especially the last, to lie with our heads where our heels do, or at least to make the bed high at feet and low at head.

His list was not exhaustive: impotent men were urged to urinate through wedding rings; barren women were enjoined to touch the hand of a hanged man. (Birth, marriage and death were recognised as boundaries of a like kind.) According to some authorities, the stars had a part to play. John Case, author of *The Angelical Guide*, published in 1697, advised the reader who wanted 'an heir or man-child to inherit' to 'observe a time when the masculine planets and signs ascend, and [are] in full power and force, then take thy female, and cast in thy seed, and thou shalt have a man-child'. Notice his use of the familiar 'thou' and 'thy' in place of the more formal 'you' and 'yours'. Sometimes a range of strategies was deployed in parallel: at the beginning of the eighteenth century Elizabeth Blundell, the wife of a Lancashire landowner who could trace his ancestors back the best part of six hundred years, took the waters at spas on the Continent on medical advice and made pilgrimages to the shrine at Holywell in Wales in a prolonged and unsuccessful effort to procure a son and heir.

## CONTRACEPTION

Court records provide evidence of ill-founded folk theories about conception. Thus faced with a paternity suit in 1563, John Cotgreve responded: 'Cock's wounds! . . . Can a man get a child standing? For I never had anything to do with her but standing'. The armoury of effective contraceptive strategies available to married and unmarried couples included (most effective, of course) abstinence; sexual activities which stopped short of full intercourse – masturbation and *coitus interruptus*, a practice mentioned and condemned in the Old Testament – but also, and perhaps more surprising to readers new to the study of seventeenth-century England, chemical and barrier methods. West Country villagers were familiar with the herbs and spices which were believed to bring on 'late periods'. According to one authority, honeysuckle juice, 'drunk of a man by the space of 37 days together, will make him that he shall never beget any more children'. Sheaths, made of such natural substances as fish skin, seem to have been used principally to protect men from sexually transmitted diseases.

Because lactation inhibits ovulation, mothers who breastfeed are less likely to conceive. Biblical references endorsed the observable connection between breastfeeding and diminished fertility. It was after she had weaned her daughter that the wife of the Old Testament prophet Hosea conceived 'and bare a son'.

A study of Somerset mothers indicates that the 'fourteen rich women' in the sample (rich women did not customarily suckle their infants) 'had an overall fertility . . . twice as high as . . . the Minehead mothers overall'. Since baptisms, not births, were registered in seventeenth-century England, this conclusion is based on the analysis of indirect evidence. Nevertheless, the figures are striking enough to stand up to scrutiny.

The high yet unpredictable toll of premature deaths as a result of illness and accident made it impossible to assess the number of sons needed to secure a family from extinction. At the same time the cost of rearing children was recognised by parents and the ratepayers who footed the bill for supporting the orphans and abandoned offspring of the poor. Mary Boyle (born 1625), daughter of a rich and socially ambitious man whose earldom was his own achievement, married a younger son in spite of her father's disapproval. As she recalled in the autobiography she wrote after her conversion to a pious way of life:

> when I first married and had my two children so fast, I feared much having too many, and was troubled when I found myself to be with child so soon out of a proud conceit I had that if I childed so thick it would spoil what my great vanity then made me to fancy was tolerable (at least in my person) and out of a proud opinion, too, that I had, that if I had many to provide for they must be poor, because of my lord's small estate.

Her husband Charles Rich shared her concern, 'he would often say he feared he should have so many as would undo a younger brother'. There were ominous signs of divine disapprobation of their worldliness. Their daughter died in infancy. When he was 3, their son Charles was struck by a sudden desperate sickness. Mary 'begged of God to restore my child; and there did solemnly promise to God if he would hear my prayer, I would become a new creature'. Young Charles' recovery was miraculously swift. In the late 1650s the Riches' fortunes were transformed. As so often happened, death conferred wealth and title on a younger son. In February 1658, 'by a preposterous fate inverting the usual methods of mortality', her husband's elder brother's son died before his father or his grandfather. The grandfather did not long survive him and the father died the following May. Thus, as Mary observed, 'By the death of all these three above-named endeared relatives of my husband, he in about a year and four months came to be Earl of Warwick'. Their son, now heir to the earldom, married an earl's daughter. Then, in May 1664,

> the eighth day of that month, my dear and only son fell ill, and it proved to be the small-pox . . . I shut myself up with him, doing all I could both for his soul and body; and though he was judged by his doctors to be in a hopeful way of recovery, yet it pleased God to take him away by death on the 16th of May, to my inexpressible sorrow. He wanted about four months of being of age . . . . I was (as well as my lord) very desirous (if God saw fit) to have more children.

Mary was still under 40 but her prayers were in vain. She submitted meekly to the chastisement: 'the just hand of God in not granting our petition' and 'withholding that mercy from us when we so much needed it, being that we were unthankful for them [the children] we had and durst not trust to his good providence to provide for more, if he saw fit to give them to us'.

## BIRTH: THE MOTHER

A woman's experience of birth was shaped by her marital status, social rank, physical build and health and the gender of her child.

The plight of the small minority of women who gave birth outside marriage was bleak. Unless she had a powerful protector, the single mother was at the mercy of parish officers anxious to avoid responsibility for maintaining her and her child. Her supporters risked prosecution in the Church courts: in 1608 John Phelips of Stratford-upon-Avon found himself in trouble when he took his pregnant daughter in.

As several documents in the dossier suggest, childbearing was a focus of anxiety. Nicholas Culpeper's prescriptions include many to remedy the great and little problems of pregnancy and delivery. Married women could expect indulgences – on 3 June 1647 the thrifty parson Ralph Josselin 'brought home some cherries . . . early fruit', in the belief that the 'faintness' which troubled his wife was a symptom of a pregnancy dating from the New Year.

Birth, like death, was a domestic event. In most households, women managed it. Although this has been represented as a manifestation of resistance to male authority, it seems more likely that the care of the mother and her new-born child was seen as women's work because women had responsibility for the physical welfare of their households in sickness and in health. A snug, dark environment was preferred. Perceval Willughby, one of the few male obstetricians, and the author of the most comprehensive account of the theory and practice of childbirth written in seventeenth-century England, subscribed to this orthodoxy. Of the difficult labour of one of his patients, he noted: 'Her chamber was too great, and too light, at the time of her labour I could not obtain the favour to have it darkened. Her husband feared the knocking in of nails would spoil the windows'.

Medical men might be brought in to assist when complications arose or were anticipated – the Chamberlen family guarded the professional secret of forceps delivery – but birth was essentially women's work. The mother's attendants, female friends and relations and, whenever possible, an experienced, but not formally qualified, midwife, sought to quiet her fears and relieve her pains using a combination of the practical – massage, drinks of warm spiced wine or ale, lubricating the birth passage with oils or butter – and the ritual – unlocking doors and untying knots to ease the baby's entry to the world. Attempts to speed the delivery by internal manipulation increased the risks of infection and injury to mother and child. Willughby makes a powerful case for leaving well alone, contrasting the damage done by 'hauling' midwives with the well-being of women who gave birth unattended. He cited the histories of

> a poor fool Mary Baker, wandering for sustenance, wanting clothes to keep her warm, having gone barefooted for many years, was, in an open, windy, cold place [she gave birth in February] nigh to a house of office [a privy], delivered by the sole assistance of Dame Nature, Eve's midwife. . . . This poor creature, leaning with her back against a wall, was quickly delivered and more easily than many have been by midwives in warm places. She and the child lived.

Then there was 'a woman, big with child, which followed her husband, who was a soldier' in Queen Elizabeth's army in Ireland.

> The poor woman, finding her labour upon her, retired to the next thicket; and alone by herself, without any midwife, or other preparation, brought forth twins, which she presently carried to the river, and there washed both herself, and them, which done, she wrapped the infants in a coarse cloth, and tied them to her back, and that very day marched along with the army twelve miles together barefooted, and was never the worse for the matter.

In households of high rank or pretension, the rituals associated with childbirth lasted a month, stretching beyond the christening and often, indeed, the baby's departure for a foster home. According to custom, the newly delivered woman customarily rose from childbed ('made her upsitting') 'on the fourth day' after giving birth but, for the whole of her month, she was expected to stay within the four walls of the house, though she received visitors bearing gifts and good wishes. Lancashire mothers were 'presented' with, among other things, 'groaning cakes'. Because of the value placed on sons, it was generally 'the glad mother of a jolly boy' who earned the warmest congratulations. The ceremony of 'churching' marked her return to the world. Veiled and accompanied by women, she was required to attend the parish church to give 'hearty thanks' to God. From 1661 the words prescribed in the Book of Common Prayer emphasised the perils and pains of labour.

Although recent calculations suggest that women of childbearing age were more likely to die as a result of unrelated illnesses or accidents, accounts of childbirth echo the language of the Prayer Book. Nicholas Assheton, a sporting, tippling squire born at the end of the sixteenth century, praised God for a mixed blessing. His wife's

> delivery was with such violence that the child died within half an hour, and, but for God's wonderful mercy, more than human reason could expect, she had died; but he spared her a little longer to me and took the child to his mercy; for which, as for one of his great mercies bestowed upon me, I render all submissive hearty thanks and praise.

Despite the child's death, relations and friends came 'presenting', an indication that the mother's survival, independent of her child's, was a matter for congratulation.

After the birth of her son John in 1659 Elizabeth Carey, Viscountess Mordaunt, thanked God for her 'safe delivery'. Without his help, she was 'nothing but a dead dog'.

In humbler households arrangements were undoubtedly simpler. Dwellings were cramped, cash was short and a wife could not always be spared for so long from her duties. Peppered water took the place of more costly cordials and the interval between delivery and the resumption of everyday life was almost certainly curtailed. The husband of another of Willughby's patients kept an alehouse. His wife's delivery had been complicated by the eruption of a rash, 'small arisings . . . all over her body'. However, 'she seemed to recover, and, by all, she was thought to be past danger of death, being cheerful and comfortable for a night and a day'. In view of her improved state of health, and since her husband had 'but few rooms to entertain his guests, her chamber was made a place to receive them'. 'The ensuing night, being disquieted with drinking companions . . . she died'.

Nevertheless, since the wives of landowners and parsons were purveyors of charity and medical expertise to their communities, it might be argued that the essential ceremonies were observed when 'deserving' women were brought to childbed. A number of cases point in a contrary direction. The 'poor fool' and the soldier's wife represent not only those whose wandering way of life deprived them of the bonds of neighbourliness but also those women of higher rank and with fixed abodes whose labour pains seized them unaware. And there are fragments of evidence to suggest that neighbourly help was freely given only to those who were in a position to return it. The pastor Henry Newcome described the predicament of Ann Haslome, married in the 1650s to 'a sad husband' who 'spends all he gets'. By Newcome's account she was a godly, grafting woman. (Readers familiar with the story of the Nativity in the King James translation of the Bible, published in 1611, may pick up echoes of its phrases in the passage which I quote.)

> She hath several children, and they are little ones; yet they card and she spins and have much to do to get bread. Sometimes, when they have worked hard

all day, they ask whether there be anything for supper, and she sometimes hath nothing. Why then, they will say, pray mother take the book, and go to prayer, that we may go to bed, and God may send us something in the morning; and so they contentedly go to their beds. . . . When she was with child . . . a neighbour . . . promised to lend her some clothes for the child. And when the time drew near that she should be delivered, she sent the wench to Bury [Bury in Lancashire] for a farthing candle, a farthing in pins, and a farthing in pepper etc. The candle was lest she should labour in the night, the pins to hold the clothes on the child etc. When the girl came there, the woman said she owed two pence already, and they could not let her have no more pennies. When she was in labour, she sent to two or three goodwives [her better-off neighbours] and they were not well, and said they could not come. She sent to her that promised to lend the clothes, and she could not spare any. When she had all these returns together, she said, 'Lord, wilt thou do all thyself?' And so indeed it came to pass, she was brought to bed by daylight, and needed no candle; two of the women sent for made shift to come; and the woman that promised the clothes repented her denial and sent the clothes, and all was well.

Bastard-bearers and others likely to become a charge on the rates were liable to harsh treatment even in labour. Communities threatened by the arrival of a poor woman in the last stages of pregnancy sometimes used force to expel her. Ralph Josselin, whose concern for his own wife's welfare in pregnancy is manifest in his diary, thanked God when, in February 1657, 'a travelling woman' went into labour 'but one quarter of an hour' after quitting his parish.

## BIRTH: THE CHILD

Many babies died very young. Those who had been baptised were believed to have a passport to heaven – consequently a child whose life was in danger might be christened even before it was fully delivered. Although there was an expectation that, in normal circumstances, the ceremony would be performed in the parish church as soon after birth as might be, privileged parents sometimes opted to have their infants privately baptised at home. Other means of protection were not neglected. Some parents took astrological influences seriously. A clergyman has passed on the tale of a Warwickshire father who instructed the midwives attending his wife to 'hold their hands' when, having 'consulted his books', he discovered the unfavourable 'aspect of the stars' at the time when she was due to give birth. Coral was a good-luck charm, well-wishers brought branches of it for the teething child to chew on and beads for him to wear.

New-born infants were tightly swaddled in strips of cloth – like the baby Jesus in pictures of the Nativity. This bandaging protected the baby from draughts and probably helped to keep him passive. It did not, as people of the time believed, make the baby's limbs grow straight. It is not clear to what extent the babies of poorer parents were swaddled. Like swaddling, purpose-made nappies were probably confined to the better off. However, by the end of the seventeenth century 'Hamburg sleazy', a fine, soft, cheap fabric was being used to make napkins, or 'clouts', as they were known. 'Warming the clouts' was a suitable task for the new mother's less experienced supporters.

There was no satisfactory substitute for breast milk. The prospects of orphans and babies whose mothers could not feed them were therefore greatly enhanced if a wetnurse could be found to suckle them. Among those who could afford the choice, opinion was divided between those who favoured employing a wetnurse as a matter of course and those who advocated mother's milk. The wives of devout clergymen were prominent among those who chose to nurse. Henry Newcome (born 1627) and his wife came to recognise that maternal nursing was a spiritual duty only after their first child had been handed over to a wetnurse:

> My first child, a daughter . . . was inconsiderately [thoughtlessly] nursed out . . . where it pleased God to bless her that she prospered well; though after we were sensible of the neglect of duty in not having her nursed at home, which made her mother resolved to endeavour to nurse, if the Lord gave her any more children.

When a fifth child, Peter, was born in 1657, 'his mother was hardly put to it to nurse him' but 'it pleased God to send in Margaret Neild'; this godsend lived in the Newcomes' house 'and with my wife and her the child was comfortably nursed'.

Among landowners and their imitators, wetnursing seems to have been by far the commoner option. Since a breastfeeding mother was less likely to conceive for physiological reasons and because of the apparently widespread expectation that nursing women should abstain from sexual intercourse, couples anxious for heirs had good reason to hire a nurse. Those who associated lactation with the beasts of the field were disgusted at the prospect of their own womenfolk making cows of themselves. Some wives played an indispensable part in the family business: disturbed nights made them less effective partners; infantile sounds and smells could put customers off. The unwholesome atmosphere of the town strengthened the case for finding a foster mother in the country. But it is likely that, for the most part, parents followed the custom which prevailed in their own circle without undue deliberation.

Household accounts demonstrate that wetnursing was an expensive option. A nurse who lived in might expect to eat as well as the child's natural mother; the wages paid to nurses who lived out were on a scale which would enable her to do the same. Wetnurses were chosen with care. It was believed that temperamental traits were passed on – 'engrafted . . . and imprinted' – by the nurse's milk. When the Plymouth surgeon James Yonge (born 1647) and his wife 'put' their son John 'to nurse to Susan Slanning', they chose a woman they knew well. Before her marriage Susan had been a servant in Yonge's father's house; indeed it was at her wedding that he and his wife 'became first acquainted'. Mary Verney gave precise instructions for her baby's journey to its foster home: the nurse's husband should carry 'the child before him . . . tied about him with a garter, and truly I think it will be a very good way, for the child will not endure to be long out of one's arms'. Nurses became attached to the babies in their care. When a 'nursery' in her care (almost certainly an orphan or bastard child farmed out by the parish) died in 1681, a Bedfordshire woman was observed to be 'almost distracted with the grief of it'. Women who suckled the infants of the rich had a financial interest in the baby's survival; many received substantial tips from the parents and their friends on top of their wages.

Children were breastfed for many months. Robert Sibbald (born 1642) 'sucked till [he] was two years and two months old, and could run up and down the street, and speak'. His parents justified this evidently exceptionally 'long suckling' on the grounds of his health – he was 'a tender child' – and the early deaths of their older children. Their caution appeared to pay dividends since Robert survived fourscore [eighty] years. Weaning was a milestone. It was an event of particular significance when it coincided with the baby's separation from his nurse's home and breast and the need to adjust to his or her parents' unfamiliar regime but the bacteria which lurked unrecognised in the beakers, bowls and spoons made of metal, wood or horn threatened the weaned child's health wherever he or she might be.

## INFANCY

After weaning, walking and talking were important landmarks. Pictures and written references to leading strings and walking frames tend to confirm the suspicion that, at least in the families of the better sort, young children were discouraged from going on all fours like a beast. Speech was another attainment that set humankind apart from animal creation. The active, speaking child acquired a history, the child 'intended for a Jane' became one Jane in particular. It was the developing personality that made the death of a child harder to bear as time went on. Here, in full, is the obituary which Adam Martindale, a Presbyterian minister born in 1623, wrote for his seventh child. By the time this baby was born, Martindale and his wife had buried a daughter and two sons.

> January 11 1660 [in our notation 1661] God was pleased to bestow upon us a gallant boy, which was sweet company to his poor mother in mine absence, and a refreshing [refreshment] to me at my return. We called him John, after his toward brother that died the year before; though we were afterwards troubled that we had done so (fearing lest we had offended God by striving with his Providence to have a John) when he was taken from us, May 21 1663.

He was a beautiful child, and very manly and courageous, for his age; of which this may pass for a specimen: we had a wanton tearing calf that would run at children to bear them over. The calf he would encounter with a stick in his hand, when he was about two years old (for he lived not to be much older), stand his ground stoutly, beat it back, and triumph over it, crying 'Caw, caw', meaning he had beaten the calf. I do not think one child of a hundred of his age durst so much.

## FURTHER READING

Fildes, Valerie (1986) *Breasts, Bottles and Babies: A History of Infant Feeding*, Edinburgh
——(1988) *Wet Nursing from Antiquity to the Present*, Oxford
McLaren, Angus (1984) *Reproductive Rituals: The Perception of Fertility in England from the Sixteenth Century to the Nineteenth Century*, London
McLaren, Dorothy (1985) 'Marital Fertility and Lactation, 1570–1720' in *Women in English Society, 1500–1800*, Mary Prior (ed.), London
Wilson, Adrian (1985) 'Participant or Patient? Seventeenth-century Childbirth from the Mother's Point of View' in *Patients and Practitioners: Lay Perceptions of Medicine in Pre-industrial Society*, Roy Porter (ed.), Cambridge

# CHAPTER 4

# Childhood

## THE DEBATE: THE DISCOVERY OF CHILDHOOD?

The outcome of the recent debate about past attitudes to childhood is a salutary instance of the merits and pitfalls of a common-sense approach to historical problems. Philippe Aries' pioneering and influential *L'Enfant et la vie familiale sous L'Ancien Régime* (1960), which launched the controversy, came out in England in 1962. Aries claimed that, from the end of the sixteenth century, the offspring of the better-off were 'subjected to a special treatment, a sort of quarantine, family and school together removed children from adult society'. Building in part on Aries' work, J. H. Plumb set out to paint 'a dark picture of childhood in seventeenth-century England'. Plumb discerned a 'new attitude to children' emerging as, towards the end of the century, 'a social morality' displaced the war on 'the old Adam', epitomising the undisciplined, sinful, wilful nature of fallen man. Lawrence Stone argued that, as this 'new type of family' which 'evolved' among 'the upper bourgeoisie and squirearchy', 'more and more time, energy, money and love of both parents were devoted to the upbringing of the children, whose wills it was no longer thought necessary to crush by force at an early age'.

To the non-historian it may seem incredible that the existence of childhood could ever be questioned and, in due course, this thesis was indeed challenged by Linda Pollock, who analysed material from 236 British diaries, 144 American diaries and thirty-six autobiographies. She concluded that

> children formed an integral part of the family from at least the late 16th century. Parents were undoubtedly aware of the individuality of their offspring, of their varying needs and dispositions and endeavoured to suit their mode of childcare to each particular child.

She found 'the amount of paternal concern for children', even babies, 'of particular interest'. Pollock was especially critical of the claim that parents in general were emotionally cold and physically violent.

Most recent writers have endorsed Pollock's common-sense conclusion that childhood was a recognised stage in the human life cycle. But, as Keith Thomas pointed out, while the 'affection and concern' felt by parents 'was no less great' than in the present, their '*methods*' of child rearing 'may have been different'. Thomas' emphasis on methods reflects his reservations about Pollock's case. He concluded that, like 'adults in a servile condition', a category which included many male plebeians, children were often beaten – by their parents, by their employers and, most often perhaps, if they went to school, by their schoolmasters. And coroners' records describe children so terrorised by their parents that they did away with themselves rather than face another bout of brutal treatment.

## THE CHARACTERISTICS OF THE CHILD

It was, however, evident, then as now, that children were physically weak, inexperienced in the ways of the world, and morally unformed. Thomas Wright (born 1561) held that children 'lack the use of reason . . . following nothing but that pleaseth their senses, even after the same manner as brute beasts do, for as we see beasts hate, love, fear and hope, so do children'. In contrast 'men, by reason, take possession over their souls and bodies'.

At the end of the seventeenth century the philosopher and writer on education John Locke characterised children as 'travellers newly arrived in a strange country of which they know nothing'. He also noted, as a thing he had

> frequently observed . . . that, when they have got possession of any poor creature, they are apt to use it ill. They often torment and treat very roughly young birds, butterflies and such other poor animals which fall into their hands and that with a seeming kind of pleasure.

Such unthinking cruelty extended to unfortunate human beings: 'There was in a town in the west a man of a disturbed brain whom the boys used to tease'.

The child's amorality was recognised in law, in the words of Chief Justice Hale, whose work *Pleas of the Crown* was published in 1682:

> An infant kills a man . . . no felony. But, if by circumstances it appeareth that he could distinguish between good and evil, it is a felony – as he hide the dead, make excuse, etc. But in such case execution in prudence respited to obtain a pardon.

## THE EXAMPLE OF JACK CREMER (BORN 1700)

The opening pages of the autobiography of 'Rambling Jack' Cremer, who went to sea at the exceptionally young age of 8 – most of the other boys on Her Majesty's ship *Dover* were 14 or 15 years old – puts flesh on these theoretical bones. What Rambling Jack called the 'Rodamantaram ['rodomantading' means bragging] Historey' of his life, written when he was 68, is so graphic that it is worth quoting at length. His idiosyncratic spelling gives an idea of how he might have sounded as he sat reminiscing in his retirement.

As he recalled, he

was born in East Lane in Rotherif [Rotherhythe] in the Parrish of St Marie Mardelins [Magdalene], Bourmonce [Bermondsey] in the Subberbs of London.

My father was a Master of a Marchant-man . . . . He died and left a Widow with four Children, boys . . . .

My father's Aunt, his Mother's sister . . . took a fancy to me in my cradle, and beged my father to send me down to Plymouth – I then being on or about two Years of age. My father condesended [consented]; he having so maney of us, and having so many Troubles of being taken prisoner and losing his Wife's fortin . . . .

My Unkle Alsop [his aunt's second husband] was very fond of me, and put up with many of my Childish Actions, which children are proane to. I verey well mind he removed me from the Clark of the parrish, he being too sevear [a schoolmaster], and put me to one Mrs Strong's writting School. And in a small time afterwards he dyed, to my great los and grief. And by letter, afterwards, came word from London that my father was Dead.

My Aunt was in much grief, and lived a Molincholey Widow. And I lived a year or moore with her; till always complaint against me for fighting and quareling with other boys and rude with girls, and not altering anything for the better, my Aunt ofen told me she would send me home to my Mother in London.

I begun to be outraggoes, and not minding at all the threts, would go to play when I pleased, not minding my prayers. She always kept me very strickt, and was continually giving me good advise . . . . My Aunt could bear it no more. I grew wers and wers . . . .

When I came to London, I was brought to my mother, who received me verey indiferent. I did not know her, nor she me, and indiferent boath sides; only they told me that was my mother and the three boys my brothers. Soe afterward I was called by them their West-Cuntry brother or 'Hickmundrowdell Jack', which youst to inrage me so that I was always fighting them and other boys. This my mother could not stand and made her not love me as the other children, which I too plainly seaid.

My mother's brother-in-law [her step-brother] came to see my poor Mother in her Distress; and we four sons being all at home, he took a liking to me, being the most Mischeafyous and prety active. He wished to take me, only he was afraid I was too young to go to sea; but he said 'Neck or Nothing' – if I lived, all would be well, and if I were knocked on the head, theair would be one short in the Family, but I had the chance to live and make a brave man . . . .

My Unkle put his man-Sarvant to take care of me till he came himself; he gave him pirtikular order to me verey careful of me as being so young, for me to lay with him, and he was to keep me clean, reminding him that I was but a child, and to be tender of me, nor to let me be as little as possible out of his sight.

This I partly remember what he ordered his man in my hearing, and gave me a crown [five shilling] piece for the man to buy me what I should long for from the bomboate people [bumboats were the maritime equivalent of the market stall]. And he gave me a large stock of gingerbread, and sent me aboard among the crue . . . .

Thus I begun my Troubells.

. . . The fellow got all my Unkle's things on board and took possession of his cabin, putting everything in order against my Unkle's coming on board. And he got a duble hammock for himself and me on the Ollop [the Orlop or lowest deck] among the Midshipmen, wheair I youst to be left sometimes the hole day with a cuple of biskets and a bit of Cheese or stinkin butter, pityed by the midshipmen and the quartermasters. While the vilanous fellow lodged himself with a woman in my Unkle's cabin, and I lay by myself severall Nights with my cloaths on, either on the cables, or in the hammock, if any would lift me into it out of compassion for my littleness . . . nor could I get upon Deck without some poor fellow was kind anuff to help me up and then, boroakin-harted, hardly able to get down again.

Jack's uncle clearly regarded him as too young to look after himself; Jack's troubles underline the differences in physical scale between the small boy and the youth.

## GOOD AND BAD PARENTS

There are indications that parents, including plebeian parents, who are inevitably under-represented in Pollock's sample, were and were expect-ed to be concerned about the welfare of their offspring. In his spiritual auto-biography, the travelling preacher John Bunyan, a tinker by trade, exclaimed

The parting with my wife and poor children hath . . . oft been to me . . . as the pulling the flesh from my bones . . . . [I] have often brought to my mind the many hardships, miseries and wants that my poor family was like to meet with . . . especially my poor blind child, who lay nearer my heart than all I had besides. O the thoughts of the hardship this might go under would break my heart to pieces.

When a child died, parents were expected to grieve. Mental and physi-cal symptoms of distress were regarded as normal. The Revd Richard Napier, a physician who specialised in the treatment of mental disturbance, did not think that Ellen Craftes, one of his humbler patients, was mad when 'she took fright and grief that a door fell upon her child and slew it. Presently [at the moment] head and stomach ill; eyes dimmed with grief that she can-not see well'. By contrast, a woman's failure to love her children was a sign of mental disorder. Here is a list of Elisabeth Clark's symptoms: 'Careth not for her children; can take no joy of her children; tempted to hang her-self'.

If he or she was not mad, the negligent parent was wicked. One of the most striking examples relates to an Englishman living on the other side of the Atlantic. The evidence assembled in the early 1650s to support the charge that Hugh Parsons, a brickmaker and woodsawyer of Springfield, Massachusetts, was a witch emphasised his failure to respond in the expected ways to the illness and death of his child:

> George Colton stood forth to testify on oath that coming to Hugh Parsons's house where his wife was sitting by the fire with the child in her lap . . . she said though my child be so ill and I have much to do with it yet my husband keeps ado at me to help him about his corn . . . . It was evidenced by George Colton upon oath that he showed no natural sorrow for the death of his child when he first heard of it in the Long Meadow.

In his defence,

> Hugh Parsons desired that Goodman Cooley would testify whether he was not affected with the death of his child when he came to speak to him to go to the burial of it, he saith he could not speak to him for weeping.
>
> Hugh Parsons saith that when his child was sick and like to die, he run barefoot and barelegged and with tears to desire Goody Cooley to come to his wife because his child was ill.

Yet, as Thomas's comments suggest, it is misleading to play down the differences between the circumstances and outlook of today's parents and children and those of their predecessors in the sixteenth, seventeenth and early eighteenth centuries. Bunyan's love for his children speaks to us over the centuries. All the same, his duty to God weighed more heavily with him than his responsibilities to his 'poor children'. Children were not routinely confined to school: many went to work at a very early age. There were deserted or orphaned children who struggled to get by without adult support. Orphans, much commoner then than now, were notoriously at risk of neglect and mistreatment. Preachers' exhortations and individual case histories testify to the difficult relationships between step-parents and -children and between half-brothers and -sisters.

Henry Newcome's autobiography tells an incomplete but disturbing story of the inability of family and friends to protect a small girl from abuse at the hands of her father and step-mother. The child, his own granddaughter, was born on 16 April 1678. On 7 May she was baptised Jane. Her mother died three days later and, before Christmas, her father Daniel had remarried. The first child by his second wife, a son, was born in October 1679; two more followed, the younger born posthumously in April 1684. Recalling the matters which troubled him in the autumn of 1682, Newcome listed: '1. Daniel's unwise absence from his home and affairs that require his presence. 2. His wife's sickness in his absence. 3. The renewed ill-usage of Jane'. Of the early weeks of the following year, he noted:

> About this time we had great affliction about little Jane, who was badly used; insomuch as we were clamoured upon that no course was taken about her. And, after much contesting, Mr Wilson [Daniel Newcome's patron, 'his best

friend'] fetched her away . . . and placed her from them; which, though it caused great distance amongst us, yet it was a thing necessary to be done . . . . Daniel and his wife carry wretchedly and rudely after their shameful abuse of the child. It is an affliction and shame to me.

As a minister of religion, Newcome was peculiarly sensitive to accusations that he fell short of the conduct that became a Christian.

In February 1684 Daniel Newcome died after several weeks of illness. Jane, back in the care of her step-mother Sarah, survived until April 1686. That month James II eased the restrictions on congregations which, like Newcome's, refused to conform to the doctrines and ceremonies of the Anglican Church. Jane's sad end soured his happiness:

It was a great allay to my present great content in the liberty that Jane Newcome, daughter to my son Daniel, about eight years old, my grandchild, should fall ill, and continue so unaccountably handled and died 30 May.

Richard Gough's many revealing stories about the Shropshire community of Myddle include the chilling tale of Thomas Elks who 'hired a poor boy to entice' his orphaned nephew

into the corn fields to gather flowers. The corn was then at its highest. Thomas Elks met the two children in the fields; sent the poor boy home and took the child in his arms into the lower end of the field where he had provided a pail of water, and putting the child's head into the pail of water he stifled him to death, and left him in the corn.

The child was reported missing; the poor boy owned up to his role in luring Elks' victim into the fields and men were set on the wicked uncle's trail. They caught up with him near Mimms in Hertfordshire. Their attention was attracted by two ravens perched 'on a cock of hay, pulling the hay with their beaks and making a hideous and unusual noise'. Confronted, Elks, 'being tormented with the horror of a guilty conscience, confessed that these two ravens had followed him continually from the time that he did the fact. He was brought back to Shrewsbury, and there tried, condemned and hanged on a gibbet on Knockin Heath'.

## ILLNESS, ACCIDENTS AND DEATHS IN CHILDHOOD

As many harrowing accounts make clear, the most concerned of parents were powerless to safeguard their children from illness or injury. Smallpox raged in Manchester in 1680

and was very mortal, several hopeful children taken away by them. Mr Edward Greaves's eldest son died December 3rd. Mr Barlow's eldest son died December 6th, Richard Hanson had but one son, and he died; William Booker buried a very hopeful son December 15th. Little Sarah Leech, a pretty sweet child of precious Jo. [John] Leeche's, deceased, was buried December 21st. February

15th Mr Higinbotham had a little son died also of the same disease. Martha Taylor's son March 2nd. William Hibbert had a child also died of the same distemper April 2nd . . . . March 4th (Friday) Rose [Newcome's infant grand-daughter] was suddenly and dangerously taken this day. Others are taken away by the like or less beginnings, as a daughter of Mr Butter's this week. March 25th (Friday) Matthew Greaves was buried who died of the smallpox . . . . April 6th (Wednesday) Little James [Daniel Newcome's posthumous son] began to be unwell, and it proved to be smallpox after a time. He had them comfortably, and they were kindly, and he came through them well. At the same time the Lord visited both the children at Hulme and four children at Dr Banne's and all escaped. The Lord dealt severely with three families: Mr Hooper's, Mr Butler's and Michael Pimlett's in taking away two apiece, it being all their present stock.

Adam Martindale (born 1623), a farmer's son, was struck down with smallpox in the late summer of 1632. When he 'first began of it', his mother and elder sister were already dead from the disease. He was in St Helen's Chapel

and was so violently sick that I could not abide the sermon out, and was with much difficulty got home by my brother Henry. After some little (I being kept warm) the smallpox broke out very thick, upon which some of my friends [the seventeenth-century definition of 'friends' includes relatives] dressed mine eyes with saffron to preserve my sight, and perhaps it did me good, for, though I was blind several days through the closing up of mine eyelids, my head and body wholly overspread first with pox and after with scabs, it pleased God to preserve both mine eyes and (which was the greater wonder, though less material) though my face, when the scabs were peeled off, remained for a long time full of red spots, it was not at all pitted . . . but in time as clear and smooth as ever it was.

Temporary blindness was a not uncommon side-effect of smallpox. Nicholas Saunderson (born 1682), one of a large family with little money, was permanently blinded when he was 2. A child of prodigious memory and great linguistic and mathematical ability, Saunderson is said to have 'taught himself to read by tracing out the letters with his fingers on the gravestones in the churchyard' of his home village in Yorkshire – he eventually became Lucasian Professor of Mathematics at the University of Cambridge.

Children were also at risk from accidental injuries and death. Adam Martindale described two life-threatening incidents in his childhood.

The first occurred when I was so young that I cannot remember it but I can easily believe them that told me of it because I shall carry the mark of it to my grave. There was set upon the floor for some use or other the bottom part of a broken earthen pot . . . with water in it, of which some being spilt upon the floor made it very slippery and I being a little stirring lad playing about it, my feet slipped and down I came with violence, hitting my little tender head against an ugly sharp corner of the broken pot which gave me a deep and dangerous wound.

By God's blessing 'and care taken in dressing the gaping cut' he made a complete recovery.

Worse was to come.

> This had somewhat of danger in it but the next boded no less of present [instant] death. My elder sister having some business to do at a marl pit [created by the excavation of limy clay to spread on arable land as a fertiliser] not far from the house (which served as a watering pool, fish pond and other uses, as to wash, scour or the like), I being a little boy in coats [that is not yet in breeches] but so grown up that I can well remember it, reaching at something that grew upon the pit's brink, fell in and before she was aware (being intent on her business) I was almost quite drowned, being senseless and seemingly dead when she drew me out; but being laid on a cushion by the fireside with my face downwards, I began after some time to come to myself again, having vomited up a great quantity of water. Afterwards being got to bed and carefully tended I was quickly well again.

Godly parents interpreted illnesses, accidents and their outcomes as marks of divine disapprobation or favour. Ralph Josselin and his wife, 'pulling down a tree with a rope' in August 1644, 'with our pulling all fell together but no hurt, God be praised'. The incident reminded him of his children's similar lucky escapes. Some time earlier Mary, who was 2, had fallen 'out of the parlour window with her face against the bench and had no hurt; a strange providence, all the wit of the world could not have given such a fall and preserved from hurt. To God be the praise'. In the following October, by the grace of God, she survived unharmed when a horse kicked her. On 21 May 1650, when she was 8 years old, Mary Josselin fell ill; she 'talked idly' and 'began to sweat'. The day after she was 'very weak' and passed 'a stool with three great dead worms'. A restless night followed; on the 24th she was 'very near death'; by the 26th 'all hopes of Mary's life was gone' and the next day, in her father's words,

> a quarter past two in the afternoon my Mary fell asleep in the Lord, her soul passed into that rest where the body of Jesus and the souls of the saints are, she was 8 years old when she died . . . who was our first fruits . . . it was a precious child, a bundle of myrrh, a bundle of sweetness, she was a child of ten thousand, full of wisdom, woman-like gravity, knowledge, sweet expressions of God, apt in her learning, tender-hearted and loving, an obedient child to us, it was free from the rudeness of little children, it was to us as a box of sweet ointment which when it's broken smells more deliciously than it did before. Lord, I rejoice that I had such a present for thee. It was patient in sickness, thankful to admiration [wonderfully thankful], it lived desired and died lamented.

Mary Josselin was buried the next day in her father's church at Earl's Colne in Essex.

For children, as for adults, death often came as a release from suffering. At the same time it was widely believed that the earth was an antechamber to heaven and hell and that the eternal destiny of the dead – man, woman or child – was determined by the manner of his or her life and death. When a child died, godly parents strove to transmute raw, bitter grief first into resignation and ultimately into the confident expectation of a joyous reunion. While the child lived, however, it was the godly parents' duty to set his foot securely on the narrow path to salvation. The rod spared might result in a child damned. Fear of hellfire and damnation fuelled by sermons and works like Janeway's *A Token for Children* – there are extracts in the dossier – gave children nightmares. Images of heaven were perhaps less potent: when he was 11 Tom Josselin (born 1644) 'dreamed he saw a wonderful house in the air, very fine and shiny like the inside of an oyster shell'. John Locke, often identified as the chief promoter of a new regime for children, differed from earlier authorities less in the ends or means he advocated than in his terms of reference, which relate to this world rather than the next. It may be that the critical shift which affected the behaviour of a minority of parents, and in particular of cultivated men towards their children, was less a discovery of childhood than a blunting of the conviction that hellfire awaited the disobedient child.

## How long did childhood last?

As Chief Justice Hale's definition of the child's liability for his action in terms of capacity rather than age suggests, there were in real life no clear-cut boundaries between infancy and childhood or between childhood and youth. Gender and family circumstances determined the allocation of time between play, school and work.

## Play

In Keith Thomas's view, historians, concentrating on adult attitudes, have made an oblique approach to the history of childhood. To penetrate the world of the child, he argues, we must analyse the games, tricks, rhymes and stories, material of the sort which Iona and Peter Opie took as their agenda for the life work of collecting, editing and interpretation. This is a debatable strategy.

The Opies gathered the current versions from living sources in school playgrounds; much of what has come down to us from the seventeenth century survives because it was acquired by highly educated and sophisticated adults – men like Samuel Pepys, whose books were deposited as *Bibliotecha Pepysiana* in his old Cambridge college in 1724, and John Moore, whose collection was incorporated into the Public Library of the University of Cambridge a decade or so earlier. With such a pedigree it is difficult to argue that Tom Hickathrift's exploits or Poor Robin's jokes were the exclusive property of the young.

The case for songs and stories as child's play, let alone as evidence of the differences between child- and adulthood remains unproven. However, it remains the case that even the sternest of seventeenth-century moralists was prepared to concede, on biblical authority, that children should, within carefully controlled limits, be permitted to play. Charles Hoole's *Vocabularium Parvum* 'for the use of little children that begin to learn the Latin Tongue', published in 1666, listed 'bandy, battledore, shuttlecock, quoits, bowls, tops, scourges, whirlgigs, knucklebones, dice, draughts, chess, cards, merrytotters [swings or seesaws]', 'fox to thy hole', hide and peep, blind man's buff, 'how many plums for a penny?' and 'a duck a drake and a water snake' among his target readers' 'sports'. Hoops, stilts and ninepins are mentioned elsewhere. Locke referred to 'scotch hoppers'. Then as now, children mimicked adult doings. On 10 August 1712 the daughter of a Lancashire squire, Mally Blundell, who was rising 8, and her sister Fanny, who was approaching her sixth birthday, held a doll's funeral. In their father's words: 'My children buried one of their babies with a great deal of formality. They had a garland of flowers carried before it, and at least twenty of their playfellows and others were at the burial'.

For almost every child, play was soon overshadowed by the business of earning, vocational training or book learning. Scattered evidence suggests that, in plebeian families in particular, girls graduated from babyhood to baby-minding and other household chores.

## Schooling

Formal education was largely a male preserve. There seems to be no doubt that the majority of boys who went to school to learn to read and write in English were destined for better-regarded and better-rewarded occupations in which the ability to make and consult written records was needed day in, day out. In consequence, 'to write . . . and read well' was 'a pretty stock for a poor boy to begin the world with'.

Some men and more women took their first steps towards literacy in their teens or even later. Thomas Tryon (born 1634), whose career as a working child is described in the next section (pp. 71–2), paid for his own schooling. When he was 13, 'thinking of the vast usefulness of reading', he

> bought a primer and got now one, then another to teach me to spell and so learned to read imperfectly, my teachers not being ready readers. But in a little time, having learned to read competently well, I was desirous to learn to write, but was at a great loss for a master, none of my fellow shepherds being able to teach me. At last I bethought myself of a lame young man who taught some poor people's children to read and write; and having by this time got two sheep of my own, I applied myself to him and agreed with him to give him one of my sheep to teach me to make letters and join them together. But I was as much at a loss for time, being forced to get my fellow shepherds, now and then, to look after my sheep whilst I went to learn.

For boys born before the end of the seventeenth century illiteracy was not a barrier to success in some plebeian trades. Tryon's *Memoirs* imply that reading and writing were not a prerequisite for an apprentice in the building trade. An analysis of probate records has demonstrated that, in Shropshire at any rate, a small minority of the men called on to value the goods and chattels of their dead neighbours were unable to make a written record of their estimates. Alan Pickering, an expert on cattle and horse flesh, who served as an assessor on no fewer than twenty-one occasions between 1680 and 1741, is perhaps the outstanding example. By this time, letters and words on sign boards and almanacs and other cheap books had become commonplace, at least in urban environments, and witnesses who were unable to sign their names to legal documents frequently marked not with an X but with a recognisable initial. By the end of Pickering's career his inability to record his own valuations must have made him a conspicuous figure.

In theory schoolmasters were licensed by the Church. Thus in February 1587 Thomas Cullyer of Norwich was authorised to teach 'boys and infants the ABC, art of reading, writing, arithmetic and suchlike'. Too often, teaching in a petty school was 'left as a work for poor women, whose necessities compel them to undertake it as a mere shelter from beggary'. The age at which children first went to school was not fixed. Charles Hoole, the author of *A New Discovery of the Old Art of Teaching Schoole*, published in 1660, believed that it was 'usual in cities and great towns to put children to school about four or five years of age, and in country villages, because of further distance, not till about six or seven'. The standard practice was to teach reading first: many teachers used a horn book, a sheet printed with the alphabet and the Lord's Prayer, mounted on a board with a handle and protected from damp and grubby fingers with a film of horn. When a child knew his letters and could spell out simple words, he was ready to tackle a text in English. A child who was kept at his books until he was eight would normally have learned to write as well but, because school was not compulsory and parents suited their plans to their own and their children's needs, reality was untidier than Hoole's model.

After a false start under 'an old school dame who lived at the very next door', James Fretwell (born 1699) was taught to read by his mother and, 'though she had a large family to oversee and provide for', she did the same for her other younger children. When James 'could read in his Bible', she enrolled him at the school at Kirk Sandal, four or five miles away. There 'she had the pleasure of seeing [him] removed out of the horn book class' which the master 'upon first sight . . . thought most suitable'.

At my first going to Sandal I walked it every day, but was not able to hold it long, it being too far for such a child to go daily, for I was not quite five years of age, and some boys who went with me, being much older, hurried me too fast, and sometimes left me behind, so that I came home weeping, therefore, after a short time my father boarded me out at Sandal with one Mary Stanniforth, a widow woman, who took good care of me and I usually came home every Saturday.

Shortly before Adam Martindale's sixth birthday his godmother gave him an ABC.

> I, by the help of my brethern and sisters that could read and a young man that came to court my sister ... quickly learned it .... Then of mine own accord I fell to reading the Bible and any other English book.

Thereafter things went less well:

> About the middle of January 1630, when schools began to be revived after Christmas, I was sent to the free school of St Helen's almost two miles from my father's house, a great way for a little fat short-legged lad as I was to travel twice a day; yet I went it cheerfully .... Had not great crosses befallen me in this septennium [seven-year period] of my life, a good teacher might well have fitted me for the university .... My hindrances were many, as first, many teachers (five in fewer years). Secondly, these none of the best. Thirdly, a long tedious method then and there used. Fourthly, dullards in the same class having power to confine me to their pace

and, fifth, a series of domestic crises including his father's illness – 'a most violent and raging fever ... which lay much in his head and made him rage and ramble strangely'; the deaths of his mother and sister and his father's subsequent mental breakdown – 'almost overwhelmed with grief ... he fell again to be much disordered in his head'.

Even without such afflictions, attendance was often irregular. The author of a textbook intended for students of Latin *Pueriles Confabulatiunculae ... or dialogues fit for children*, which was published in 1617, included examples of the excuses which might be offered by latecomers and absentees in the hope of escaping a beating which suggest the tension between the demands of school and duties at home, a tension which increased with the boy's age and ability to give a hand in the family business. Thus:

> My father commanded me to go into the field that I might know whether the ditchers were there.
>
> I was presently to knead the dough: that labour endured almost an hour and a half and afterwards whilst I am washen, whilst I dry me whilst I ... get myself ready the time goeth away.

The cane, the birch and the ferule, a flat board also used to beat children and 'adults in a servile condition', were the teacher's badges. In his *School Pastime*, published in 1669, John Newton castigated the 'whipping masters' who 'used greater severity to their scholars than our laws prescribe for common rogues and vagabonds'. He evidently expected that parents would favour his proposals for a tender regime designed to cajole young children into learning and, indeed, parents with the means to employ a tutor or the leisure to take on the task of teaching themselves often seem to have preferred to keep their young sons at home rather than to entrust them to the master or dame of the petty school.

'Pictures', John Newton argued, 'are the most intelligible books that children look upon' and therefore

> an alphabet with the picture of some creature annexed whose name beginneth with the letter with which it is joined, their eyes being delighted with the picture, they may very probably be induced to take notice of the form of the letter with which the name of the creature doth begin.

If pictures were 'made into cards' and the children gathered 'about a little table', the teacher could

> throw down the cards containing the letters which make the syllable or word in the spelling whereof he would instruct them, surely they would learn the thing much sooner and with more delight than by pointing . . . to the letter in a book, and more of them would learn also.

Hoole, who called these the children's 'playing years', described other ingenious and entertaining methods devised to make reading a game:

> Some have got twenty-four pieces of ivory cut in the shape of dice, with a letter engraven upon each of them, and with these they have played at vacant hours with a child, till he hath known them all distinctly.
>
> Some have made pictures in a little book or upon a scroll of paper wrapped upon two sticks within a box of isinglass [a firm semitransparent gelatinous substance from the air bladders of freshwater fish] and by each picture have made three sorts of each letter, with which its name beginneth [perhaps examples of English, Roman and Italic letters or a mixture of fonts and upper and lower cases], but those being too many at once for a child to take notice on, have proved not so useful as was intended.
>
> Some likewise have had pictures and letters printed in this manner on the back side of a pack of cards to entice children that naturally love that sport, to the love of learning their books.
>
> Some have writ a letter in a great character upon a card, or chalked it upon a trencher [a wooden bread or chopping board would be the equivalent today], and by telling the child what it was, and letting him strive to make the like, have imprinted it quickly on his memory, and so the rest one after another.
>
> One having a son of two years and a half old, that could but even go about the house, and utter some few gibberish words in a broken manner; observing him one day . . . to be busied about shells and sticks and such like toys which he himself had laid together in a chair, and to miss any one that was taken from him . . . devised a little wheel with all the capital Roman letters made upon a paper to wrap round about it, and fitted it to turn in a little round box, which had a hole made in the side of it, that only one letter might be seen to peep out at once. This he brought to the child and showed him only the letter O and told him what it was. The child, being overjoyed with his new gambol [game], catcheth the box out of his father's hand and runs with it to his playfellow, a year younger than himself, and in his broken language tells him there was 'An O, an O.' And when the other asked him where, he said, 'In a

hole, in a hole', and showed it him, which the lesser child then took such notice of as to know it again ever after from all other letters.

This cascade of examples, the last confused enough to suggest that it was based on a real experiment in education, is further evidence that parents saw their children as individuals and that some at least sought to devise or adopt methods of learning through play that would not be out of place in a progressive infant school in our own day.

The obituary John Evelyn (born 1620) wrote for his son Richard, 'a prodigy of wit and understanding' who died in January 1658 at the age – which his father gives with the touching precision shown in many diaries and memorial inscriptions – of 'five years and three days old only', gives an indication of the curriculum followed by the most promising sons of intellectual fathers, the 'child of extraordinary towardliness and having a teacher at home', as Hoole put it: 'At two and a half years old' Richard Evelyn 'could perfectly read of any of the English, Latin, French or Gothic letters, pronouncing the first three languages exactly'. Before he was 5 he could translate from English to Latin and vice versa, he 'had a strong passion for Greek' and 'a wonderful disposition to mathematics'.

At all social levels less attention was paid to teaching girls to read and write. Elizabeth Grace, an Essex widow who made her will in 1573, made provision for her grandchildren: both were 'to stay at school in learning, the boy to write and read and the girl to read and sew till they shall be fit and of age to go to service'. Note the dual qualification: the right stage of development and the right age seem to be equally important. For landowners' daughters, learning to write was not necessarily a higher priority than learning to sew or dance. Mally Blundell, whose father Nicholas was a Lancashire squire, was born in September 1704. Her father's diary suggests that she began her education with her needle rather than her pen: in May 1710 she 'went first time to school to Ellin Whithead to learn to sew'. A year later she and her younger sister Fanny (born 1706) started dancing lessons. By this time, according to her father, Mally was able to read 'pretty well in the spelling book so we left it off and she has now begun to read'. (Nicholas Blundell's diary confirms that the theory described in print was applied in real life.) On 24 April 1712 Blundell 'began to teach Mally to write'; on her eighth birthday she 'began to join in writing' and the following March 'writ two letters . . . the first she writ with the intention they should be sent'.

Women were known for their poor spelling which was often attributed to their lack of familiarity with Latin from which so many newly coined English words were derived. In fact, into the second half of the seventeenth century English spelling was unstable – judged by later convention, the published work of men like John Newton and Charles Hoole who represented themselves as experts on education abounds in errors. 'Smoak', 'carret', 'weesel', 'hee and shee goat', 'stomack', 'gyant', 'neece', 'colledge', 'cobler', 'shoomaker', 'salt celler', 'candle-wyke' and 'sope ' all appear in Hoole's *Vocabularium*. Nicholas Blundell (born 1669), who had been educated by the Jesuits at St Omer in Flanders, spelled phonetically. On 11 January 1709 he noted that 'Mr Aldred and I had a deal of discourse about fatoning of Kattle and Sheep'; later the same month he recorded a visit 'to Leverpoole' where he was 'treated . . . with Jocolet [chocolate]' and 'payed all that [he] ought [this could represent either "owed" or "was obliged to"] to Mr Allanson and to Mr Hirst and cleered of all accounts . . . for Brass and Puter [pewter]'.

## Work

As their strength and experience increased, the child who had been a nuisance underfoot among the work people became a handy member of the team, able to make a measurable contribution to the household income in kind or cash.

In his survey of the farming year in the East Riding of Yorkshire in the middle years of the seventeenth century, Henry Best refers in passing to children's work. When the sheep were washed in early June, before shearing there were 'always children, boys and girls, with bushes and whins [gorse] made fast to the ends of sticks' ready to catch wisps of loose wool as it 'swam' downstream. Later in the month when the sheep were clipped the farmer employed girls, one 'to keep the fire under the tar pot' – tar was used to mark the sheep to indicate ownership – 'and the other to gather up the locks of wool that are scattered and to carry the best of them and put them within the fleeces before they be lapped up and to put the worst sort of them into the other leape [basket], viz., [that is] such as are hairy and tarry'. The wives and children of the harvesters gleaned the corn that fell from the sheaves on to the ground. At the beginning of 1710 Nicholas Blundell hired children to pick out the bad corn from the good.

In the second half of the sixteenth century, apparently quite suddenly, the craft of knitting was taken up in many of the wool-producing districts of England. When Elizabeth I visited Norwich in 1578 she took a special interest – 'particularly viewed' – a demonstration of knitting and spinning put on in St Stephen's parish: 'Upon the stage there stood at one end eight small women children [girls] spinning worsted yarn and at the other end as many knitting of worsted yarn hose'. Twenty years later it was claimed that 'by knitting of fine jersey stockings every child [was] able at or soon after seven years of age to earn four shillings a week'. The oldest extant English knitting pattern comes from *Natura Exenterata or Nature Disembowelled*, published in 1655. It seems more likely that the original 'single sentence three pages long, punctuated erratically with commas' was intended as a curiosity not as a practical guide. The knitting children of Norwich may well have learned from and worked to shanties like those William Howitt (born 1792) heard in knitting schools in the Yorkshire dales.

The spinners who accompanied the St Stephen's knitters represent the older tradition of textile crafts. Thomas Tryon (born 1634) was the son of a tiler and plasterer. By his son's account Tryon senior was 'an honest sober man of good reputation'.

But having many children, was forced to bring them all to work betimes . . . .
The first work my father put me to was spinning and carding wherein I was
so industrious and grew so expert that I could spin four pound [of wool] a
day . . . . This work I followed close till I was ten or eleven years old. But then
I began to be weary of the wheel and was strongly inclined to betake myself
to the flocks and on Sundays . . . I would voluntarily keep sheep for a penny
or two while the shepherd went to church or to some feast or cudgel-playing
or other merry meeting, as they called it.

In textile-producing districts, when trade was good, their was work for all
including the very young. Daniel Defoe published his *Tour through the Whole
Island of Great Britain* between 1724 and 1726, though some of his observations were based on material collected as much as a quarter of a century
earlier. Around Halifax he found the people 'all full of business; not a beggar, not an idle person to be seen'. The workmen's 'women and children
[were] always busy carding, spinning, etc. so that no hands being unem-
ployed, all can gain their bread, even from the youngest to the ancient,
hardly any thing above four years old but its hands are sufficient to itself'.
(Then as now, of course, journalists' conclusions should be treated with
some caution.)

The work expected of Martha Love, an orphan apprenticed to an innkeeper and his wife in 1695 to learn the craft of housewifery or of a mother's
helper or a farmer's boy working alongside his father was less monotonous
but, as William Stout's description of his sister Elin's childhood suggests,
perhaps even more strenuous. School did not exempt a boy from labour.
Although their parents took book learning seriously enough to send their
sons away to school, the Stout boys were recalled whenever extra hands
were needed on the family farm.

## FURTHER READING

Cressy, David (1980) *Literacy and the Social Order: Reading and Writing in Tudor and
   Stuart England*, Cambridge
Plumb, J. H. (1982) 'The New World of Children' in *The Birth of a Consumer Society:
   The Commercialisation of Eighteenth-century England*, Neil McKendrick, John Brewer
   and J. H. Plumb (eds), London
Opie, Iona and Peter (1959) *The Lore and Language of Children*, Oxford
——(1969) *Children's Games in Street and Playground*, Oxford
——(1985) *The Singing Game*, Oxford
Pollock, Linda (1983) *Forgotten Children: Parent–Child Relations from 1500 to 1900*,
   Cambridge
Thomas, Keith (1989) 'Children in Early Modern England' in *Children and their Books:
   A Celebration of the Work of Iona and Peter Opie*, Gillian Avery and Julia Briggs (eds),
   Oxford

# CHAPTER 5

# Youth

It was the business of youth to acquire the knowledge and skills which would be needed in adult life. These, of course, varied with gender, rank and intended vocation. During this stage in their career young men and women were regarded as socially immature; they were expected to remain unmarried and subject to the tuition and domestic authority of the householder under whose roof they lived. In some cases this was their father, more often a master acting *in loco parentis*. Widowed mothers and widowed employers stood in for their husbands. The relationship between master and servant was peculiarly powerful. When Pall Pepys came to live in her brother Samuel's household, 'not as a sister . . . but as a servant' in January 1661, he underscored her altered status by refusing to let her 'sit at table' with him and his wife. Most young people were obliged to perform menial tasks for those in authority over them. Of young men, only the richest undergraduates, who engaged poorer students as their servants, were exempt. For the majority of English men and women, such dirty, and therefore demeaning, work would form a part of their daily routine until they were too frail to carry on but students and apprentices brought up in well-off families and destined for the upper ranks of urban society were unaccustomed to cleaning, fetching and carrying and were inclined to be resentful.

## DURATION

Although it was conventional to divide life into seven-year spans, as Adam Martindale did when he described his schooling, in practice, chronological age was of less importance than 'capacity'. Accident often played a part – Ann Harrison's carefree youth ended when her mother died: at 15, she recalled, she was catapulted from the schoolroom into the full responsibilities of adulthood. She had to fling 'away those little childishnesses that had formerly possessed me and, by my father's command, took upon me the charge of the house and family'.

For training in some occupations, physical size and strength were prerequisites: boys born in the seventeenth century were almost certainly less well-grown than most boys of their age in our own time; there is some evidence that, in the past, boys matured later than they do today, that they were older when their voices broke and that young men were still growing in their twenties. Not surprisingly, rank seems to have influenced the age at which physical maturity was reached. In other cases, skills – such as counting and penmanship – were the essential qualifications: at 14 William Stout (born 1665), who had seven years of schooling behind him, 'went to a scrivener [writing master] to learn to write ... and arithmetic' before starting his apprenticeship to a Lancaster ironmonger. In three weeks he 'got a good entrance into arithmetic', which he enjoyed, but, being 'naturally left-handed' and incapable of being 'steady in [his] right hand', in writing he 'made not much improvement'. It could take many parents time to scrape together the wherewithal needed to support a son at university or law school.

In fiction and in fact young women are less conspicuous than young men; the range of occupations open to them was dramatically narrower.

## TAKING LIBERTIES WITH AUTHORITY

Social immaturity was one of youth's defining characteristics. As yet unburdened with the obligations of householding, which they would assume on marriage, young men and, to a lesser extent, young women had a name for irresponsibility. The story of the Prodigal Son, who wasted his fortune on riotous living was a favourite of decorators: wall-hangings survive and paintings at Knightsland Farm near South Mimms in Hertfordshire. Youthful rowdiness was an expected feature of Shrovetide – the few days before the onset of the imposed solemnity of Lent – and May Day.

At Oxford in the 1630s Anthony Ashley Cooper (born 1621) exploited his rank and wealth to become 'leader of all the rough young men' of his college. As he recollected, Exeter College was full of 'tall raw-boned Cornish and Devonshire gentlemen' who pitted their 'famous . . . courage and strength' in contests with their rivals from Christ Church which sound like the ancestors of rugby scrums, 'making a great noise with their feet, they hissed and shoved with their shoulders'. Anthony Ashley Cooper was 'often one of the disputants and gave the sign and order of the beginning, but, not being strong of body' – and there was a good chance that the losers would be pushed downstairs – he 'was always guarded by two or three of the sturdiest youths'. He repaid his henchmen by 'giving them leave ... to eat upon his expense' in college when they were broke, buying off the farmers whose geese and turkeys they had stolen and bailing them out when they ended up in prison.

Apprentices and servants were also predisposed to misbehave. They could not be trusted to conduct themselves properly even in church unless they were in their masters' sight.

Samuel Pepys constantly complained of the conduct of the young people who worked for him: in the 1660s his footboy, his clerk, his maid-servants. Boys got into fights. Coming back from a shopping trip in January

1663, he discovered that his footboy Wayneman Birch had struck his neighbour's boy down 'in the dirt, all over dirty, and the boy [the victim] taken by a gentlewoman into a house to make clean but the poor boy was in a pitiful taking and pickle'. Boys were easily distracted from their tasks. One evening during supper he sent Wayneman out for mustard to go with the tongue they were eating: 'the rogue stayed half an hour in the streets, it seems at a bonfire'. Will Hewer, his clerk, who was about 17 when he joined the Pepys household, walked 'with his cloak flung over his shoulder like a ruffian'; he often stayed out late; once he came home drunk and was sick before he went to bed; he was bawled out for 'corrupting the maids by his idle talk and carriage'. Maids were sacked for stealing, drinking and answering back. Jane Birch, Wayneman's elder sister, who served the Pepyses on and off from 1658 to 1669, was a tease. On one occasion she cut off 'a carpenter's long mustachio' and got him into serious trouble at home – 'his wife would not come near to him a great while believing he had been among some of his wenches'. She upset Lady Batten, who lived nearby, by taking off the way 'she called "Nan" to her maid within her own house'. Pepys spoke for many householders responsible for the young men and women under their roof when he lamented of 'the inconvenience that doth attend the increase of a man's fortune, by being forced to keep more servants, which brings trouble'.

Youthful pranks endangered life and property. On 2 November 1660, just before Gunpowder Treason Day on the fifth, Samuel Pepys' footboy Wayneman Birch found himself in trouble with his master when he 'let off some gunpowder'. The powder was in his pocket and he put 'a match carelessly with it, thinking it was out; and so the match did give fire to the powder and had burned his side and hand that he put into his pocket to put out the fire'. A servant of Rachel Russell's inadvertently put a candle with a gunpowder squib buried in it (it was intended for a fellow servant) on her ladyship's table. One evening towards the end of January 1724 four young people congregated in William Stout's shop in Lancaster: his own nephew and maidservant, and two outsiders, a youth and a girl. When the visiting 'lad . . . begged a pipe of tobacco', young Stout 'put a little gunpowder in it, unknown to the lad, but did not take care to shut the drawer he took the powder out of . . . . A spark flew into the powder drawer and set fire to three or four pounds' of explosive. The blast 'scorched and beat down' the joker, his intended victim and his audience – 'a wonder none of them was slain' and the house 'escaped . . . firing'. Powder burns were common enough for prescriptions for ointment to cure them to appear in housekeeping manuals. Mrs Woolley's *The Gentlewoman's Companion*, published in 1675, included 'a very good receipt for one hurt with gunpowder' – its chief ingredients were goose and chicken dung, 'as much . . . of the newest that can be got'.

Other irresponsible acts exposed the young person to moral rather than physical danger. When an outbreak of plague in London brought refugees to the neighbourhood in Lancashire where the Martindales lived their

daughter Jane was dazzled by their glamour. She was determined to follow them to the city though 'she had no friends in London to go to'. Her
parents were heartbroken at the prospect but

> Having her father's spirit and her mother's beauty, no persuasion would serve,
> but up she would to serve a lady, as she hoped to do, being ingenious with
> her needle. Moneys to carry her up and subsist upon awhile [were] . . . fur-
> nished. [In London] her money grew very low. Then with the prodigal she
> thought oft upon the plenty of her father's house, yet knowing upon what
> terms she had left it, she concealed her straits from us. Only . . . she writ for a
> goose pie to make merry with her friends; and a lusty one was immediately
> sent her, cased in twig work; but before it could reach her (the carrier being
> three weeks in coming down and returning) or the money that was sent with
> it to make her friends drink as well as eat, that the goose might swim without
> her cost, her money grew so near to an end that she had thoughts to sell her
> hair which was very lovely both for length and colour.

The disturbing possibility that she might have sold her body hangs in the
air.

But before she was reduced to utter destitution, Jane Martindale found
a husband in London, a young man of good family and no fortune and,
with assistance from her parents, they took an inn.

## OPPORTUNITY AND RISK

Family circumstances, birth order and, perhaps above all, gender influenced the scale and nature of the risks and opportunities of youth. The dif-
ferential in treatment and expectations between the elder brother and his
juniors was greatest in landowning families though others, and in particular farmers, had worked out the consequences of dividing their holding
and had taken the hard but rational decision to pass their business on to
one son. There are indications that the predicament of the younger sons of
landowners was particularly difficult in the seventeenth century. The traditional career of service in a nobleman's private army had disappeared, a
regular military career in the service of the state was not yet an option.
Apprenticeship had become less attractive, perhaps because of the rising
costs of setting up in a superior trade. The Church, still subject to period-
ic upheavals which resulted in ejections and resignations, was a less appeal-
ing option than it would become in the eighteenth century. John Aubrey
(born 1626), himself an elder son, took it for granted that younger sons
would behave badly: 'He was pretty wild when young, especially addicted to common wenches. He was a second son'. Or again: 'He was (I take
it) a younger brother, a mad fighting young fellow'. The reaction of some
of their contemporaries suggests that Freeman Sondes' murderous attack
on his elder brother in 1655 was, if not excusable, thoroughly understand-
able.

In *Industry and Idleness,* a series of prints published in 1747, William Hogarth depicted parallel episodes in the divergent life histories of fellow apprentices, Francis Goodchild and Tom Idle. Their names reflect their nature – and perhaps the virtues or vices each youth had learned at his mother's knee – and foreshadow their destinies. The diligent apprentice, Goodchild, marries their master's daughter and ends up Lord Mayor of London. Idle, a waster from the outset, is eventually betrayed by his prostitute lover and hanged at Tyburn as a thief and murderer.

The lessons derived from the adventures of the heroes of crudely printed chapbooks published in the seventeenth century are, perhaps surprisingly, more subtle than the emphatic moral message of *Industry and Idleness.* In the world inhabited by Tom Hickathrift and Dick Whittington fate played as great a part as merit in the lottery of life. In his early youth Tom Hickathrift, whose tale is retold in the dossier (p. 217–18), was a layabout, idling by the fire while his aged, widowed mother worked her fingers to the bone to satisfy his heroic appetite. His fortune was an undeserved reward for his prodigious strength and a foolhardy decision to take a shortcut through a giant's domain. The real-life Richard Whittington (born circa 1360) was the younger son of a Gloucestershire knight who came up to London to make his fortune as a mercer and financier (he supplied kings of England with cloth of gold and princesses with their wedding dresses). He married Alice, the daughter of Ivo Fitzwaryn, a mercer a generation older than himself – the records do not tell us whether or not he was Fitzwaryn's apprentice. Whittington died in 1423; his many benefactions – almshouses; a refuge for unmarried mothers; a prison rebuilt (a work of charity because the old gaol was 'over little and so contagious of air that it caused the deaths of many men'); libraries; clean water for the poor; latrines – fixed his name in the memory of Londoners. The version of his biography which became popular in the seventeenth century radically recast his early life. His wealth and good marriage were not earned by industry or initiative. Far from it. Dick is the least venturesome of heroes, as passive as Cinderella or Sleeping Beauty and, unlike them, not a victim of malice:

> This Richard Whittington was so obscurely born that he could scarcely give account of his parents or kindred, and being almost starved in the country, necessity compelled him up to London . . . . To beg he was ashamed, to steal he did abhor. Two days he spent gaping upon the shops and gazing upon the buildings, feeding his eyes but starving his stomach. At length mere faintness compelled him to rest upon a bench before a merchant's gate.

He was taken in, fed and – at the insistence of the daughter of the house, Mistress Alice – given work, running errands and drudging in the kitchen, 'making of fires, scouring kettles, turning the spit, and the like'. The lowliest member of the household, he lived on scraps from the servants' table. His bed was in the garret. There he 'was troubled with rats and mice insomuch that he could not sleep . . . they ran over his face' so, with a penny he had been given 'for going of an errand or for making clean boots or shoes', he bought the cat that was to transform his life. Puss was the only friend Dick knew and he shared his food with her. It was the custom of the house that Fitzwarren's servants should invest in their master's voyages and, when the time came for a ship to set sail, poor Dick, unwilling to accept an advance from Mistress Alice, had nothing to 'adventure' except his cat and, much against his will, he was persuaded to part with her. The kitchen maid added to his wretchedness by picking on him, 'sometimes beating him with the broom, sometimes laying him about the shoulders with a ladle, the spit or what next came to her hands'. Unable to bear any more, he resolved to run away – only to be stopped short by 'a merry peal from Bow Church' ringing out the familiar injunction: 'Turn again, Whittington, Lord Mayor of London'. When his ship came in, loaded with caskets of jewels and pearls' allotted to him as a reward for the Puss's campaign against the rats and mice of the Barbary Coast, 'there was a strange and sudden metamorphosis'. With the aid of tailors, shirtmakers and the barber, 'out of a smoky and dirty kitchen drudge there appeared a proper and well-proportioned man', the ideal match, as Alice Fitzwarren and her father both recognised, for his master's daughter.

Some real-life histories had more in common with the tall story than with Hogarth's moral tract. George Villiers, born in 1592, the second son of the second marriage of a Leicestershire gentleman, was orphaned at the age of 13. According to the stories current at the time, his mother had been a poor relation whose 'ragged habit could not shade the beautiful and excellent form of her person'. As a youth, Villiers had little money – he turned up at 'a horse race in Cambridgeshire' in a tattered black suit, unable to afford a bed for the night. His charm and good nature, fine face and figure were his fortune. He was 'the handsomest man of England, his limbs were so well-compacted and his conversation so pleasing and of so sweet a disposition'. Dangled before the susceptible king, James I, by cynical backers, he became the most powerful man in England, loaded with profitable offices, lands and honours, the first man outside the royal family to be raised to a dukedom since the middle of the sixteenth century.

Apprentices and servants benefited from similar good luck. In 1545 Edward Osborne rescued his master's baby daughter from a watery grave (a careless nursemaid had let her fall into the Thames). Seventeen years later he married her and, with her, acquired her father's fortune. Their great-grandson became the first Duke of Leeds. William Lilly (born 1602) was a grammar school boy whose parents could not afford to apprentice him. He went into domestic service in London, performing much the same tasks as the legendary Dick Whittington:

> My work was to go before my master to church; to attend my master when he went abroad; to make clean his shoes; sweep the street; fetch water in a tub from the Thames (I have helped to carry eighteen tubs of water in one morning); weed the garden (all manner of drudgeries I willingly performed); scrape trenchers etc.

Lilly died a wealthy man. A bold proposal of marriage, described in the next chapter (see pp. 104–5), was the basis of his fortune.

The youthful careers of Wayneman Birch and Daniel Newcome and, especially, Jack Sheppard foreshadow Tom Idle's. 'A pretty well-looked boy', Wayneman Birch joined the Pepys household in 1660. By his master's account he was a likeable rogue whose persistent lies and defiance drove adult after responsible adult to wash his hands of the boy. In 1663 he was shipped off to Barbados as an indentured servant, a temporary slave. Pepys had concluded that 'to keep him here were to bring him to the gallows'. Twice, as a very young child, Daniel Newcome (born 1652) narrowly escaped drowning. As time went by, his father must have feared that he was born to be hanged. Apprenticed to a London master, he ran away (a most serious act, as we shall see). 'The poor child was gotten linked with vile knaves that . . . made a prey of him . . . so that to tarry in the city was no way fit'. If he returned to the country, idleness would ruin him. The best advice was to 'send him beyond the seas' to Jamaica. Letters brought 'much good news from a far country'. In 1672 he came home. His marriage shortly after signalled his entry into the adult world but the manner of it boded ill. In money trouble, 'unknown and unsuspected' by his father, 'he privately married' an heiress, who 'wanted of her age'. Their daughter Jane's sad story is told in Chapter 4.

Jack Sheppard's early life gave no hint of the shape of things to come. He was born in Spitalfields, in the East End of London, in 1702, the second surviving son of Thomas Sheppard and Mary his wife. In 1708, following the deaths of her husband and her youngest child, Mary Sheppard went into service in the household of William Kneebone, who kept a draper's shop at the sign of The Angel in the Strand. What became of her elder son Thomas is not known. Eight-year-old Jack was placed in the workhouse school in Half Moon Alley off Bishopsgate; the boys wore a russet-brown uniform with the badge of a boy and sheep. A couple of years later, Mr Kneebone took him out of Half Moon Alley to bring him up under his own roof; when Jack was 15, Kneebone apprenticed him to a carpenter. He was 21 and almost out of his time when he ran off and took to a life of crime. Many people blamed bad company for his downfall. Edgworth Bess, a soldier's wife, whom he came across at the Black Lion, a rough alehouse near his master's home in Drury Lane, was responsible, they said. Jack met Bess in the spring of 1723; he was hanged at Tyburn eighteen months later, an object of horrified fascination to the press and public of London. What grabbed their attention was not so much the recital of his 'many robberies' as his record of gaol-breaking.

*The History of the Remarkable Life of John Sheppard*, which came hot off the press on 19 October 1724, offered:

> A particular account of his rescuing his pretended wife [Bess] from St Giles's Roundhouse. Of the wonderful escape himself made from the said Roundhouse. Of the miraculous escape he and his said wife made together from New Prison,

on the 25th of May last. Of his surprising escape from the condemned hold of Newgate on the 31st of August. Together with the true manner of his being retaken; and of his behaviour in Newgate till the most astonishing and never to be forgotten escape he made from thence, in the night of the 15th of October.

A fortnight later he was back in Newgate. What purported to be *Jack Sheppard's Last Epistle* appeared on the front page of *The Daily Journal* on Monday, 16 November, the day he was hanged. The doggerel verses, spiced up with thieves' cant, end with a flippant description of the execution. He was 'ambled from Whit' – Newgate, so-called because Sir Richard Whittington had left money for its reconstruction – to Tyburn.

> The gownsman [clergyman] comes there to me
> And talks a long time of repentance
> I am up the jagger [gallows] dubbed [tied] tight . . .
> My peepers are hid from the light
> The tumbler [cart] wheels off and I Morris [dance].

## TRAINING: GRAMMAR SCHOOLS

The grammar school was the entry gate to the professions and superior trades (categories which overlapped, as we shall see). The mother tongue was the business of the petty schoolmaster or dame; the grammar in question was Latin and Greek, though mastery of these ancient languages was achieved by only a minority of pupils. The traditional view that in the grammar schools of 'Shakespeare's England', the England of the late sixteenth and early seventeenth centuries, 'the cleverest boys of all classes were brought up together' has been modified. Boys brought up on farms and boys who lived over their fathers' shops did go to school with the parsons' sons and the squires' but there were fewer of them than the old optimistic picture suggested. Many of the 'Free Grammar Schools' charged fees. At Lavenham in the second half of the seventeenth century the five bursaries set up by Richard Peacock had been usurped by 'certain bourgeois families'. At Shrewsbury, where tuition fees seem to have been introduced in the eighteenth century, entry fees were charged on a sliding scale. Here, and at Bury St Edmunds, boys from the town were in a minority. At Colchester between 1637 and 1642, of 165 boys admitted, eighteen had free places, and even they had to pay a premium on entry and charges for candles, heating and writing lessons. Elsewhere arithmetic and modern languages were treated as extras. And, as so often happens, the chief beneficiaries of scholarship funds were the sons of better-off and more assertive fathers. Thrift was not the only motive for monopolising free grammar school places.

John Aubrey argued against educating the sons of county gentlemen cheek by jowl with the sons of artisans:

A cobbler's son may have a good wit and be a good man, but he could not be a proper friend for a person of honour. It is of ill consequence for a youth to be sent to a great school in his own country [neighbourhood] which contracts an acquaintance never to be shaken off, and this will be . . . troublesome . . . school fellows know one another's foibles, as they say, and some come to be their servants who were their playfellows at school.

In advocating educational segregation, Aubrey may be reflecting a suspicion that low-born intellectuals were potential fomenters of discontent, an attitude that was perhaps commoner in the later seventeenth century than it might have been before the Civil Wars.

## TRAINING: UNIVERSITIES AND LAW SCHOOLS

Oxford, Cambridge and the Inns of Court served as finishing schools for the sons of wealthy gentlemen and as training schools for youths destined for the Church and the higher branches of medicine and law.

It would be strange to suppose an English gentleman should be ignorant of the Law of his country. This, whatever station he is in, is so requisite that, from a Justice of the Peace to a Minister of State, I know no place he can well fill without it. I do not mean the chicane or wrangling and captious part of the Law.

John Locke's observation – which makes the distinction between the gentleman and the professional clear – comes from his *Thoughts Concerning Education*, published in 1693.

Locke was not alone in taking the universities' dual functions for granted. 'When the senior fellows [of Exeter College] designed to alter the beer of college which was stronger than other colleges', the aristocratic gang leader Anthony Ashley Cooper

hindered their design. This had put all the younger sort into a mutiny. . . . I advised all those . . . intended by their friends to get their livelihood by their studies to rest quiet and not appear and that myself and all the others that were elder brothers or unconcerned with their angers

should take part in a demonstration – the destruction of the records of students' consumption of food and drink, on which their college bills were calculated.

University education was not cheap. In the years between 1687 and 1695 Thomas Brockbank's father, a Westmorland parson, spent on average a sum equivalent to around three-quarters of his annual income on keeping his son at Oxford. Fifty years earlier Ralph Josselin 'went up to Cambridge to Jesus College . . . under Mr Thomas Lane, my loving and I hope godly and honest tutor; he dealt lovingly with me, but I was forced to come from Cambridge many times for want of money and lose my time in the country'.

His father had died in 1636 and quarrels with his stepmother about money made the situation worse. In 1640 he took his MA. 'Charges there and for my gown and cassock' – his parson's robes – amounted to £19 18s 'and somewhat upward, this was a hard pull'.

As Ashley Cooper's reminiscences suggest, the structure of college society mirrored that of the world outside. At the top of the undergraduate hierarchy were the fellow commoners, who, as their title indicates, ate with their tutors and shared many of their privileges. At Trinity College, Oxford, for instance, the president and senior fellows dined at high table with the sons of peers and knights. At Lincoln College, Oxford, the gentlemen commoners were excused from lectures: an acknowledgement that few of these youths came to university with the intention of taking a degree. The poor students at Lincoln, working their way through college as 'servitors', waited at table, made up fires, acted as gatekeepers and knockers-up. In 1587 Bryan Twyne wrote to his father from Oxford to ask permission to hire a servitor to carry wood up to his room, deal with the ashes from his fire and slop out his chamber pot. It was 'intolerable and too base for a gentleman to do such things for himself'.

Geography and access to patronage strongly influenced the opportunities of boys from poor or humble homes. In Cambridge local boys, the sons of tradesmen connected with the university and, especially, sons of senior college servants stood a much better chance of a university place than boys of roughly similar rank in other market towns. William Peters, son of the college butler, entered Caius (said 'Keys') in 1661; Christopher Green, son of the college cook, followed him six years later; he ended up as Regius Professor of Physic. Jeremy Taylor (born 1613), chaplain to the Archbishop of Canterbury and the King before the Civil Wars and, after them, a bishop, was the son of a Cambridge barber and churchwarden; young Taylor went to Caius from the newly founded Perse School.

Girls were not admitted to the grammar schools. There were no female undergraduates or law students.

## TRAINING: APPRENTICESHIPS

Boys from all but the grandest of landowning families spent their youth as apprentices. Country gentlemen, great merchants, professional men, farmers and craftsmen all paid premiums to apprentice their sons to occupations appropriate to their rank. While the universities and the Inns of Court, the London law schools, trained the medical and legal elite, the physicians and future judges; the surgeons, apothecaries and attorneys, who occupied the less prestigious, but often very profitable, branches of medicine and law served their time as apprentices or articled clerks. The overseers of the poor used apprenticeships to provide for the maintenance and close supervision of poor orphans and the troublesome children of pauper parents.

The prestige and profitability of trades were reflected in the scale of the premium charged. The trades to which pauper apprentices were put would never make them rich. In placing its hero in the kitchen of his master's house the rags-to-riches tale of Dick Whittington is realistic, in this respect at least – no starveling country lad would have entered a great merchant's household as his apprentice. By the beginning of the eighteenth century Leeds merchants were able to charge apprenticeship premiums in excess of £300, significantly more than it had cost the Revd John Brockbank to support his son for eight years at Oxford. And to the premium there had to be added the investment necessary to set a young man up in business at the end of his time.

The ranking of manufacturing trades, to take examples from just one sector of the economy, was determined by the cost of raw materials, the physical effort required to work them and the complexity of the processes involved. The closely related opportunities for profit were also significant. The goldsmith ranked much higher than the blacksmith who worked iron; the ordinary cobbler, who produced the basic footwear which all but the poorest could afford to buy new, was outranked by his neighbour the tailor whose services could be afforded by many fewer. The rank order of trades shifted across time. A list of mayors in which a run of, say, butchers is succeeded by a run of, say, innkeepers suggests that political and economic ascendancy in the locality had passed from one to the other.

Boys intended for the lowliest trades became apprentices as soon as they were physically able. Entrants to the superior trades, where strength was normally less important, were often much older – if nothing else, they needed a good grounding in reading, writing and arithmetic on which to build the accounting skills essential to the efficient running of a complex business.

The terms of apprenticeships were laid out in a written contract designed to protect the interests of both parties – provided that they were of equivalent rank. If his master abused him, the pauper apprentice had little hope of redress. The indentures, to give these contracts their proper name, were two-part documents which spelled out the obligations of each side to the bargain. They took their name from the jagged edges made when the sheet of parchment on which they were written was cut in two. If the need arose, the authenticity of the document could be tested by the 'bite' of the 'teeth'. The metaphor is entirely appropriate: indentures closed on master and servant like the jaws of a trap, it was extremely difficult for either party to extract himself unilaterally from his undertakings. The guilds, associations of masters with a monopoly of trade in the ancient chartered towns, had a vested interest in the number of young men recruited to their crafts and the quality of the training they received. Ratepayers slept easier in their beds knowing that the pauper lads were in a master's charge. The state, which was concerned to ensure that young men were kept in check, treated runaway apprentices with exemplary severity, punishing them as vagrants and returning them to their masters.

These contracts spell out the activities and premises from which the apprentice was barred. By contrast, the skills he was expected to acquire and his master's duties as an instructor are described in the most general terms. Trade secrets, or 'mysteries' as they were often called, were not to be betrayed. At the start of an apprenticeship, the youth and his sponsors got the better of the bargain. As the years passed, the balance shifted so that by the end of his time, well able to run a branch of his master's business but still working for no more than his keep, he was a considerable asset. At this stage it was the need to satisfy the requirements of the guilds and achieve the freedom to set up on their own account that kept apprentices in servitude. Young men from the provinces, who came up to London to train rather than to settle, tended to return home before their time was up. At both ends of the process the apprentice was likely to resent the situation in which he found himself. To many young apprentices the menial tasks they were required to perform about the house and in the work place were irksome – they were servants' chores. Young men on the verge of independence watched unhappily as the profits they had made were dropped into their masters' coffers.

In the course of the seventeenth century the proportion of young men who served apprenticeships regulated by guilds declined. At the end of Elizabeth I's reign apprentices made up perhaps 15 per cent of the population of London, by the time Queen Anne came to the throne at the beginning of the eighteenth century no more than 5 per cent of the population of the capital were apprentices. The guilds' power to control entry to their trades was limited to the well-established trades in the ancient boroughs. As new crafts like stocking-knitting were introduced, as new centres of manufacturing grew up in the countryside outside the jurisdiction of the guilds, more young people entered their employers' households without the protection they afforded. However, the declining importance of the guilds did not mark the end of apprenticeship. Individual masters and, later, firms continued to take on apprentices; parishes went on using apprenticeships as a means of getting pauper children off their hands.

## TRAINING: SERVICE

Although the experiences of university students and apprentices are more familiar and better documented, three or four hundred years ago more young men – and the great majority of young women – went into service. In general, male servants came from poorer families. Theoretically, servants were protected by the law of the land but, in practice, authority rarely interfered in the relationship between master and man. The contracts they entered into were shorter than the apprentices'.

Landowners, and better-off townspeople with pretensions to fashion, kept male domestics, most of them adults. The youngest and cheapest was the 'boy' or 'footboy' whose principal outdoor functions were to run errands and escort his master when he was out and about. The anecdotes about William Lilly and Wayneman Birch which appear earlier in this chapter give a flavour of the domestic servants' experience.

Farm servants, servants in husbandry as they were known, were engaged from harvest to harvest. A boy moved on from the kind of casual work described in Chapter 4 to living-in service when the farmer judged that he would get an adequate return on his investment in board and lodgings; money wages were a smaller item in his accounts than these payments in kind. The canny farmer was well aware of the times when his servants sat down to eat without having done a day's work; there was a growing tendency to save money by hiring labour by the day or by the task. Servants found new berths at hiring fairs which were held at the end of the harvest year, at Michaelmas (29 September) in the south and at Martinmas (11 November) further north. The little evidence we have suggests that farm servants moved around a fairly restricted area. Both employers and hired hands seem to have preferred to enter into bargains with people they knew personally or by reputation. Local loyalties were strong in this period, a man's shire was his 'country'. Crops and stock, and with them, the necessary skills varied from region to region.

The longer-term prospects of servants in husbandry were determined in large part by their family background. Those who had expectations of land or money could look forward to setting up on their own account. The stockman had skills which would keep him in work all year round – beasts, like servants, needed to be fed day in, day out. A shepherd could build up a flock. A man who could thatch could also expect to find work outside the haytime and harvest when demand for labour was at its peak. Less fortunate, or less calculating, youths could hope at best to patch together a precarious living as a day labourer. If that did not appeal, they had the option of taking to the road in search of work. With no money and no fixed home, they were liable to be prosecuted for vagrancy.

## MASTERLESS MEN

The powers charged with the maintenance of the social order – the landowners, clergymen, magistrates and substantial landowners – saw a world of difference between, on the one hand, the high-spirited and occasionally unruly apprentices and students, whose masters and tutors stood *in loco parentis* and who would themselves, before long, be metamorphosed into sober householders, and, on the other, the rootless and hopeless who had neither a stake in society nor a master to keep them in check. Acts of Parliament passed in the sixteenth century demonised the masterless man as a rogue, a sturdy beggar who used stealth, menace or actual bodily harm to deprive the law abiding of goods or cash. A well-founded fear of thieves and muggers coloured reactions to the young man on the tramp, dossing down in barns and doorways, picking up an odd day's work and, when he found none, getting by in whatever way he could. Vagrants, men or women on the road or in a strange town or village without the means to pay their way, were liable to be arrested, flogged and despatched to the parish, usually their place of birth, which had responsibility for them. The printing press fed an apparently insatiable appetite for illustrated accounts of the wrongdoings and exemplary punishments of notorious rogues from Nicholas Jennings, an Elizabethan trickster and master of disguise, to Jack Sheppard.

## THE LESS-VISIBLE WOMEN

Rich and well-born brides were, of course, among the glittering prizes awarded to the heroes of chapbook tales but, on the whole, in fact as in fiction, young women are less visible than young men. The chapters of house-holding and old age give examples of widows who successfully managed estates and other family businesses but the assumption was that men would lead and women would back them up, stepping into the breach as the need arose. The law did not recognise a married woman as a person in her own right. The training provided for young women reflected these expectations. Girls were not admitted to the grammar schools, the universities or the Inns of Court; they were not formally trained in law or medicine (though female practitioners, particularly midwives, were common). The range of apprenticeships which girls entered was restricted.

## THE EDUCATION OF THE ELITE

Girls born into a tiny minority of the most culturally pretentious noble and ministerial families in the 1520s and 1530s followed an academic syllabus which closely resembled their brothers' – Elizabeth I was among them. The fashion passed and, even in those decades, many more of the daughters of courtiers, country gentlemen and the merchants and professional men who mimicked aristocratic style as far as it was within their means were brought up to be accomplished rather than learned.

Anne Murray (born 1623), whose father was tutor to Charles I and whose mother was governess to the younger members of the royal family, was educated by 'paid masters' who taught her and her sister 'to write, speak French, play the lute and virginals and dance'. A gentlewoman was 'kept to teach us all kinds of needlework'.

In the opinion of Anne Harrison (born 1625), her 'mother's education of me . . . was with all the advantages that time afforded, both for the making of all sorts of fine works with my needle and learning French, singing, lute, the virginals and dancing'. But sports were her real passion – she 'loved riding in the first place, and running and all active pastimes'; she was 'what we graver people called a hoiting [boisterous, noisy] girl'.

These accounts tally with the printed advice in circulation later in the century. Hannah Woolley, self-styled arbiter in the field of female education, compiled *The Gentlewoman's Companion or Guide to the Female Sex* (1675), which contained 'directions of behaviour in all places companies and conditions from their childhood down to old age'. To Woolley's mind, 'reading furnisheth them with agreeable discourse'; the ill-read 'country gentlewomen' were liable to be overcome in polite company and stand around 'like so many mutes or statues'. And, because 'our English tongue is of late very much refined by borrowing many words from the Latin', women without a smattering of the language were inclined 'to stare about like so many distracted persons', hearing the sound of English spoken by more sophisticated companions and yet recognising only the odd word here and there. For similar reasons, a nodding acquaintance with French and Italian was also desirable. As for writing, Hannah Woolley maintained,

> you should so practise them in their pen as not to be ignorant in a *point de Venise* [a type of lace work] and all the productions of the needle with the obvious devices of wax work, rock work, moss work, cabinet work, bugle work etc. And in due time let them know how to preserve, conserve, distil with all those laudable sciences which adorn a complete gentlewoman.

The repertoire of handicrafts Mrs Woolley decreed appropriate for a young gentlewoman in the late seventeenth century remained current for two hundred years after her death.

Such accomplishments were not necessarily acquired at home. In her mid-teens Hannah Woolley had opened a school before being, by her own account, 'greedily' snapped up by a noblewoman anxious to give her daughter every educational advantage. There were clusters of girls' boarding schools in the villages around London – Bow, Chelsea and Hackney among them – their pupils drew sightseers to the Sunday services in the churches they attended.

The daughters of Catholic landowners like Nicholas Blundell were educated in convents on the Continent. These communities were very much homes-from-home for English girls. Five of Blundell's sisters and most of his aunts were nuns. The nuns and their boarders, or 'pensioners' as Blundell called them, were not cut off from the outside world: friends and relatives visited and 'treated' them to coffee. During his sojourn in Flanders as a refugee from the anti-Catholic reaction which followed the abortive rising in favour of the Stuart pretender James 'III' in 1715, Blundell pottered about the convent grounds and buildings much as he did in his house and gardens in Lancashire, decorating, pruning trees, setting traps for rats and mice. In 1716 he placed his 11-year-old daughter Fanny in the care of his aunt Alice with the Poor Clares at Gravelines; his sister Winnie took charge of 13-year-old Mally, who was settled in the English Benedictine convent at Ghent. The girls remained in Flanders until 1723 when they were brought home – Mally much against her will – to marry and provide their father with a grandson to inherit the estates which had been in the family since the Middle Ages.

## FEMALE APPRENTICESHIP

Few young women were admitted to craft apprenticeships. Taking up an apprenticeship implied an intention to pursue an independent career: women were expected to marry and a majority did. The law observed God's decree that man and wife were 'one flesh'; the bond between them was uniquely potent: her marriage extinguished a woman's legal personality for its duration. Female apprentices were most commonly found in the fashion trades: milliners, who provided women of taste with 'hats, hoods and caps . . . gloves, muffs and ribbons . . . neckaties and ruffles' and mantua-makers, who supplied the loose gowns, without stays, which fashionable ladies wore when they were off-duty relaxing at home with their families and close friends. Apprenticeships to 'the art and skill of housewifery' were a means of providing for a 'poor fatherless child' like Martha Love, who was bound out to an innkeeper from Littleport and his wife in 1695.

## SERVICE

The poultry yard and the dairy were female territory. There was a very limited market for fresh milk before the advent of refrigeration and the heat treatments that prolonged its shelf life: salt butter and cheese were the staple products of the dairy. Of course, like every other household, farms needed women to cook and clean and mend clothes and linen. And, as in other family businesses, the women were called on to give a hand with men's work when the demand for labour was at its peak.

Although the accomplishments Hannah Woolley describes were primarily intended to add lustre to a father's establishment and, in due course, a husband's, almost any young woman, as Woolley emphasised, might be left to fend for herself – 'riches had wings' and the death of her parents could throw a girl on to the reluctant charity of friends and relations. A thoroughly accomplished young woman might seek employment as a 'waiting woman' to 'a person of quality', the wife of a nobleman, for example. As such, she would be expected to 'dress well, preserve well and write a legible hand . . . have some skill in arithmetic'. The broad lines of Woolley's prescription are confirmed in Samuel Pepys' accounts of the duties of his wife's waiting women. Elizabeth Pepys' companions were the daughters of 'decayed merchants' and the like. They accompanied their mistress on shopping trips and went with her to the theatre; they played cards with her; helped her to dress and undress and do her hair – perhaps surprisingly they performed similar services for their master.

Woolley also outlined the qualifications and tasks of chambermaids, nurserymaids and head- and under-cookmaids in prosperous households. In the best households, a chambermaid's primary task was the care of fine and costly linens and lace, which required expert washing, starching and mending. In more modest establishments her duties extended to plain needlework (before there were sewing machines every shirt, shift and sheet was stitched by hand); the more refined branches of cookery – making raised pies, sauces, pickles and garnishes – shopping for the raw materials for meals; and waiting at table.

Woolley warned her readers against the common but mistaken assumption that children are 'easily pleased' and that the nurserymaid's was therefore 'an easy kind of life, void of labour and painstaking'. A nurserymaid should be 'naturally inclined to love young children . . . not churlish or dogged towards them, but merry and pleasant, and contrive and invent pleasant pastimes agreeable to their age, keep their linen things always mended; get their breakfasts and suppers in good and convenient times' and, in particular, 'take heed that they get no falls by your carelessness': children dropped by their nursemaids often grew up 'irrevocably lame or crooked'; the use of prams and pushchairs must have reduced the number of injuries caused by letting babies and small children fall. Woolley had particularly shrewd advice for maidservants of all sorts; cookmaids, for example, were advised to ask for higher wages rather than taking 'cook's perks' in kind, a course that made for bad housekeeping and dishonesty.

Woolley differentiates the responsibilities of the waiting woman, the chambermaid, the nurserymaid and the cookmaid and while these distinctions can be seen in practice in the relative status and rewards they enjoyed, the lines of demarcation were inevitably blurred in times of domestic crisis and when an unmechanised household confronted major chores. The preparations for a great feast, and the infrequent big wash were tasks of this order so too, in the Pepys household in London in the 1660s, for example, was cleaning up the stinking mess left behind by the too often postponed emptying of the privy. And tried and trusted servants like the Pepyses' long-serving maid Jane Birch were given special responsibilities. Threatened by the advance of the Great Fire which swept through London at the beginning of September 1666, Samuel Pepys stripped his house of valuables; their restoration took a good deal of effort. He and Jane were kept up late 'setting' his much prized books in 'perfect order'; Jane, 'whom I have confidence in' was roped in to help him stow away money and plate when the rest of the household was safely asleep.

The diaries of Samuel Pepys, which describe fashionable life in London in the 1660s, and of Nicholas Blundell, which reflect patterns of behaviour in rural Lancashire in the first quarter of the eighteenth century, both suggest that maids moved readily from household to household in search of a more congenial job, higher wages or simply a change of scene. Although there was a suspicion that a maid whose family lived close by might be disposed to be light-fingered, employers preferred to engage maids they knew personally or through the recommendation of a friend or acquaintance. By their husbands' accounts, Elizabeth Pepys and Elizabeth Blundell were both short-tempered women given to sacking their maids or driving them out of the household. Since a very large proportion of her earnings came in kind – food, shelter, cast-off clothes – a young woman who left her place or was dismissed without another to go to ran the risk of using up her savings – Woolley advised young women against putting all their wages on their backs; instead they should 'lay something up against sickness and a hundred other casualties'. Indeed, the 'young wench . . . runaway out of service' to escape a 'sharp mistress' was a type of vagrant familiar from the sensational pamphlets about rogues and vagabonds which became popular with English readers from the 1560s.

Sexual jealousy was high on the list of provocations offered by maidservants to their mistresses. According to Hannah Woolley, every maidservant, even the cookmaid, disfigured by the sweat and grease of the kitchen, had to be on her guard against the lascivious attentions of gentlemen for, 'as hungry dogs . . . eat dirty puddings', 'a brave gallant' might lower himself to seduce 'the wench of the scullery'. Richard Gough, a Shropshire man who wrote *The History of Myddle*, his own parish, at the beginning of the eighteenth century, told the story of Mr Osmary Hill, who

> kept a very flourishing school at his own house, where many gentlemen's sons of good quality were his scholars . . . . He had several daughters, who were servants to gentlemen whose sons were his scholars. He had one daughter who was servant to a gentleman who lived near Wellington, and as this young woman was holding water for her master to wash his hands in the kitchen, he cast a little water from off his finger into her face, which the mistress (who was present) seeing, and conceiving it too familiar an action, she in a rage took up the cleaver, and gave her such a blow on the head that she died.

Entries Samuel Pepys made in his diaries in 1668 and 1669 describing the flowering and harsh ending of his liaison with his wife's waiting woman Deb Willet paint perhaps the frankest picture we have of a romance between a prosperous householder and a young woman in his employ. Pepys describes the consequences of the physical and emotional temptations which beset both him and Deb in this household where the social distance between master and servant was slight. Their story appears in this chapter rather than in the chapter on courtship because the outcome of an affair between a man and his wife's maid was an almost foregone conclusion: discovery and, for the maid, following discovery, dismissal and disgrace.

To protect his privacy, Pepys wrote his diary in shorthand. He further cloaked descriptions of his sexual adventures outside his marriage by his use of 'foreign' words and phrases. From the middle of June 1668, Pepys' editors tell us, the entries 'display the effects of . . . eyestrain . . . . The symbols and lines are more widely spaced, and the handwriting larger . . . . The MS [manuscript] is also less impeccable: the symbols often less neat sometimes incomplete and blots and errors more frequent'.

The entry for Saturday 11 January 1668 ends, 'and then home to supper, and so by the fireside to have my head combed [for lice], as I do now often do, by Deb, who I love should be fiddling about me, and so to bed'. One evening at the end of March Pepys

> called to Deb to take pen, ink and paper and write down what things came into my head for my wife to do, in order to her going into the country; and the girl writing not so well as she would do, cried, and her mistress construed it to be sullenness and so was angry, and I seemed to be angry with her too, but going to bed, she undressed me and there I did give her good advice and beso la [kissed her], ella weeping still and yo did take her, the first time in my life, sobra mi genu [on to my knee] and did poner mi manu sub her jupes [put my hand up her skirts] and loca [touch] her thigh, which did hazer [give] me great pleasure; and so did no more, but besando-la went to my bed.

Early in August, 'This day yo did first with my hand tocar la cosa [touch her "thing"] de our Deb in the coach – ella being troubled at it – but yet did give way to it'.

The presence in the coach of both her mistress and 'an old man, a guide' to the route through Surrey – Pepys was on his way to Portsmouth on Navy Board business – may help to explain her lack of resistance. The pair escaped detection until Sunday 25 October.

> After supper, to have my head combed by Deb, which occasioned the greatest sorrow to me that ever I knew in this world; for my wife coming up suddenly, did find me embracing the girl con my hand sub su coats; and, indeed, I was with my main in her cunny. I was at a wonderful loss upon it, and the girl also.

The gravity of the situation was only too clear. On Monday morning Pepys set off 'by water to Whitehall but with my mind mightily troubled for the poor girl whom I fear I have undone by this, my wife telling me that she would turn her out of door'. Summing up the month, as he habitually did, Pepys wrote of October 1668:

> So ends this month, with some quiet to my mind, after the greatest falling out with my poor wife, and through my folly with the girl, that I ever had; and I have reason to be sorry and ashamed of it – and more to be troubled for the poor girl's sake; whom I fear I shall by this means prove to be the ruin of – though I shall think myself concerned both to love and be a friend to her.

Inevitably Deb left. At the last Elizabeth Pepys prevented her husband from speaking to her or handing over the money he planned to give her. The day Deb went, her master set off

> to the office with my heart sad and I find that I cannot forget the girl and vexed that I know not where to look for her – and more troubled to see how my wife is by this means likely for ever to have her hand over me, that I shall ever be a slave to her.

Deb Willet's subsequent history is not known. Many maidservants out of place found themselves forced into prostitution. Courtship, with marriage as a possible outcome, is the theme of the next chapter.

## FURTHER READING

Beier, A. L. (1985) *Masterless Men: The Vagrancy Problem in England, 1560–1640*, London

Ben-Amos, Ilana Krausman (1994) *Adolescence and Youth in Early Modern England*, New Haven, Conn. and London

Clark, Peter (1983) *The English Alehouse: A Social History, 1200–1830*, London

Kussmaul, Ann (1981) *Servants in Husbandry in Early Modern England*, Cambridge

Thirsk, Joan (1984) 'Younger Sons in the Seventeenth Century' in Joan Thirsk *The Rural Economy of England: Collected Essays*, London

# CHAPTER 6

# Love and the business of marriage

Marriage was, conventionally, the final stage in the metamorphosis from irresponsible youth to adult maturity and, with it, the assumption of the rights and heavy responsibilities of householding. The sorry picture of marital discord between Goodman Tomson and his Goodwife, recorded by John Smyth of Niblet in Gloucestershire in 1639, is evidence of the acknowledgement of distinctions routinely made between the child and the youth and the youth and the married man.

> This Jacky Tomson, so called till sixteen, and after John Tomson, till he married at twenty-four.... After his marriage (humours at home not settling well between him and his wife) he lost his mirth and began to droop .... One of his neighbours ... demanded ... the cause of his bad cheer and heavy looks. Whereto, he sighing, gave this answer: 'Ah neighbour, if once again I were either Jacky Tomson or John Tomson, I would never be Goodman Tomson while I lived'.

At the extremes of society, the conventional link between marriage and setting up a household did not apply. Among the great landed dynasties and the paupers and delinquent poor marriage and the creation of an independent household did not coincide. For the grandee's heir, often married young to secure the succession, the critical event was not marriage but his predecessor's death. In the eyes of their betters, paupers and the delinquent poor never achieved social maturity and were disposed to make imprudent marriages or cohabit without incurring the costs of a church ceremony.

The preacher and writer William Gouge described the married couple as 'yoke-fellows'. To people who regularly saw, and often managed, ploughs and wagons drawn by horses or oxen the image was more telling than it may be today. An ill-matched pair was ungainly, uncomfortable and inefficient; they made heavy work of their joint task. In a letter to his wife, Dudley Ryder (born 1691), a merchant's son and, at the time of writing, a senior law officer of the Crown, described the relationship between man and wife, using comparable images drawn from the world of business:

> I look upon matrimony, as it really is, not only as a society for life in which our persons and fortunes in general are concerned, but as a partnership wherein

our very passions and affections, our hopes and fears, our inclinations and aversions, all our good and ill qualities are brought into one common stock.

According to the laws of Church and state, marriage created a relationship between man and wife which was exclusive and dissoluble only by death. The roles were complementary: a woman was her husband's other half. Their union was life long and took priority over any other tie including the bond between parent and child. Therefore, as Gouge put it, in order 'that matrimonial society may prove comfortable, it is requisite that there should be some equality betwixt the parties that are married in age, estate [wealth], condition [rank], piety', as well as 'mutual liking'. And indeed in practice, for the devout, piety had an important place in the checklist of requisites alongside rank and wealth. The inscriptions in the sample of seventeenth- and eighteenth-century wedding rings displayed in the Ashmolean Museum in Oxford emphasise God's part in making marriages: 'To God's decree we both agree', 'None can prevent the Lord's intent', 'Providence divine hath made thee mine', 'God's decree well pleaseth me' are typical of the sentiments.

The minister John Angier (born 1604) was among the godly men and women who accepted that divine providence shaped his life. In 1628 he married Ellen Winstanley (born 1605). As his son-in-law and biographer Oliver Heywood expressed it: 'it pleased God to knit Mr Angier's heart to her and hers to him'. God, as Angier would have acknowledged, works mysteriously – the Angiers' life was marred by Ellen's 'troubled spirit'. 'Being of a melancholy constitution, Satan took great advantage in casting his darts into combustible matter, which occasioned much affliction both to herself and to her husband'.

Ellen died just as the Civil War broke out,

> giving intimation to her husband who it was she desired might succeed her, which in convenient time he complied with and about a year after did marry her. It was Margaret Mosley of Ancoats, a very prudent, gracious gentlewoman. They were married very publicly in Manchester Church in the heat of the wars, which was much taken notice of as a great act of faith.

The church's register supports Heywood's story: in 1641, ninety-three marriages were recorded in the church, in 1642, sixty and in 1643 only eighteen.

Concern about unequal marriages led Charles I to write to the Vice-Chancellor of the University of Cambridge and the heads of the Cambridge colleges in 1630, no doubt at their prompting, to reinforce the University's old 'charters against women *de malo suspectas* [of ill fame]'.

> Whereas we have been informed that, of late years, many students of that our university, not regarding their own birth, degree and quality, have made divers contracts of marriage with women of mean estates and of no good fame in that town to their great disparagement, the discontentment of their friends and parents and the dishonour of the government of that our university,

in future:

> If any taverner, innholder or victualler or any other inhabitant of the town or
> within the jurisdiction of the university, shall keep any daughter or other
> woman in his house to whom there shall resort any scholar of the university
> of what condition whatsoever to misspend their time or otherways misbehave
> themselves, or to engage themselves in marriage without the consent of those
> who have the guardiance and tuition of them

if, after due investigation, the charges were confirmed, the offending woman
was to be banished. If she refused to go, she was liable to be summoned
before the Lords of the Privy Council for contempt.

For good measure graduates were also banned from frequenting taverns
and other places of entertainment 'to eat, or drink, or play or take tobacco
to the misspending of their time and to the corrupting of others by their ill
example'.

Three or four hundred years ago, therefore, the choice of a husband or
wife was a decision of the utmost significance for the individuals concerned,
for their families and for the wider community. The personal qualities,
material resources, social, economic and political connections that a partner brought to the marriage influenced individual and family fortunes to
an extent that is inconceivable today. In many occupations, marriage was
a business partnership. Let one instance from the lower margins of society
serve to illustrate the proposition: the petty criminals who populated the
London underworld in the early eighteenth century commonly operated
in what were, or amounted to, man-and-wife teams: male thieves relied on
female accomplices to handle the goods they had stolen.

Parishes, the building blocks of English society, were composed of households, themselves societies in miniature. Since marriages gave rise to the
great majority of households, well-regulated families were the foundations
of the social order. As William Gouge argued, 'good members of a family
are likely to be good members of church and commonwealth'.

## AGE AT MARRIAGE

Since the end of the Second World War historians' understanding of the
timing of marriages in Elizabethan and Stuart England has changed dramatically. Until the 1960s it was believed that, three or four hundred years
ago, many people married very young. G. M. Trevelyan, a historian with
a great gift for conveying a sense of the past to a wide readership and to
listeners to the BBC, summarised the conventional picture of courtship and
marriage:

> The love marriage was more frequent by the end of the Tudor period, but child
> marriage were still all too common: in this matter the reformed church was at
> first as much in fault as the mediaeval. In 1582 Bishop Chaderton married off

his only daughter, Joan, aged nine to a boy of eleven. The result was bad. On another occasion John Ridmarden, aged three, was married in the arms of a clergyman who coaxed him to repeat the words of matrimony to a bride of five. Before the end he struggled to get down, saying he would learn no more that day; but the parson said, 'You must speak a little more and then go play you'. . .

Among the poor, it is probable that marriage choice had always been less clogged by mercenary motives. We have but slight evidence on the subject, but we may presume that among the peasantry . . . Dick and Nan walked together in the wood and afterwards to church for reason of love liking, added to the belief that Nan would make a good mother and housewife, and that Dick was a good workman, or 'had a pig put up in the sty'. . . . Marriage to legalise the consequences of incontinence was exceedingly common especially in the lower ranks of society where maidens could not be so carefully guarded at all hours.

These assumptions were not unfounded. They were based on evidence of court cases heard in the diocese of Chester between 1561 and 1566 and published by F. J. Furnivall in 1897 under the title *Child Marriages and Divorces*: about the ages at which aristocrats' heirs were married; and, as Trevelyan makes clear, on the plots of plays and stories – Shakespeare made Juliet 13.

The very different picture universally accepted today – that the majority of first marriages involved couples in their middle twenties – is a product of the painstaking work of a group of Cambridge-based historians who organised the collection of many thousands of entries in parish registers, analysed the returns made by a huge team of volunteer recorders and published the results of the joint enterprises in articles and books designed for fellow academics, individuals researching the history of their own family or community and the general readership of students and others interested in the everyday experience of past generations.

The project mounted by the Cambridge Group for the History of Population and Social Structure focused on the registers of a tiny fraction of parishes – fewer than 5 per cent of the total – which had been well kept over a very long stretch of time. Local studies covering shorter time spans have qualified the broad statistical picture. Christopher Haigh's work on Tudor Lancashire, published in 1975, confirmed that child marriages were indeed common in landowners' families in the north-west of England: 'it would be possible to quote large numbers'. A study of the London marriage market at the beginning of the seventeenth century has uncovered revealing variations in the ages of brides. Like landowners, wealthy Londoners married their daughters young, often in their late teens, and normally, of course, to men of their own rank, who expected the bride's family to supply her with a handsome dowry. The marriages of young women who had come into London to work and depended for their dowry on their own savings were postponed until they were in their middle twenties; their husbands-to-be were much the same age, often not long out of their apprenticeships and looking for a partner to manage their household and support them in their trade.

## MIXING AND MATCHING

The expectation that the rank, resources, values and occupational background of a couple should be compatible narrowed the field from which an appropriate choice of wife or husband might be made. Parents and masters who stood *in loco parentis* to young unmarried men and women – their students, apprentices and servants – sought to prevent contacts which might lead to clandestine courtship. In practice it was difficult. The majority of the small population of undergraduates lodged in single-sex colleges or hostels but most other young people living under their parents' or their masters' roofs encountered potential partners indoors as well as in the neighbourhood in the normal course of their daily lives: other members of the household, visitors or customers. Servants made acquaintances while running errands, fetching water, marketing. The sons and daughters of the very great met in London, in and around the court. The families of lesser landowners participated in the seasons of social events which grew up in London and the county towns in the later seventeenth century. None of these environments was effectively policed by responsible adults.

Then there were the opportunities afforded by local high days and holidays: weddings, the many days of celebration during the Christmas season, Shrovetide, Easter, May Day and Whitsun; the parish feasts and fairs. (Richard Baxter thundered against 'voluptuous youths that run after wakes and May games and dancings and revellings'. Dancing which provided opportunities for groping, kissing and dishonest embracing was the target of much godly disapproval.) Roger Lowe's diary, written in the 1660s, reminds us of another perennial chance for a young woman to encourage a potential suitor. Margaret Wright, a maidservant, persuaded Lowe to see her home – 'I went and she made much of me', he noted with satisfaction.

A description of a Twelfth Day party attended by the sons and daughters of prosperous and respectable London tradesmen in 1716 suggests a very free and easy atmosphere. As Dudley Ryder noted, the young people, friends and cousins, 'passed the afternoon and evening at cards during which we were very merry'; the young men kissed their partners 'very much'. Then they 'played at blind man's buff and puss in the corner' and 'more kissing' went on. Ryder's brother William had a particular way with 'the contrary sex'. He talked with them

> with the greatest freedom but without any guard upon his tongue. His talk with them is prodigiously silly and sometimes a blunt thing comes out from him that is affronting and yet, by what I can perceive, though they despise him for his parts, they love his company because he is free with them and kisses and tumbles them about and makes a mighty noise with them.

For these young men, at least with women of their own rank, kissing seems to have been the limit to which propriety would stretch. When sexually aroused, as he was by a discussion with male friends about 'the inclination of women to venery [lust]' and polygamy, Ryder sought out prostitutes in the street on his way home: 'I was so raised with our discourse about women that I was extremely inclined that way and looked for a whore with a resolution not to lie with her but to feel her if I could'. Feeling rather than intercourse seems to have been his habit on such occasions. Self-reproach followed.

The dazzling possibility of securing a glittering marital prize blinded some young women (and occasionally their parents) to the odds against pregnancy trapping a lover into matrimony. Sarah, Duchess of Marlborough recounted the sad and salutary tale of Mary Trevor, a maid of honour at Charles II's court, whose mother persuaded her

> to trust Mr Thynne and go to bed with him because he said he would not marry anybody till he knew whether he could have a child. This design succeeded but he did not keep his word. And I saw myself this woman go out of the gallery where the maids lived with infamy, wringing her hands and saying her mother had undone her by her advice.

Mrs Trevor may have had in mind the eventual triumph of Anne Hyde, who twenty years or so earlier had allowed herself to be seduced by James Duke of York, the King's brother on the strength of a written promise of marriage. When James attempted to back on his word, the King had held him to it. Of course, Anne Hyde had the advantage over poor Mary Trevor of an influential father, the King's chief minister, Lord Clarendon. Servant girls, their judgement clouded by sweet talk, sweetmeats or other trivial gifts, were most susceptible to the blandishments of men of superior rank.

The scanty evidence which survives suggests that the degree of physical intimacy customarily permitted to courting couples was most generous among the plebeians, but a woman whose 'quiver was open to every arrow' would have met disapproval at every social level. Chapbooks, which had a wide circulation among hearers as well as readers, and which often take young plebeians as their heroes and heroines, give the impression that all was well as long as lovers were seriously committed to each other and married in the end. Take, for example, the conclusion of the story of the courtship of the apprentice William and his sweetheart Susan, who was a serving maid:

> So being night they went to bed
> Not making any strife
> He did obtain her maidenhead
> Before she was his wife
> But afterwards they married were
> As lovers ought to do
> And now they live at heart's content
> And long may they do so.

## THE CHOICE OF A MATE

For property owners, marriage was the occasion for a substantial transfer of wealth between families and between generations. The dowry a bride brought into her husband's family was balanced by the pension in cash or kind which a widow was entitled to draw from his estate. Too much rode upon the marriages of the heirs and daughters of property owners to permit them a free choice of wife or husband. Mercenary and dynastic considerations often took precedence over the personal preferences of the younger generation. The square footage of parchment covered by the contracts spelling out the terms of marriage settlements expanded in the course of the seventeenth century as their terms became more elaborate. Their physical size serves as a testament to the scale and significance of the transfers of property which hung on the marriages of inheriting sons and daughters of major landowning families.

The landowner's heir was married young to a young bride with the intention of securing the succession, to augment the family's fortunes and cement alliances, and to protect the family's interests from the hazards associated with a landowner's premature death. Until 1641, when Charles I, under acute pressure from critics of his policies, yielded up this and other unpopular prerogatives in a successful attempt to buy off some of his more moderate opponents, the custody of heirs under the age of 21 and of unmarried heiresses, regardless of age, passed to the Crown, which exploited their wardship as a source of revenue. Guardians had the right to profit from the marriage of their wards, provided that the proposed match was *absque disparagatione*, without disparagement, or to put it positively, provided that the match was fitting. Impediments included mental and physical disabilities; being too young or too old to have children; inferior birth – a comprehensive category embracing bastards, foreigners and, in women, those who had lost their virginity. Prerogative wardship encouraged speculation on the outcome of fathers' illnesses: in Elizabeth I's reign John Symons petitioned his employer, the Master of the Court of Wards, Lord Burghley, for the grant of a ward to replace one who had slipped from his grasp, the son of John Gascoigne, who had been 'in some extremity of sickness' but had, to Symons' dismay, 'recovered'.

To argue, as some historians have done, that landowners became progressively more sympathetic to their children's wishes is to oversimplify a complex picture. Parents' priorities varied and changed. Richard Boyle (born 1566), the first Earl of Cork, a self-made man who won his fortune unscrupulously in Ireland, was determined to see his daughters peeresses (he provided them with dowries generous enough to compensate for their undistinguished ancestry). Alice married Viscount Barrymore, Sarah Lord Moore's eldest son and then, a widow at 14, Lord Digby; Joan's husband was the Earl of Kildare. Their marriages were an integral element in his strategy to implant himself and his heirs into the aristocracy. But, having achieved a number of satisfactory alliances, he was prepared to yield, with an ill grace, to his seventh daughter Mary's sustained resistance to the match proposed for her and eventually allowed her to throw herself away on an earl's younger son. Mary (born 1625) was intended for Lord Clandeboye's heir. She stubbornly refused to engage herself to him. As her father wrote in November 1639:

> My daughter Mary did this day, as she had many times before, declare a very high averseness and contradiction to our counsels and commands, touching [concerning] her marriage with James Hamilton, the only child of the Lord Viscount of Clandeboye, although myself and all my sons and daughters . . . and all other her best friends, did effectively entreat and persuade her thereunto and I command.

Note the distinction Cork makes between the influence of friends and the authority of a father.

'For her disobedience in not marrying Mr James Hamilton' her father 'detained [his] promised allowance' and for over a year 'gave her not one penny'. She got, defiantly, into debt. Accepting defeat, the Earl came up with a number of other 'great and advantageous offers' but in the meanwhile Mary had been introduced to Charles Rich, the Earl of Warwick's younger son, by her brother Francis' new wife, who had been a maid-in-waiting to the Queen. As Mary's acquaintance with Charles Rich ripened, she 'began with some seriousness to consider what I was engaging myself in'. Her father, she knew, would 'never endure it'. And she recognised that she was

> too expensively brought up . . . to live contentedly with Mr Rich's fortune. . . . Upon these considerations I was convinced that it was time for me to give him a flat and final denial . . . but when I was upon readiness to open my mouth to utter these words, my great kindness for him stopped it . . . which convinced to me the great and real possession he had of my heart.

Mary adopted a compromise position. Though she would not marry without her father's consent, she was 'resolved not to marry any other person in the world' if she could not have Charles Rich. The Earl of Cork capitulated. He offered to 'see and be civil to Mr Rich' and accept him as a son-in-law. As a punishment for her stubbornness, Mary's dowry was docked.

Parents who had themselves made love matches did not necessarily favour them for the next generation. Rachel Wriothesley took a younger son as her second husband but, in her widowhood, she proved hard-headed when it came to settling the futures of her three children. Born in 1637, Rachel Wriothesley was left a childless widow when her first husband, the Earl of Carbery's heir, died of the plague in 1667. Her father's death a couple of months later made her one of the greatest prizes in England. Her portion of his estates, shared out by lot with her two sisters included Bloomsbury, as yet undeveloped. As a wealthy widow without a father or brother to interfere, she had an unusually free choice. She fell in love with William Russell, the Earl of Bedford's younger son, and married him apparently uninhibited by the disparity in their fortunes – though she cannily safeguarded her financial interests. The bulk of her property remained outside his control thanks to a trust drawn up to preserve it for her use. Lady Russell's letters to her husband contain some of the most delightful snapshots of family life in seventeenth-century England. In 1677 she wrote:

> Miss Rachel [their elder daughter, born in 1674] has prattled a long story but Watkins [the house steward] calls for my letter so I must omit it. She says papa has sent for her to Wobee [Woburn] and then she gallops and says she has been there, and a great deal more; but boiled oysters call, so my story must rest.

And in 1681: 'Boy asleep, girls singing abed'.

This evidently very happy marriage did not convince Lady Russell that she should encourage or permit her children to marry for love. They were married young and all the evidence suggests that they were passive pawns in their mother's strategy; she had a reputation as a tough negotiator. Of one potential father-in-law, she wrote: 'I have a well-bred lord to deal with yet inflexible, if the point is not to his advantage'.

Rachel (born 1674) was married off to the Earl of Devonshire's heir in 1688; Katherine (born 1676) to the Earl of Rutland's heir in 1693 and the heir to his grandfather's estates and titles, Wriothesley (born 1680), to Elizabeth Howland, a great mercantile heiress in 1695. Indeed Wriothesley's marriage was one of those cited by Trevelyan as evidence of the persistence of the cynical trade in child marriage. It may be that as an older mother (she was nearly 60 when Wriothesley married) Lady Russell was particularly concerned to settle her son and daughters early and well. She had the satisfaction of seeing her three children achieve ducal rank.

Business and professional families also invested heavily in their children's marriages. Prudence dictated that merchants, lawyers and medical men should defer their marriages until they were established in their trades or professions and that they should ally themselves with women whose dowries would add, as Dudley Ryder phrased it, to the 'common stock'. Ryder (born 1691), who kept a shorthand diary from June 1715 to December 1716, was the second son of a prosperous linen draper. He was educated at the Universities of Edinburgh and Leyden – as a dissenter he was excluded from the English universities. During the period covered by his surviving diaries he was a law student living at home in London. Marriage is a running motif of the entries. In August 1716 Ryder and his cousin Joseph Billio

> talked about matrimony and agreed in this that the sorrows and cares and burdens to which it exposes a man don't seem to be sufficiently balanced by the joys and pleasures one can expect from it. I wish I could reason myself into an easy state of mind under the thoughts of being never married, but I feel a strong inclination towards it, not from any principle of lust or desire to enjoy a woman in bed but for a natural tendency, a prepossession in favour of the

married state. It is charming and moving, it ravishes me to think of a pretty creature concerned in me, being my most intimate friend, constant companion and always ready to soothe me, take care of me and caress me.

Ryder had clear views about the qualities desirable in a wife: her temper should be 'meek, humble and modest', she should be prudent and affectionate, 'capable of advising with and consulting upon any difficulty or occurrence'. But he was swept away on a tide of infatuation. In April 1716, riding alongside the coach which was taking his sister on the first stage of her journey to Bath, Ryder set eyes on Mistress Sally Marshall for the first time. (Mistress is a courtesy title, denoting her rank not her marital status; she was the daughter of a reasonably well-off Highgate tailor.) He was immediately and agreeably struck by her appearance and 'therefore kept as close to the coach side as possible and took all the opportunities I could of looking into the coach and talking to her. . . . The more I looked, the more I felt myself moved and pleased with her looks and it was something of a pleasure to me now and then to meet her eyes and catch them turned upon me'.

Prudent though he set out to be, Ryder was hooked. In August he rehearsed a proposal of marriage in his diary:

> I thought I would talk to her in this manner – 'Madam, when a man is really in earnest and serious in his addresses, it is all in vain to make a great many protestations and use many words to declare his love. I come now to tell you that I think you the most agreeable woman living and have ever since my acquaintance with you been extremely touched with your beauty. I have had an opportunity of not only seeing your person, which has all the charms one could wish or imagine, but I have often with a great deal of delight and pleasure observed an extraordinary prudence and good humour and good sense in you and whatever qualities are useful to make a man happy in your affection and possession'.

Dudley Ryder was, nevertheless, aware that, as a man hardly even yet on the threshold of his career, his 'circumstance were not proper at all for matrimony'. If Mistress Marshall had 'but a small fortune it would ruin me to marry her, keep me low in the world and prevent my rise. And if she has a considerable fortune, her father would never consent that I should have her without a proportionate fortune'. The cost of setting his brother William up as a married man had depleted their father's savings and seemed likely to 'quite destroy' his own prospects of marriage in the foreseeable future. His father, well informed about the Marshall family's relatively modest resources and equally aware of the cost of establishing a household, was, none the less willing to 'make up the match with Mr Marshall' if Dudley 'was so deeply engaged in love as to interrupt my study or that I could not be easy without her'. In the event Dudley Ryder determined to wrestle with his emotions; he waited until he was well into his forties and an eminent lawyer before he finally took a wife.

It would be unwise to assume that calculation was a peculiarity of landowners and their dowagers or men of business. Travelling in Essex at the start of the eighteenth century, Daniel Defoe picked up the tale of the much-married men of Benfleet and the other malaria-ridden parishes in the Essex marshes. According to their own version ('they fibbed a little'), cynical men married women not 'seasoned' to the 'fogs and damps' of the marshlands and might bury anything between a credible five and an improbable fifteen wives, pocketing a dowry with every victim. Cynicism was not a male prerogative. In 1562 Ellen Gardiner, pregnant and unmarried, uncertain of the child's paternity, was reported to have told an acquaintance how she intended to provide for herself and the coming baby: 'Clare hath a house and Holt hath none, therefore Clare shall be the father of my child'.

Adam Martindale was only a young boy when his eldest brother jilted a woman of substance and went to the altar with 'a wild airy girl' who brought a much smaller portion with her. The stir caused by this apparently irrational act stuck in Martindale's mind. The first choice:

> had seven-score pounds [£140] to her portion (as I have often heard) of very suitable years and otherwise likely to make an excellent wife. But, when things were near accomplishing, he on a sudden slights her, and sets his affection upon a young, wild, airy girl, between fifteen and sixteen years of age, an huge lover and frequenter of wakes . . . and merry-nights where music and dancing abounded. And, as for her portion, it was only £40. This was a great surprise upon us, and we were all full bent against it. I was then under ten years old but was, either of myself, or by impression of others, apprehensive of the difference between these two matches. But say and do what we could, he was uncounsellable, have her he would, and at last with much ado, procured my father's unwilling consent and married her. 'Tis true indeed she proved above all expectation . . . an exceeding good wife.

The diary which Roger Lowe, an apprentice mercer (dealer in textiles), of Ashton-in Makerfield in Lancashire, kept in the 1660s, gives us a picture of courtship in which prudence and calculation generally seem to play a less significant part than liking. But in this community too, among young people who could expect to become householders of substance within their communities, examples of formal matchmaking can be found. Ellin Marsh, a local woman who 'had a house and a living' of her own, identified Lowe among the field of potential husbands and engaged 'a private mediator to intercede' with him on her behalf. However, it may be that Lowe's diary tells us more about him as an individual than about seventeenth-century Lancashire apprentices in general. William Stout, who was born in the 1660s and apprenticed to a Lancaster ironmonger when he was in his teens, took a profoundly cautious attitude to marriage. He remained a bachelor and used his wealth to reward those of his nieces and nephews who made prudent marriages.

When Roger Lowe's diary opens, Mary Naylor was the object of his affections. May 1663 'was the first night' that ever 'he stayed up a-wooing in his life'. (Occasional references to night-courting suggest that sitting up late or even cuddling up in bed, usually under the watchful eyes of friends or relatives, was one of the ways in which young plebeian couples got to know each other.) In the courtship of Roger Lowe and Mary Naylor, there were frequent fallings-out and reconciliations. On 8 May Mary 'said she would have nothing to do with me, and was highly displeased with me, but in conclusion she was pleased'. A month later the couple 'engaged to be faithful unto death'. In July they still appeared to be of one mind: 'Said she, "Am I not a wise wench to engage myself thus?"'. Lowe's affections 'ran out violently after her' and he was 'never contented' unless he saw Mary every day. There was, however, another serious contender for his hand, as he indicated in his entry for 13 November 1663.

> I was at this time in a very fair way for pleasing my carnal self for I knew myself acceptable with Em Potter, not withstanding my love was entire to Mary Naylor in respect of my vow to her and I was in hopes that her father countenanced me in the thing.

Em did indeed succeed Mary Naylor as his sweetheart. Their romance ran no more smoothly: Em had another admirer and, in 1666, Lowe noted, she expressed misgivings about the damaging rumour that 'my mother bore me a bastard'. There is no record of his marriage but the circumstantial evidence suggests that it was Em Potter who eventually became his wife. The skill and concern which she showed in nursing Lowe when he was taken ill early in their acquaintance may have helped to persuade him that she would make a reliable partner. In his case too, caution had a part to play when the time came to settle down.

Below the level of the literate village craftsman, evidence of courtship is likely to come from hostile witnesses – the ratepayers (including the parson) who regarded the wives and children of irregularly employed labouring men as an almost certain charge upon their pockets. Nevertheless, as the example of thieves and fences quoted earlier in the chapter suggests, those at the margins of society looked for partners they could rely on.

## UNEQUAL MATCHES

Mary Boyle, in matching herself with Charles Rich, and Rachel Wriothesley, in matching herself with William Russell, went against William Gouge's precept that there 'should be some equality betwixt the parties that are married' in respect of wealth. Their husbands were, however, broadly similar in rank and age. Some marriages were made in absolute defiance of propriety.

William Lilly's account of the courtship which led to his first marriage gives us some idea of the motivations, manoeuvrings and anticipated reactions associated with the making of an unequal match. William Lilly (born 1602) was a grammar school boy whose father's poverty forced him into menial service in London. He had done well there; before he was 25 his conscientious service in the household of Gilbert Wright (died 1627) had earned him an annuity of £20, an income much greater than a servant could expected to receive in wages. However, his wife to be, Wright's widow, whose given name we do not know, was older, much richer, his employer. Lilly's description of the steps which led to their marriage is revealing:

> My mistress had been twice married to old men . . . she was of a brown ruddy complexion, corpulent but of mean stature, plain, no education, yet a very provident person . . . . She had many suitors, old men, whom she declined [the implication is that she was looking for a sexually-satisfying union]; some gentlemen of decayed fortunes, whom she liked not, for she was covetous and sparing. By my fellow servant [evidently a woman] she was observed frequently to say, she cared not if she married a man that would love her, so that he had never a penny; and would ordinarily talk of me when she was in bed. This servant gave me encouragement.

But he was in a dilemma:

> I was much perplexed hereat, for should I attempt her and be slighted, she would never care for me afterwards. But again, I considered that if I should attempt and fail, she would never speak of it. [N]or would any believe I durst be so audacious as to propound such a question, the disproportion of years and fortune being so great betwixt us. However, all her talk was of husbands, and in my presence saying one day after dinner, she respected not wealth, but desired an honest man, I made answer, I thought I could fit her with such a husband. She asked me, 'Where?' I made no more ado but presently [straightaway] saluted [kissed] her and told her myself was the man. She replied I was too young. I say, 'Nay'. What I had not in wealth, I would supply in love; and saluted her frequently which she accepted lovingly; and the next day at dinner made me sit down with my hat on my head [a privilege reserved for the mostly highly ranked man present] and said she intended to make me her husband. For which I gave her many salutes . . . .
> I was very careful to keep all things secret, for I well knew, if she should take counsel of any friend, my hopes should be frustrated therefore I suddenly procured her consent to marry, unto which she assented so that upon the 8th day of September 1627 [less than four months after her former husband's death] at St George's Church in Southwark, I was married unto her, and for two whole years we kept it secret.

According to Lilly, the marriage turned out well and 'during all the time of her life, which was until October 1633' they 'lived very lovingly'.

Early in the 1670s Gilbert Burnett (born 1643), the son of a Scots lawyer, married Lady Margaret Kennedy, eighteen years his senior and the daughter of an earl. They too kept their marriage secret for a long time. In his autobiography Burnett described how 'Lady Margaret, being young and in a frolic of divination by letter, GB came up to her as the letters of her husband's name'. Long after, in her middle forties, as she explained to Burnett after their marriage, this 'had gone a great way to determine her to it'.

## TYING THE KNOT

A marriage could be made with remarkable ease. From the Middle Ages until the English laws of matrimony were finally clarified in 1753 all it took was for an eligible couple to exchange a solemn promise phrased in the present tense. Proposals for a radical revision of the law of marriage surfaced several times in the second half of the sixteenth century but all that came of them were the Canons of 1604 which, in theory, required parental consent for marriage under the age of 21 or by licence. However, even such marriages contracted without parental consent were, in law, irregular rather than invalid.

William Gouge defined 'the things which are absolutely necessary to make a person fit for marriage with another': 'being of the same kind' – a human being could not marry an animal; 'of the contrary sex' – male or female; 'beyond the degree of consanguinity and affinity' – the ties of blood and marriage – 'forbidden by the Law of God . . . and explained in the table appointed to be hung up in every church'; 'of age' – legally 12 for girls and 14 for boys; and 'free: nor married nor betrothed to another'. Gouge underlined the binding nature of betrothal: 'So firm is a contract as the law calleth a betrothed maid a wife'. However, a 'handfast' marriage, based on a private undertaking, although binding, was unsatisfactory in the eyes of the Church and the secular courts. A regular marriage, in a church before witnesses, created legal rights and responsibilities: the wife's property and income passed into her husband's control; he was responsible for her debts. None of this applied to handfasted couples.

There are, nevertheless, accounts of couples exchanging private vows. In 1566 John Brotherton engaged himself in marriage with these words, 'I take thee, Alice, to be my wife, and none other woman, God help me, and the contents of this book [the Bible]'. Alice was not satisfied with this formula so John elaborated: 'Here I take thee, Alice Ince, to be my wife, before all other women. So God me help and holidame [Our Lady], and by this book'. And kissed the book, holding her hand still in his.

At Romford in 1607 William Jefferson was the involuntary witness of the handfasting of Richard Harrison and Anne Bayle. As Jefferson recalled it, Harrison said: 'Anne, I, before this man, do take thee to my wedded wife, forsaking all other, keeping myself to thee, as long as we both shall live'. Anne responded in similar terms and then 'in confirmation of the said contract . . . he the said Richard did give and deliver unto the said Anne an angel of gold [a coin] as a pledge, as he had betwixt them'.

To mark their betrothal, suitors normally gave their brides-to-be keepsakes according to their condition and estate. Two halves of a penny, one kept and one given, were tokens of the unity to come. Rings, beads and combs were popular and available at prices to suit any pocket.

In contrast to the private handfasting, a regular marriage was the outcome of a public process as befitted what Gouge called a 'public action' by which 'families are erected and church and commonwealth increased and continued'. Though not 'absolutely necessary', a public betrothal before 'sufficient witnesses' was the desirable beginning of a marriage. Gouge offered his readers a script:

> First the man taking the woman by the hand to say: I A take thee B to my espoused wife, and do faithfully promise to marry thee in time meet and convenient. And then the woman again taking the man by the hand to say: I B take thee A to be my espoused husband and do faithfully promise to yield to be married to thee in time meet and convenient.

An interval between the betrothal and the wedding allowed time to draw up any legal settlement that was needed and to assemble the appropriate resources for the new couple's household: a roof, a bed and a cooking pot were the barest essentials. When the 'time meet and convenient' arrived, the banns were called three times in the churches in the parishes to which the parties belonged on days, usually Sundays, when a good congregation could to be expected to hear the announcement and to bring to light any impediment to the marriage. Although poverty was not a legal bar to marriage, in some parishes the very poor found it hard to persuade the parson to call the banns or perform the wedding ceremony, as a woman from Nether Compton in Dorset discovered in 1628. The incumbent noted: 'She hath no house not home of her own and very likely to bring charge on the parish, and therefore will hardly be suffered to marry in our parish'.

It was common, especially in better-off families, to avoid the calling of banns by obtaining a bishop's licence to marry without banns. On 18 April 1637

> There appeared personally Richard Cooke, of the parish of Cirencester, innholder, before the right worshipful Francis Baber, Doctor of Laws and Chancellor of the diocese of Gloucester, and alleged that there is a marriage intended between Robert Heath of the same diocese, singleman, and Margaret Cooke of the [parish of] Siddington in the diocese of Gloucester, aged 25 years or thereabouts. And saith further that there is no lawful let or impediment by reason of any precontract, consanguinity or affinity to hinder this intended marriage. They have the consent of their parents thereto. Of the truth of which promises he maketh faith.

The public solemnisation, the final stage of a regular marriage, which took place in the presence of an officiating priest and witnesses, combined 'a religious consecration' and 'a civil celebration'. A record of the marriage was entered into the parish register.

A comparison of marriage and baptismal registers demonstrates that, in many parishes, one in five of the plebeian women who married between

1600 and 1640 were pregnant. Trevelyan's words imply that parsons and prospective in-laws had very often to chivvy reluctant grooms to the altar. Today, historians are more inclined to interpret prenuptial pregnancy as evidence of the solemnity and force of the betrothal. Betrothed women, who, after all, faced severe penalties if they gave birth to a bastard child, made love and risked pregnancy confident that the public process of marriage would be completed. Sometimes, of course, their plans went wrong; the young man died, left the area involuntarily or changed his mind late in the affair. Disapproving parsons, supported by ratepayers whose pockets bore the cost of supporting any woman whose confidence proved misplaced, used prosecutions for fornication to put pressure on the marriageable members of the community. Couples who brought their first child to the font within six or eight months of their marriage faced the prospect of confessing their sin in the parish church, possibly before their neighbours, perhaps clad only in the white sheet of penitence, plus a hefty fine. Women who bore bastard children were liable to be whipped, both as a punishment for immorality and as a warning to other young women disposed to follow their example. For such women, the prospects of marriage were poor.

Although regular marriage came to prevail over handfast unions in face-to-face village communities, there was a continuing demand from poorer artisans, sailors between voyages and runaway couples for a valid form of marriage which was cheap, quick to arrange and discreet. Marriages performed by a clergyman without banns or bishop's licence, clandestine marriages as they were called, passed the lawyers' test. A handful of English churches claimed a traditional right of issuing marriage licences on their own authority, without reference to the diocesan courts: it has been calculated that in the fifty years between the 1640s and the 1690s more than 70,000 marriages took place at two London churches where this ancient privilege was asserted. Legislation, primarily designed to raise taxes for a war against France by introducing a tax on marriage licences, put a stop to this activity. The clergy involved in the practice balked at the prospect of paying a heavy fine at the first conviction for officiating at a wedding, followed by suspension from office for the second offence. The trade in clandestine weddings, simply shifted to the neighbourhood of the debtors' prison, the Fleet, where thousands took place every year under the protection of the prison authorities before the law of marriage was finally put into order when Hardwicke's Act came into force in 1754.

Regardless of the legal situation, in the view of the community a wedding was incomplete without a party. Perhaps surprisingly, John Angier (born 1605), whose biographer depicted him as a model for the godly life, shared the view.

> When his daughter was married to a Yorkshire minister [his biographer, Oliver Heywood] they were contracted in the close of a solemn day of fasting and prayer in his study. . . . And about a month after that they were solemnly mar-

ried before a numerous congregation . . . and then feasted above a hundred persons of several ranks, ages and sexes. He usually said he loved to have a marriage like a marriage.

Henry Best, writing in Yorkshire in 1641, described the 'fashions at our country weddings'. Once the wedding day was fixed:

> which may be about a fortnight or three weeks after . . . they get made the wedding clothes, and make provisions against the wedding dinner, which is usually at the maid's father's. Their use is to buy gloves to give to each of their friends a pair on that day; the man should be at the cost for them; but some-times the man gives gloves to the men, and the woman to the women, or else he to her friends and she to his; they give them that morning when they are almost ready to go to church to be married. Then so soon as the bride is tired [attired; dressed], and that they are ready to go forth, the bridegroom comes and takes her by the hand and saith, 'Mistress, I hope you are willing', or else kisseth her before them, and then followeth her father out of doors; then one of the bridegroom his men ushereth the bride, and goes foremost; and the rest of the younger men usher each of them a maid to church. The bridegroom and the bride's brothers or friends tend [wait] at dinner.

Sixty-odd years later, in 1712, a landowner's daughter, Dorothea Trotman of Siston Court in Gloucestershire, married her cousin Samuel Trotman. Their wedding festivities were observed by John Sanders, whose employ-er was Dorothea's aunt. The couple were accompanied from the bride's home to church by two bridesmaids and two bridemen plus eight coachloads of near relations – this was a wedding very much within the family. On their return from the church: 'As the bride and groom entered the hall, four gentlemen held a large damask cloth over the bride and bridegroom's head whilst there was a noble large cake broke over their heads'.

The custom of breaking a cake, which was probably more like a biscuit or oatcake than a modern wedding cake, over the head of the bride per-sisted until the nineteenth century. The bride's unmarried friends used the pieces in rituals designed to predict the identity of their future husbands.

> A set of musicianers being placed in a gallery over the great stairs welcomed the bride and bridegroom home in the best manner they could and played up the dinner which was very splendid and great, so much to be particularly named. There were twenty-four dishes on the table at the first course besides the pasty, venison and roast beef on the sideboard. . . . The third course had three large pyramids of the finest and best sort of dried sweetmeats and besides they had sixteen large china dishes of wet sweetmeats and jellies and fruits and other things which made the dessert as noble as the dinner.

Dancing and cards followed. At supper time the family was served with 'two rich sack possets in noble large silver basins and a rich large bride-cake garnished on top with fine dried sweetmeats stuck very thick in it. All the family, servants included [Sanders received one himself], were presented with favours – probably ribbons – from the bride'. On the second day neighbouring gentry came to dinner, on the third the labourers were entered. After that the 'foreign man cook' brought in for 'the three grand festival days' retired. The fourth day, Sunday, was marked by a wedding sermon.

Along with the 'religious consecration' and the civil recording of the ceremony, the customary feasting of family and friends associated with weddings, like that which marked baptisms and burials, commemorated the chief actors' entry into a new stage in the human career. (An anthropologist would call this a rite of passage.) It also served to affirm the ties which bound individuals and their families to the wider community. And, as superstition predicted and experience confirmed, weddings bred weddings.

## FURTHER READING

Davies, Kathleen (1981) 'Continuity and Change in Literary Advice on Marriage' in *Marriage and Society: Studies in the Social History of Marriage*, R. B. Outhwaite (ed.), London

Elliott, Vivien Brodsky (1981) 'Single Women in the London Marriage Market: Age, Status and Mobility' in *Marriage and Society: Studies in the Social History of Marriage*, R. B. Outhwaite (ed.), London

Gillis, John (1985) *For Better, for Worse: British Marriages, 1600 to the Present*, Oxford

Ingram, Martin (1981) 'Spousals Litigation in English Ecclesiastical Courts' in *Marriage and Society: Studies in the History of Marriage*, R. B. Outhwaite (ed.), London

Spufford, Margaret (1981) *Small Books and Pleasant Histories: Popular Fiction and its Readership in Seventeenth-century England*, London

Stone, Lawrence (1992) *Uncertain Unions: Marriage in England, 1660–1753*, Oxford

# CHAPTER 7

# Householders

For all but the grandees, who married too young to be entrusted with the responsibilities of independent housekeeping, and very poor couples, who lacked the means to set up even the most rudimentary establishment of their own, the consequence of a successful courtship was a new household. Between 80 and 90 per cent of those who survived into adulthood married, thus householding was the normal condition of mature men and women.

There was a powerful relationship between the rank or occupation of the householder and the size, structure and material circumstances of the household. The largest, headed by great landowners, had well over a hundred members, the smallest were those of solitaries, often widows without children or servants. Landowners, professionals and businessmen, many farmers, shopkeepers and craftsmen, even some labourers, had employees living under their roofs. Their number and function was a gauge of the household's status, prosperity and pretensions. At all social levels, the size and composition of households altered as children were born, left home or died. Husbands and wives died. Widows and widowers remarried. Kin moved in to support the bereaved.

## HOUSEHOLD FUNCTIONS

Three or four hundred years ago the functions of households were much more extensive than they are today. In a society in which the welfare and the good order of the community depended primarily on the vigilance of parents and employers, the practical and moral responsibilities borne by heads of households were recognised as onerous. A widow without an adult son was expected to step into her husband's shoes and add his agenda to her own responsibilities. In spite of a feminist tendency to put a positive interpretation on instances of women doing men's jobs, for many widows the combination must have been more exhausting than empowering. Her contemporaries would not have envied Widow Scarlet of Romford who earned a pittance carrying loads of sand and timber.

The household was the normal place to be born, the natural place to die. Households provided care, discipline and vocational training for children and young people. Masters stood in for the natural fathers of the undergraduates, apprentices and servants who lived under their roofs; when he referred to his family, a householder included these surrogate children. It was in the household that the sick and the dying were nursed. Institutions to house those physically or financially incapable of fending for themselves – orphaned children, disabled adults, the frail and elderly – were rare. Even in 1720 London had only a handful of notable refuges. Defoe singled out the Bluecoat Hospital, which catered for orphans, Bedlam, for 'lunatics', Bart's and St Thomas', for 'sick and maimed people', and the 'new and noble' foundation which Defoe rightly anticipated would be called 'Guy's Hospital', after Mr Thomas Guy who 'built and endowed' it.

Older unmarried people, perhaps especially men without close or effective kin, recognised that they might eventually depend on the services of strangers: thus, when he made his will in 1578, Thomas Horseman of Romford in Essex included a bequest to 'the goodwife of the house in which it shall fortune me to die'. And thus, in 1658, when Thomas Cley, a weaver of Wigston Magna in Leicestershire, and Joan, his wife, decided that they could no longer cope on their own, their solution involved a deal with a neighbouring householder. The Cleys made over property to Robert Smyth and his heirs and, in return, Smyth agreed that 'at all times hereafter during the natural lives of Thomas Cley and Joan his wife for the life of the longer liver of them' he would

> well and sufficiently provide for, maintain and keep the said Thomas Cley and Joan his wife with good wholesome meat, drink, lodging, fire, washing, starching, clothes (both linen and woollen), hose, shoes and all other necessaries and things convenient and fitting for people of their qualities and condition.

The agenda set for Robert Smyth must be considered in the knowledge that this was an unmechanised society and that all the, often complex, household tasks enumerated or taken for granted – harvesting, purchasing and preparing food, cooking, fetching water and fuel, making fires, washing, starching, making and mending clothes – were both time consuming and physically demanding.

Many householders 'lived over the shop', in or close to their places of work. This was true of landowners, farmers, of many craftsmen and shopkeepers and providers of services – innkeepers and barbers, for example. However, a very significant and probably increasing proportion of householders went out to work: professional men – lawyers, for instance – and craftsmen and labourers who worked for wages. In many of the poorest households only the women and young children worked at home for money – the rougher end of the textile trade depended on homeworkers who carded wool, span and knitted. Knitting and carding required very simple equipment; the spinning wheel, which had taken over from the more primitive (and much cheaper) spindle was often supplied, along with the wool, by the dealer who employed them.

In great households the senior officers were often highly qualified men, the executives of what were, in effect, some of the biggest businesses in England. Chapter 5 reflects the experience of the many men and women who spent their teenage and early twenties in their employers' households, acquiring the skills which would enable them to earn an independent living. Farming, manufacture and retailing depended on male and female servants in husbandry and on, predominantly, male apprentices. Servants also cooked, washed and cleaned, they ran errands, minded children and tended the sick.

William Lilly's account of his first mistress' 'death and occasion thereof by means of a cancer of the breast' is a powerful illustration of the extent of responsibilities which might be laid on a member of the household 'family', in this case a trusted servant. In 1620 Lilly (born 1602) left his home in Leicestershire to work for a Leicestershire-born man and wife who needed 'a youth to attend [them] who could write'. (Gilbert Wright, though wealthy, was illiterate.) In 1622 Mrs Wright

> complained of a pain in her left breast, whereon there appeared at first a hard knob no bigger than a small peason [pea]; it increased in a little time very much, was very hard and sometimes would look very red. She took the advice of surgeons, had oils, searcloths, plates of lead and what not. In 1623 it grew very big, spread all over her breast then for many weeks poultices were applied to it, which in continuance of time, broke the skin and thence abundance of watery thin stuff came to suppuration, but never any great store issued forth. It was exceeding noisome [stinking] and painful. From the beginning of it until she died, she would permit no surgeon to dress it but only myself. I applied everything unto it and her pains were so great the winter before she died that I have been called out of my bed two or three times in one night to dress it and change plasters.
>
> In 1624, by degrees, with scissors, I cut the whole breast away, I mean the sinews, nerves etc. In one fortnight, or little more, it appeared mere flesh, all raw so that she could scarce endure any unguent [ointment] to be applied. I remember there was a great cleft through the middle of the breast, which, when that fully appeared, she died.

Servants like William Lilly were utilities. Others were kept more or less for show, to add lustre to their employers' reputation. The ability to occupy servants in ceremonial duties was a badge of status. Gentlemen-in-waiting and their less aristocratic counterparts, footmen and -boys (sometimes called pages), who wore their master's livery, his badge and colours, out of doors and in the presence of strangers, were not purely ornamental. Like the servants kept in less pretentious households, they ran errands and, on escort duty after dark, carried lanterns to light their master's way. But the cost of keeping potentially productive men and boys in attendance in anticipation that their services might be required was, like their livery, a means of advertising their employers' status, wealth and stylishness.

The make-up and temper of households altered as servants came and went. Bonds that went beyond the contractual developed. Servants identified with their master's families. On 13 July 1663 Roger Lowe, an apprentice mercer noted the birth of his employer's child; twelve days later he attended 'our child's christening'. Just as masters and mistresses stood in for the fathers and mothers of their young servants and apprentices, so servants sometimes came to regard their workmates as surrogate brothers and sisters. In 1600 Daniel Reynolds made a bequest to his 'fellow servant' Agnes Rogers, 'to be paid unto her at the day of her marriage, so as she marry with a man approved of my good mistress . . . for his fear of God and honest conversation'.

## HOUSEHOLD AND COMMUNITY

Households were interdependent. Neighbouring wives supported each other in childbirth. When death approached it was very often to neighbours that the dying turned to witness and execute their wills. Almost invariably, neighbours compiled the post-mortem inventories of the goods and chattels of dead property owners.

From the point of view of local government, the England of three or four hundred years ago could be described as a federation of independent households, grouped together in about 10,000 parishes, which were to a large extent self-governing. The unpaid officials – the churchwardens, the constables, the surveyors of the highway, and the overseers of the poor, appointed for the first time in 1597 – who were collectively responsible for managing the resources of the community and for maintaining law and order, were the heads of its solvent households. At Clayworth in Nottinghamshire, in the 1670s and 1680s, a wide spectrum of village society was represented in office: gentlemen, farmers, a grocer and a weaver and a labourer served as churchwardens. Churchwardens' accounts show them discharging their responsibilities for maintaining the churchyard, the fabric of the church itself and its furnishings; for exterminating moles, hedgehogs and other vermin; for monitoring the progress through the parish of poor travellers with licences, victims of fire, shipwreck or other misfortunes, *en route* to seek assistance from family or friends. The constable had the task of policing the parish. The overseers of the poor set and levied rates to pay pensions to those who could not survive without subsidy from their neighbours. They also managed any charitable funds established to provide the deserving local poor with shelter, bread, coal and free schooling or apprenticeship premiums. The duties which these householders carried out gave them standing and influence in their communities. Occasionally women held office – at Ribchester in Lancashire female householders were elected churchwarden in two successive years. They did not serve in person (male wardens in the parish sometimes appointed substitutes): in 1674 Widow Eccles' proxy was Richard Greenwood; the following year Edward Roades stood in for Widow Townley.

The election of women to parish offices was an exceptional event but their presence in the record served as a reminder to their contemporaries, as it does to us, that, even in a society in which gender played a powerful part in defining roles, rights and obligations in the households and in the wider community, widows and other single women with property enjoyed considerable autonomy. And, therefore, when a prudent man took a wife, he sought a woman capable of acting as his stand-in.

Records compiled by William Sampson and Richard Gough, two Englishmen born in the seventeenth century, reveal the parishes, Clayworth in Nottinghamshire and Myddle in Shropshire, in which they lived as communities of households. Their methods differ. Sampson lists; Gough gossips. But both depict localities in flux as the households of which they were constructed came, went and altered in composition – a circumstance which may surprise those who imagine the inhabitants of the past rooted in the soil of their birthplace – but a disturbing fact of life to the men and women of their own day who craved stability and certainty and reconciled themselves to death because, for those who died well, death might be the gateway to an eternity not governed by time, change and decay.

William Sampson has all the credentials of a good witness. He was a local man, the son of a farmer from South Leverton in Nottinghamshire. He had been trained in accuracy: a plebeian boy who went on to university in the seventeenth century had almost certainly achieved a thorough grounding in Latin, a language in which communication depends on the precise rendition of word endings. Sampson followed his elder brother Henry to Pembroke College, Cambridge. In July 1672 William Sampson was appointed Rector of Clayworth, not far from his birth place; he preached his first sermon there a few weeks later but it was some time before he took up permanent residence in the parish. As he explained in *The Rector's Book*, in which his lists are preserved, Sampson was elected President – estates manager – of his old college only a matter of months after his appointment to Clayworth. This vote of confidence in his administrative competence 'occasioned my residence in the university and non-residence at Clayworth for three years according to the allowance [as permitted by] the Statutes of the Realm and of the University'. The tone of his note suggests that Sampson felt a need to defend himself against the charge of neglecting his flock. For much of his absence, the parish was served by a well-qualified curate, Mr John Ombler 'one of the Fellows of Benet College' (now known as Corpus Christi), Cambridge.

The enquiry which the meticulous Sampson commissioned into 'the names of my parishioners' in April 1676, barely three months after his return and compiled as the churchwardens were making a house-to-house collection on behalf of the victims of a disastrous fire in Northampton, provided the newly settled Rector with a useful alphabetical directory of the inhabitants of the village of Clayworth and the nearby hamlet of Wiseton. Twelve years later William Sampson listed his parishioners for a second time, on this occasion using the geography of the settlements as his organising principle. Why he repeated the exercise we do not know.

Great households, with a hundred or more members, were rarities: there was none in Clayworth (nor in Myddle). But Sampson's listings illustrate the association between size and high status, the gentlemen headed the biggest households in the parish. Other Clayworth households contained more children: servants made the critical contribution to the size of gentry households.

In 1676 and in 1688 Thomas Dickonson and his wife had one child and six servants – three men and three women – living with them. The statistical similarity conceals a radical change of personnel. Of the servants in the household in 1676, not one remained twelve years later. The child mentioned in 1676 was a daughter, Sarah; in 1688 the resident child was Dickonson's 'son and heir', Lacy. As this example suggests, the listings provide us with stills from the moving picture of the history of Clayworth's households. The inscription on Thomas Dickonson's memorial, which Sampson copied into *The Rector's Book* in 1699, provides further information about his family: 'He had only one wife and nine children, whereof six of them lie here interred'. In 1676 Mr Christopher Johnson, another Clayworth gentleman, headed a household of eight including his wife's niece and his own nephew. By 1688 the younger generation had departed; here again none of the servants remained in place. A third gentleman, Mr Thomas Royston, who settled in Clayworth in 1688 was head of a household of ten: himself, his wife, Anne, Thomas and William Hoggerd – her sons by her first husband; her Royston children – Mark, Anne and Margaret; their servants Joseph Hall and Martha Tonkinson – and Elizabeth Butler an 'apprentice servant', most probably a pauper child bound out as an apprentice in housewifery by overseers of the poor.

The gentry were by no means the only servant-keepers in Clayworth. Roughly one-third of households in the parish had servants, some of them were undoubtedly farmworkers, others domestics, although Sampson's list does not differentiate between them. Perhaps, as a farmer's son, he recognised that the distinction was artificial, that the labour of a household was directed to its most pressing needs, which changed with the weather and the time of year. The blacksmith, the housewright, the weaver, the tailor and the shoemaker had apprentices. The Clayworth lists exemplify the turnover of apprentices and resident servants which punctuated the histories of a substantial minority of households. Young men who were apprentices in 1676 had served out their time well before 1688 and, of the whole population of servants present in 1676, only one remained in service in the parish twelve years later and she had changed employers.

To the disruption caused by the comings and goings of servants – and, normally at longer intervals, apprentices – must be added the birth and departure of children and the more traumatic and less predictable impact of bereavement and, in particular, the death of a spouse. The Clayworth listings provide ample evidence of remarriage. Of the ninety-one households recorded in 1688, one was headed by a five-times married man and four others by men who had been married four times. The butcher John Brason had been widowed three times in twelve years: a servant when Sampson's first list was compiled in April 1676, he married for the first time later that year. With the remarriages of parents, complex and often emotionally charged step-relationships came into being. Humphrey Elton, the tailor and parish clerk, and his fourth wife Mary had living with them Robert, the son of Elton's third marriage, Mary's sons, John and Joshua Greenwood, and the couple's children, Joseph and Mary.

Evidence from other sources suggests that households which contained three generations were rare. Households which included still-married parents and already-married children were exceptional, though they are to be found in the ranks of the great landowners whose heirs married unusually young. In Clayworth a few widowed parents shared homes with their married children. In 1688 Doncaster Bett, a tenant farmer, was living with his son Thomas, Thomas' wife Anne, their daughter also Anne and a servant. Elizabeth Wright, a widow living with her unmarried children in 1676, was, in 1688, listed at the head of one of the most complicated households in the parish: the other members were her married son Benjamin, Benjamin's wife Elizabeth and their children, Elizabeth and Charles, Widow Wright's unmarried son Richard, her sister Mary and the family's servant Jane Gill.

Among the smallest, one-person, households in the parish were those of widows who were too poor to keep servants. Thomas Smith, the schoolmaster, a single man, was a lodger, a cheaper option than marrying or keeping house with a servant. Young bachelors, who had yet to attain to the status of householder, were perhaps more likely to be comfortable as lodgers than mature men who had enjoyed the householder's authority at home and abroad.

The Clayworth listings are unparalleled in English archives and we cannot immediately assume that the instability of households in the parish was typical of English communities in the 1670s and 1680s. Nevertheless, very similar tendencies are suggested in other sources which enable us to examine the particularities of individual households.

The data which Richard Gough (born 1634) amassed and preserved are very different both in conception and presentation. What they tell us is equally exceptional and precious. Richard Gough used the seating plan of the church as the organising principle of his *Antiquities and Memoirs of the Parish of Myddle*, which he began in 1700, his sixty-sixth year. In doing so, he took, in his way, as systematic an approach to his theme as Sampson. As Gough explained: 'A pew is a certain place in church encompassed with wainscot, or some other thing, for several persons to sit in together'. Some pews were divided into seats or kneelings. In Myddle, as he pointed out, 'a pew or seat does not belong to a person, or to land but to an house, therefore if a man remove from an house to dwell in another, he shall not retain his seat belonging to the first house'.

To assist his readers, Gough drew a plan 'as the church is now, 1701', with the pulpit in the top right-hand corner. 'The second pew adjoining to the south wall', on the opposite side of the church, 'belonged wholly to Balderton Hall'. His account of the owners and occupants of the Hall is a striking, if perhaps extreme, example of turnover of tenancy.

> This farm has been sold five times in little more than the space of one hundred years last past. The first owner of this farm that I can give any account of was Roger Nicholas, and of him I can only say that his wife's name was Alice and that he died AD 1572 and left behind him a son, named William, who was born AD 1550. William Nicholas built most part of Balderton Hall – viz. all except . . .

the kitchen end . . . . This William Nicholas was never married that I know of, and by his great charges in building he contracted much debt. Yet being addicted to projects, he became a timber man and purchased the timber in Kenwick's Park thinking to enrich himself by it, but it proved his ruin . . . in the end his creditors came so sharp upon him that he sold Balderton Hall . . . to Mr Chambre of Petton and went out of the country [district] and was never heard of. But some say there came an old man in beggar's habit (some years after his departure) to Balderton, late in the evening and sat under the barn wall, and was found dead in the morning, and was thought to be this William Nicholas. . . .

Mr Arthur Chambre, the purchaser, gave this estate in Balderton unto his younger son Michael. . . . This Michael Chambre was wholly addicted to idleness and therefore no marvel that he was lascivious. . . . But the worst of this Michael was that his lewd consorts were such ugly nasty bawds. . . . This Michael took no care to pay legacies [left by his father] to his sisters and, being sued by his brothers-in-law and put in prison, he and they joining together, sold Balderton Hall and the lands belonging to it to John Noke. . . .

John Noke was a wealthy draper in Shrewsbury, but running the fate of many such tradesmen,

when his business associates in London were bankrupted,

he was forced to pay great sums of money, for the raising whereof he mortgaged his estate in Balderton to Mr Webbe, another rich draper in Shrewsbury. . . . But he running the same fate as John Noke had done . . . sold it to Mr Zanky, then Rector of Hodnet.

Mr Zanky was a person much commended for his virtue and piety . . . Mr Zanky died soon after he made this purchase, and his widow came and lived some years in Balderton Hall . . . . Robert Zanky [his eldest son] a little before his death sold Balderton Hall to Matthew Lath . . . [who] had only one daughter, whose name was Jane, and she being a great fortune had many suitors. But . . . she was married to Thomas Hall . . . Thomas Hall lived at Balderton with his father-in-law and during his life he was a reasonable good husband [in both senses of the word, as Jane's partner and as the thrifty husband of the farm] but, after his decease, he let loose the reins to many disorderly courses as cocking [cock fighting], racing, drinking and lewdness. He had one bastard born in his own house, by a daughter of William Bickley. . . . By these ill courses, Thomas Hall consumed his estates. . . . He sold Balderton Hall and the land belonging to it unto Robert Hayward.

Robert Hayward . . . died December 3rd 1705.

## ORDERLY AND DISORDERLY HOUSEHOLDS

Households were miniature societies. Oliver Heywood, a Yorkshire minister, held the household of his godly father-in-law up as a model to be wondered at and, as far as a possible, emulated. He compared it to an army, a school, a church.

His government and order of his family was admirable and inimitable, I may truly say unparalleled. His family was as a well-disciplined army, where all knew their proper stations and did carefully attend their posts, yea a well instructed academy and an organised church.

As Heywood's metaphor implies, a good wife knew her place as her husband's lieutenant, backing him up and holding the fort in his absence on business. When he was at home, in a well-ordered house, he ruled the roost. As the saying went in Gloucestershire: 'For the most part it falleth out that where wives will rule all they mar all'. Children were drilled to defer not only to their parents but also to older siblings. Apprentices and servants had to submit to the authority of their seniors. When Samuel Pepys hired a maidservant he took her age and size into account. It did not do to have an undermaid who was older or stronger than the colleague whose instructions she was required to follow.

Moral lapses undermined a householder's authority. Samuel Pepys' affair with his wife's waiting woman Deb Willet was exposed in October 1668, to the great distress of the three principals. The turnover of servants meant that by the end of March 1669 the household was, in Pepys' phrase 'in a manner . . . new' and he was not at all sorry because 'the late differences . . . about poor Deb' would be forgotten. A householder who was habitually drunken or promiscuous, encouraged licentious behaviour, physically abused his children, apprentices or servants or deserted his family undermined the social order. In cases which gave rise to serious concern, neighbours were prepared to intervene.

Both adulterers and cuckolds, men with unfaithful wives, were liable to customary punishment. The cuckold was taunted with horns. He was hung up outside his house or sketched in the familiar two-fingered salute. A serenade of 'rough music', made by clattering pots and pans was a less specific demonstration of neighbourly disapproval. Ribald verses circulated. This example, which was recorded in Wiltshire in 1618 was probably part of a stock repertoire – the rhyme scheme meant that it was very easy to ring the changes on the names.

Woe to thee, Michael Robins,
That ever thou wert born,
For Blancute makes thee cuckold
And thou must wear the horn.

He fetcheth the nurse
To give the child suck,
That he may have time
Thy wife for to fuck.

Richard Gough, who wrote the history of his home parish in Shropshire, between 1700 and 1706, was in no doubt of the deleterious influence on the neighbourhood of the household of Thomas Davis, a weaver from Shrewsbury who married a local woman and settled in Myddle:

Of these two persons . . . hath proceeded such numerous offspring in this parish that I have heard some reckon up, taking in wives and husbands, no less than sixty of them, and the greater part of them have been chargeable to the parish. . . . Sina Davis and her children have for many years been a charge to us. Sina Davis was a crafty, idle, dissembling woman, and did counterfeit herself to be lame, and went hopping with a staff when men saw her, but at other times could go with it under her arm, as I myself have seen her, and she has maintenance from the parish many years before she died.

Many great families in this parish have been extinct, but this has got so many branches that it is more likely to overspread it.

In Gough's book, the Davises were not the only bad lot in the parish. There was the brood associated with Margaret Formeston 'who was married to William Chaloner of Myddle, cooper'. Formeston was

never openly defamed but she left three daughters, two of which are as impudent whores as any in this country; one of them has two bastards, and she being run out of the country, they are both maintained by the parish. The other is now (January 20 1701) great with a bastard and at Christmas last was ordered into Wem parish, where her last service and settlement was. She has fathered it on Stephen Formeston, her uncle's son and he is fled.

Margaret's brother William 'was a hatter but such an idle drunkard, that although he is a good workman, and was set up several times by his father, yet he still spent all, and sold his tools and hardly keeps clothes on his back'.

Elizabeth Kyffin, 'descended of a good, but a decaying, family in Wales', married Francis Clarke, a Myddle man.

He had but little portion with her but a sad drunken woman. He went to fetch her from the alehouse in a very dark night, but she, being unwilling to come, pretended it was so dark that she could not see to go; he told her he would lead her by the arm, and got her away almost half way home and then she pretended she had lost one of her shoes; and when he had loosed her and was groping for the shoe, she ran back to the alehouse and bolted him out and would not come home that night.

Drink was associated with thriftlessness, idleness and immorality. Among the bruising nuggets of abuse hurled at the wife of a Salisbury worthy in 1586 were 'Mistress Tosspot' and 'Mistress Drunkensoul'. Alehouse keepers were routinely criticised for their encouragement of disorder. In 1626 Henry Smith endowed a fund to provide the able-bodied poor of Terling in Essex with 'clothing, bread, flesh or fish'. 'Those that are guilty of excessive drinking, profane swearing, pilfering and other scandalous crimes or are vagrants or are idle persons or have been incorrigible when servants or do entertain inmates' were excluded from the benefits. Significantly, John Aldridge, who kept an alehouse in the same village, was charged with harbouring 'at all times such persons that do swear and dishonour God and so poor that many of them have alms of the parish and their wives and children beg in the parish'. On occasion, it was alleged, he allowed 'poor men to sit tippling and drinking in his house for the space of half a day and all night together'. A scatter of cases in the Church courts, which were responsible for punishing those found guilty of immorality, confirm that alehouses were the haunts of prostitutes and that, in some cases, the land-lady was herself a part-time whore. In some communities there were also more potent figures, substantial householders at odds with the local regime, like Roger Pouncey, the Dorchester butcher, who in the 1630s allied him-self with the ne'er-do-wells against the godly rulers of the town.

Although the broad principles of householding were consistent across region, rank and time, their application mirrored the householder's values, status and wealth, or, as contemporaries would have said, his quality and condition. The sample which follows includes households with single, married and widowed heads, with and without resident children.

## LANDOWNERS' HOUSEHOLDS

The great landowners of Tudor and Stuart England built or occupied prodi-gious houses, designed to dominate their 'country' and impress the stranger. The descriptions of Celia Fiennes (born 1662) provide an insider's view of their impact. In 1685 Fiennes, a single woman of noble birth, embarked on a series of 'journeys begun to regain [her health] by variety and change of air and exercise'. She became an enthusiastic promoter of the 'idea of England', highly critical of the 'evil itch of over-valuing foreign parts'. Her record of her journeys illustrates the prestige associated with keeping up with new fashions in house building. Woburn, begun in 1626, was to her mind, dismissable as 'an old building, low', though she admired the new gardens. She was particularly taken with the statue of 'an old weeder woman', which the Duke of Bedford had commissioned for the cherry gar-den and which was 'done so like and her clothes so well that at first I took it to be a real living body'.

Chatsworth, the Duke of Devonshire's house in Derbyshire was being remodelled when Fiennes visited it in 1697: many of the rooms 'were not finished'. She dwelt upon the

> bathing room, the walls all with blue and white marble, the pavement mixed, one stone white, another black, another of the red rance marble [spotted with blue and white]; the bath is one entire marble all white, finely veined with blue . . . . You went down steps into the bath big enough for two people; at the upper end are two cocks [taps] to let in one hot, the other cold water attem-per it as persons please [enable bathers to adjust the temperature to suit their preferences]; the windows are all private [ground] glass.

Celia Fiennes' contemporary, the prolific writer and journalist Daniel Defoe (born circa 1661) was the son of a London merchant. He celebrated

Britain as the most flourishing and opulent country in the world. Trade was the root of its prosperity: 'an estate's a pond but trade's a spring'. Yet he was a connoisseur of noblemen's houses. In his *Tour through the Whole Island of Great Britain*, published in the 1720s, he faulted Petworth's situation: 'the house stands as it were with its elbow in the town'. Like Fiennes, he favoured new buildings. William Cecil's great house at Stamford was the product of 'an exquisite fancy (as the manner of building then was)' – at the end of the sixteenth century – but recent alterations were 'infinitely to the advantage of the whole'. Words almost failed him when he attempted to describe the 'most magnificent palace or mansion house', 'noble and well contrived', which the Duke of Chandos had 'built with such a profusion of expense', 'so beautiful in its situation, so lofty, so majestic the appearance of it'.

These households were the head offices of large and often diversified enterprises concerned with the management of rural rent rolls, urban development and other investments, matrimonial and political alliances. The elaborate regulations and ceremonial which governed the conduct of the greatest households were formally set down on paper.

Although the functions of great households changed little over time, their make-up altered significantly. The nature of the change is evident; the reasons for it are less clear cut. In the sixteenth century the senior officers were recruited from the leading families of the locality; the young sons of substantial local landowners waited on their lord to do his bidding. When strangers were expected, the gentlemen of the household wore the livery which marked them as his retainers; when he travelled, they rode ahead. At home and abroad, the attendant retinue was designed to 'make show' of the noble's rank, wealth and power. Props of their lord's magnificence, gentlemen-in-waiting were barred from the drudging side of the household, the kitchen quarters and the laundry.

John Smyth, author of *The Lives of the Berkeleys*, is a witness to the stress laid on ceremony in the everyday life of the household of a Tudor landowner. He recalled how Katharine, Sir Henry Berkeley's first wife, who must then have been in her middle forties, taught him, a raw recruit to the household, 'then about seventeen', 'a boy of no desert lately come from country school and but newly entered into her service' to bow or, as he puts it, 'make a leg' with the style and grace she required of her servants. 'To show me the better how', she lifted up all her garments to the calf of her leg that I might the better observe the grace of drawing back the foot and bowing of the knee'. And, to ensure that the lesson was well learned, before he was allowed to get on with his duties, Smyth 'had to make . . . one hundred legs (so to call them) at the least'.

By the middle of the seventeenth century, the officers and attendants were of significantly humbler origin. The high-born officials had been replaced by men like William Sampson, well educated but of undistinguished birth. The gentlemen-in-waiting had been succeeded by footmen chosen for their good looks and characters. The daily ceremonial became less elaborate. The introduction of backstairs removed the servants' less decorative functions from sight.

The nature of the change is evident, the reasons for it are less transparent. A number of explanations have been put forward. The universities supplanted the noble household as finishing schools where landowners' sons could polish their minds and manners and gain access to wider networks of patronage. The memoirs of Anthony Ashley Cooper, quoted in Chapter 5 (see p. 74), demonstrate that the universities provided a young nobleman with ample opportunities for fostering local loyalties too. The coach replaced the retinue of mounted attendants as an expression of status. Cost was a consideration; with the exodus of gentlemen attendants there was less need for servants' servants. The question of domestic discipline may well have been a contributory factor. The 'orders' which Jane, second wife of Sir Henry Berkeley (born 1534), published in 1601 'to the end that none of them shall for their excuse plead ignorance', certainly suggest that the gentlemen-in-waiting were an unruly crew. They engaged in 'disorderly pastimes' indoors; made 'a great noise at dinner and supper time' and were inclined to 'scoff and rail' when asked to quieten down. Riding abroad with their lord and lady, they used such 'undecentness' as 'loud speech' and 'rude sports'. Heavy betting on cards and dice caused 'many disorders and contentions' in the household. They frequented alehouses, carousing and swearing. Disorder was not a peculiarity of the Berkeley retinue: in 1587 members of the Stanley household were reminded that dogs were to be kept out of the way during mealtimes to stop them fighting and bolting down the leftovers reserved for distribution to the poor waiting for their dole of food at the gates. Generosity continued to be a mark of nobility. As Defoe observed of the Earl of Pembroke's household at Wilton, 'the blessing' of a 'noble resident extended . . . to all the country round'.

The Russell family's fortune was founded on service to the Tudor crown. They profited from Henry VIII's persecution of the old nobility and, as the name of their principal seat suggests, from his destruction of the monasteries. In 1661 the Russells normally resident at Woburn Abbey were its head, the Earl of Bedford, his wife and two young daughters, Diana and Margaret. His other surviving children, all sons, had dispersed: Francis and William were grown up; Edward and Robert were pursuing their education abroad; James and George were pupils at Westminster School. The Earl's staff was headed by the receiver-general, chancellor of the Bedford exchequer. The funds he administered came in from the Earl's lands in Bedfordshire, Cambridgeshire, the West Country and from his increasingly valuable estates in London. George Collop was the son of a minor tenant and a lawyer by training; his background was much humbler than those of his predecessors in office. The other senior household officers were John Fox, the Earl's legal adviser, Dixy Taylor, gentleman of the privy purse, and John Thornton, tutor, chaplain and librarian. These officers had wives and family homes elsewhere but were on duty and in residence at Woburn for much of their time. The steward oversaw the indoor servants. This chain of command ran down through the house bailiff and his counterpart, the clerk of the kitchen, to the little boys like 'Tom-in-the-kitchen' who had no wages and worked for their keep alone. Responsibility for the outdoor staff was divided between the gentleman of the horse, who managed the stables, and the gardener. The great majority of the regular workforce was male. Woburn had no home farm: the estate supplied venison and rabbits for the table and, later in the century, fruit and other garden produce. The family's estate at Thorney in Cambridgeshire produced beef, game birds and fish. The household depended on London grocers for sugar, dried and candied fruits, oranges and lemons, spices – nutmegs and mace, cloves, ginger, cinnamon – Westphalia ham and the newly fashionable tea and coffee.

Among the best documented of later households is Cannons, the country house in Middlesex which James Brydges, the first Duke of Chandos, transformed between 1713 and 1725. James Brydges, the eldest son of the eighth Lord Chandos, was born in 1674. His ancestor, the first baron, had been Lord Lieutenant of the Tower of London in the reign of Queen Mary. Prisoners in his charge included the Princess Elizabeth; he oversaw the executions of Lady Jane Grey, the rebel Wyatt and a number of bishops who refused to accept the reinstatement of Catholicism. Educated at Westminster and New College, Oxford, James Brydges was an ambitious young man determined to make his fortune in the service of the Crown. On the advice of older friends, already established in public life, he invested in a suitable wardrobe and got himself elected to Parliament. In 1703 his persistent lobbying for office was rewarded; two years later he obtained the post of paymaster to Queen Anne's forces overseas. His questionable, but discreet, exploitation of the perquisites of this post – the profits which accrued from speculating with government funds in his control, commissions paid by the contractors who supplied the army's clothing and footwear, 'gratifications' from foreign princes whose troops were hired to support the English forces in the great European war against Louis XIV – made him enormously rich. To avoid drawing unwelcome attention to these unofficial dealings, he arranged that the Earldom of Caernarvon, his reward for keeping Marlborough's scattered armies supplied, should not go to him direct but to his aged and ailing father. The warrant elevating Lord Chandos was dated 15 October 1714, the day before his death. Five years later Brydges was 'enduked'.

In 1710 Brydges had bought Cannons from Warwick Lake, the uncle of his first wife Mary; he took possession in 1713, after Lake's death. Retired from public office and not yet 40, he devoted himself to making 'great alterations' to the house which he intended to accommodate part of his collection of paintings, including works by Holbein, Michelangelo, Raphael, Titian and Rubens. Over ten or a dozen years he transformed the Lakes' Tudor home into a mansion in the classical taste so much admired by Daniel Defoe. The new house had the most modern of conveniences: a marble bathing room and water closets with marble floors and basins, walls hung with Dutch tiles and lead-lined baths. The gardens were planted with exotics from the Caribbean – Chandos raised pineapples (those lucky enough to receive them as presents were asked to return the spikes for replanting) and he had ambitions to grow his own coffee. The ornamental fowl included parakeets, flamingos and ostriches. Brydges expected Cannons to make some contribution to the costs incurred by its celebrity. The house and grounds were open to the paying public. Entrance fees paid for the extra staff and equipment needed to cope with the impact of visitors. Household finances were scrutinised by an audit board chaired by Brydges with his wife, his cousin Cassandra, at his side.

On New Year's Day 1722, before the house was fully finished, the Duke, the Duchess and their niece dined at home with ninety of their officers and servants, sitting at four tables in the dining room and four more in the servants' hall. Brydges' establishment was smaller than a man of similar rank, wealth and cultivation would have retained a century or so earlier – and it was bisected socially by the relegation of the plebeian servants to a separate hall. The officers and upper servants who were entitled to eat in the dining room included the chaplain and librarian, Dr Baxter, the house steward, the secretary, who made the file copies of correspondence so valuable to historians, and the director of music – as a patron of music in his household the Duke was outdone only by the King. The musicians had their own table: the Cannons Consort was made up of singers, string and wind players (for a period Handel had been composer-in-residence). The bailiff, the wheelwright, the farrier, who shoed the horses, the ploughman, the cowman and the shepherd ate at the farmyard table in the servants' hall – cattle and sheep were driven up to Cannons from Brydges' estates in Hereford and Radnor to be finished; the brewer used the fat from their carcasses to make tallow candles and soap for use 'below stairs'. The business of conveying the Brydges, their chattels and correspondence occupied a coachman, postillions, a stableman, the postboy who rode to and from London every day on a Welsh mountain pony and the running footmen. Running footmen, 'very swift of foot' and remarkable for their stamina, were paid a special bonus if they ran to London and an additional premium for runs of over twenty miles. Craftsmen temporarily employed at Cannons were assigned places at table in accordance with their rank: painters and architects in the dining room; weavers and cabinet-makers in the servants' hall. A curfew operated: servants were required to be indoors buy nine o'clock; 'lights out' after evening prayers was enforced by the Groom of Chambers.

The histories of Rachel, Lady Russell, and Sarah, Duchess of Marlborough, cited in the chapters on Courtship and Old Age, demonstrate that, as wives and widows, women of this rank could operate confidently and effectively in the public domain. Nevertheless, the tone of landowners' letters of instruction to their wives confirms that they were generally regarded as junior partners, to be allowed little discretion. The great collector Thomas Howard, Earl of Arundel, used his wife Aletheia as his agent – this undated letter was written in or about 1615.

My dearest heart

I pray buy Robarts his two carpets and his blue quilt for that will serve your bed of Japan [your lacquered bed] exceeding well and fit for the colour [probably red]. Enquire for the hangings he promised of cloth of bodkin [embroidered] and do these things quickly for fear that they may be gone. . . .

Bid Dyx [the steward] make haste to provide that great sum of money I spake to him of, and let nobody living know the use of it.

Your most faithful loving husband.

In December 1643, fifteen months after the outbreak of the war between Charles I and Parliament, Sir Ralph Verney went into exile, taking with him his wife Mary, Edmund, who was 7, and 5-year-old Margaret; Jack, who was 3, remained in England in the company of his young Verney aunts. Verney's departure put him at odds with the Parliamentary government; he risked imprisonment if he returned to England. Three years later Mary Verney was dispatched to England in an attempt to secure the family estates from confiscation by the hostile regime. As a kinsman noted, 'women', less culpable in the eyes of the law than their husbands, 'were never so useful as now'.

Sir Ralph fired a volley of written advice across the Channel to his wife, who was, in his eyes, a novice needing instruction at every step:

Make as few visits and use as few coaches as you can; for one loseth time and the other spends money.

Your father had an excellent rule never to lend a friend money nor borrow any of it.

Almost all your letters are sealed with several seals, I pray you keep constantly to one (and tie it to your arm) that I may see if your letters are opened by the way.

I pray let nobody (though never so good friends) see any of my writings but such as I send to you to show, and then only to those I bid you . . . burn all my letters after you have fully answered them.

It transpired that Margaret was pregnant.

Now for the name. If it be a girl . . . I desire it may be Mary; but, if it be a boy . . . let it be Richard or what you please except my own name. Really, I shall take it ill if you contradict me in this.

Now for the Christening, I pray give no offence to the state . . . for so it be done with ordinary water, and that these words 'I baptise thee in the name of the father, and of the son, and of the Holy Ghost', be used with the water, I know the child is well baptised.

The baby, a boy born on 3 June 1647, was baptised Ralph a fortnight later, a nice instance of a wife, for reasons which are readily understood, defying her husband's instructions.

## WORKING HOUSEHOLDS

The working households of farmers and craftsmen were the backbone of England's economy. These were households without pretensions to sophistication or cultivated taste; success was expressed not in conspicuous consumption but in the conspicuous thrift which Thomas Tusser celebrated in his verse portrait of the model farmer's wife. Some farmers kept women servants whose main work was in the dairy or the fields but, whatever their formal role, when the need arose, maids were drafted in to back up the men. The *Remembrance* or account books kept between 1610 and 1620 by Robert Loder (born 1589), a substantial farmer from Harwell in Berkshire, expose a calculating businessman's awareness of the cost of maintaining household servants. Loder had perhaps 150 acres of arable land, plus apple and cherry orchards, extensive pasture and grazing which supported a herd of dairy cows, a large flock of sheep and pigs. Loder came into his inheritance in his twenty-first year; shortly afterwards he married Mary Andrewes, a local woman.

In 1613 his 'ordinary household' consisted of himself, his wife and their daughter, a man, Robert Earnold, a boy, Jack Andrewes, Dick the shepherd and a maid. The harvesters, hedgers, thatchers and carpenters Loder employed joined the household for the duration of their tasks. (A generation later Henry Best, who farmed in the East Riding of Yorkshire, put his harvesters up in the 'folk's chamber' or, when that became overcrowded, in the barn or one of the other outbuildings. It was his foreman's responsibility to arrange for boards for their bedsteads and straw for their mattresses.) Loder was well aware that living-in servants had to be paid whether or not they earned their master money. And they were inclined to do him down or, as Loder put it, 'play legerdemain [conjuring tricks] with their master and favour themselves'. Loder was, for instance, puzzled by the loss he made on his barley crop in 1617. 'What should be the cause hereof I know not, but it was in that year when R. Pearce and Alce were my servants, and then in great love (as it appears too well). Whether he gave it to my horses I cannot learn of them . . . or how it went away, God knows'. The memoranda he set down 'for th'end that I might see the great charges in keeping servants' convinced him that 'it were good (in such dear years) to keep as few servants as a man possibly can' and to consider other ways of getting a good return from his land.

Loder was a married man – though his wife has no more than a nominal role in his accounts. William Stout's autobiography provides an insight into the domestic options open to an unmarried tradesman. Like Loder, Stout was a frugal man, not disposed to throw money away. Born in 1665, he was the son of a thrifty farmer; he was educated at grammar school and served his apprenticeship to an ironmonger in Lancaster. When he opened his first shop in the spring of 1688 he decided to keep one of the rooms for his lodging – sleeping-in helped to deter thieves. But, although he lodged in the shop premises, he went to board with Alderman Thomas Baynes. (His rent as boarder covered 'victuals and washing'.) After a couple of years Baynes lost his housekeeper and Stout moved to board with Richard Sterzaker, 'a butcher very near my shop'. Sterzaker had several other contented clients: as Stout recalled, they all had 'very good entertainment to our good liking and satisfaction'. Stout took on his first apprentice in 1690; he too boarded at Sterzaker's. As Stout's business grew, their sleeping quarters were absorbed into the shop and, in consequence, he took a part of a 'great house' – 'the great parlour, cellar under it and three bedrooms above'. His unmarried sister Elin, who had established herself as an invaluable lieutenant in the shop, moved in with him and they 'began to keep house' together. As a bachelor, Stout never benefited from the injection of cash which a prudently chosen wife would have brought with her but his sister's decision to remain single (according to William, she had a number of suitors) kept her energies and her inheritance in the family. It may be worth observing that, in a list of households, which did not specify relationships, the household headed by William and Elin Stout composed of a pair of adults and children with the same surname would be logged as a conventional family of husband, wife and offspring.

Elin died in 1724. 'At her death my brother Leonard sent his second daughter Jennet (born 1700) to keep my house until I was otherwise provided'. Jennet kept house for the best part of three years until she married. Her younger sister Elin, 'then about twenty years of age and a servant', was drafted in to replace her. Elin's entanglement with a young Irish dragoon brought her tour of duty to an abrupt end and, with no suitable kinswoman to turn to, Stout 'gave up housekeeping', let his house and lodged and boarded with his tenants. By 1734 his youngest nieces were old enough to take responsibility for his house but Margaret found a husband and Mary's poor health made her unreliable. Once again Stout gave up housekeeping; this time he took rooms 'to lodge in' and boarded with his nephew William. In spite of his profound reservations about William's character and conduct, this arrangement lasted for some time; eventually, however, he and William parted company. Mary Bayley, a mature and very competent servant, looked after him until she too married. A great niece, 'now nigh twenty years of age and having knowledge of my way of life' – she had been living with Stout as a foster daughter – 'having no parents living . . . undertook to housekeeping upon a trial and . . . performed more to my satisfaction than I could have expected'.

The chasm which separated Stout's heart, won by a flighty young woman endowed with the glamour conferred by a London upbringing, and his canny head had kept him single but the discomfort and uncertainties he suffered in the years after Elin's death indicate the pressures on men – and women – to settle for a working compromise rather than pursue the elusive ideal life partner.

## HOUSEHOLDERS WHO WENT OUT TO WORK

Between 1560 and 1720 the number of households headed by men who went out to work grew. A minority, but an important and influential minority of these householders were professionals, administrators and businessmen whose households were vehicles for the display of their wealth and cultivation. Most of their servants were female domestics. The hiring of a retinue of adult males was a token that the householder saw himself as a member of what might be termed the urban aristocracy.

## Urban aristocrats

When they married Samuel and Elizabeth Pepys had nothing behind them. Pepys was at the start of his administrative career. His father was tailor in a small way of business; Elizabeth St Michel was the daughter of a penniless refugee from France. They made their first home in one room in the Whitehall apartment occupied by Pepys' first employer, his cousin, the Earl of Sandwich. They could not afford to keep a servant: Elizabeth did the washing and cooking herself. In January 1660 Pepys was worth £25. Six months later he was appointed to a post on the Navy Board at an annual salary of £250. Able, industrious and well connected, Pepys made rapid progress in his career: his salary was augmented by presents from naval suppliers and others who hoped to sway his judgement in their favour. By the time he closed his diary in 1669 he had amassed a fortune in the region of £10,000.

The Pepyses hired their first servant, Jane Birch, as maid of all work, in 1658. Five years later their household, accommodated in an apartment in the Navy Office building near Tower Hill, included three maids; they were, in ascending order, the scullery maid (or 'little girl'), the cookmaid and the chambermaid. A footboy was added to the household in 1660: he wore a distinctive livery, ran errands and waited on his master in public. In 1664 Mrs Pepys acquired a waiting woman for the first time. Like the footboy, the waiting woman was a token of the Pepyses' increasing wealth and commitment to a life of fashion. In 1668, after much deliberation, Pepys invested in a coach and, in consequence, added a coachman to the household.

The Pepyses' marriage was childless. In spite of his harsh treatment of his sister Pall when she entered his household, 'not as a sister but as a servant', he seems to have reconciled himself to making her sons his heirs. He had the means to support a substantial domestic establishment to serve his own needs and those of his guests and did not remarry after Elizabeth's early death. Her place as his companion was taken by Mary Skynner, to whom Pepys paid affectionate tribute in his will. Why he chose not to marry Mary Skynner (it is unlikely that the decision was hers) we do not know. At the end of the 1680s in the household the women's work was shared between a housekeeper, a cook, a laundry maid and a housemaid. Pepys also kept two footmen, a coachman and a porter. A butler and a black boy had come and gone – the black boy was sold on in 1680.

Pepys took evident delight in fitting out his home. On 18 October 1668 he spent a whole Sunday morning 'altering the places of my pictures with great pleasure'. Five weeks later he invested another Sunday morning 'knocking up nails and making little settlements' in his house. Yet there was a clear competitive edge to his spending. When they were redecorating their apartments that autumn, Pepys took his wife and her waiting woman Deb to upholsterers' shops 'to see variety of hangings', from the shops they went on to inspect the hangings in the house of one of Pepys' colleagues, 'for our satisfaction in what we were going to buy'; later the same day, at the house of a relative, he noted that 'they have hung a room since I was there but with hangings not fit to be seen with mine'. This flurry of expenditure of money and energy on home decoration coincided with the domestic turbulence generated by Elizabeth Pepys' discovery of the relationship between her husband and her waiting woman. As Pepys noted on 19 November 1668, 'This night the upholsters did finish the hanging of my best chamber but my sorrow and trouble is so great about this business that [it] put me out of all joy in looking upon it or minding how it was'.

Stylish households were to be found outside London. Celia Fiennes, a landowner's daughter who visited Bury St Edmunds in 1698, singled out a 'high house' for favourable comment.

> Except this, the rest are great old houses of timber and mostly in the old form of the country, which are long peaked roofs of tiling. This house is in the new mode of building, four rooms of a floor, pretty sizeable and high, well furnished, a drawing room and chamber full of china and a damask bed embroidered . . . a pretty deal of [silver] plate in his wife's chamber.

'This high house [was] an apothecary's'. Thomas Macro, Fiennes noted, 'was esteemed a very rich man'. Indeed so he was. As well as this house in town, he had a country house. He left a fortune which enabled his son Cox (born 1683), who owed his ludicrous name and a portion of his wealth to his mother's family, to live the life of a gentleman scholar and connoisseur.

## WAGE EARNERS

A much bigger group of households was headed by waged workers – journeymen (craftsmen paid by the day) – and agricultural workers, who were often paid by the task. Their income was uncertain: they had no cushion against ill health; when trade was slack for any reason, they were laid off. In fact the commitments involved in setting up a household – renting dwelling space, acquiring the minimum bedding and utensils – might be beyond their means. Sharing a bed was a common experience three or four hundred years ago: successful defences against charges of incest indicate that in poorer households there were always not enough beds to put unmarried men and women up separately. In 1616 John Page, a Wiltshire man, admitted that he and his daughter had slept head to toe in the same bed for many years past for want of another.

In 1579 the newly married William Thompson went north in search of work, leaving his pregnant wife in Essex with a relative who had taken her in 'for kindred sake, considering their poverty'. This kinsman's ratepaying neighbours could not be confident that Thompson would come back and resume direct responsibility for his wife and their child, who might thus become a charge on the parish. In parish accounts 'widow' seems sometimes to be used as a courtesy title for a deserted wife.

## THE NEEDY POOR

The census of the needy poor taken in Ipswich in the late 1590s confirms that small household size was linked to poverty. Ipswich solitaries were predominantly poor widows like Joan Smith and Mother Ingram, whose ages were given in round figures as 70 and 80. Women without families sometimes joined forces: 60-year-old Jane Birde and Ann Gilson, who was 42 and made her living as a 'drudge' in other people's households, lived together. Disapproval of young people living outside the authority of a natural parent or a householder *in loco parentis* comes over clearly in the terse phrasing of this late sixteenth-century list of the town's poor. Eade Hodge, 'a boy' of 17, was 'idle' – without employment – and lacked 'discipline'. The 'two sturdy maids, the children of John Mynter', both in their twenties, a spinster and a washermaid, also wanted 'discipline'. Young people, who did not have the expectation of an inheritance or the prospect of a secure position in local society to hold them in check, were perceived as a threat to the community. In the view of the sober householder, with little or nothing to lose, the like of John Mynter's daughters were bait waiting to trap unwary men, husbands and bachelors, into drinking in alehouses – the resort of discontented men, loose women and the disorderly young, vagrants – lewd dancing, adultery, fornication or ill-advised marriages. Their offspring born in or out of wedlock were likely to be a charge on their ratepaying neighbours.

Settled communities feared the mobile. In Hornchurch in Essex the parish clerk recorded forty-one people punished as vagrants in the thirty-one months between April 1628 and May 1631. The fear generated by the travelling poor, who generally passed through in their twos and threes in search of work and resorted to theft when driven by need, was a symptom of the insecurity which plagued the modest householders who were charged with the duty of relieving their destitute neighbours and preserving law and order in their parishes. To them the stolen goose was a forecast of financial ruin and the passing stranger a convenient scapegoat who could be made to shoulder the blame for unsolved crimes against people and property.

## FURTHER READING

Campbell, Mildred (1942) *The English Yeoman,* New Haven, Conn.

Clark, Alice (1972) *Working Life of Women in the Seventeenth Century* (1919), London

Davidson, Caroline (1982) *A Woman's Work is Never Done: A History of Housework in the British Isles,* London

Spurling, Hilary (1986) *Elinor Fettiplace's Receipt Book. Elizabethan Country House Cooking,* London

Todd, Barbara (1985) 'The Remarrying Widow: A Stereotype Reconsidered' in *Women in English Society, 1500–1800,* Mary Prior (ed.), London

Tusser, Thomas (1984) 'The Points of Huswiferie' in *Five Hundred Points of Good Husbandry* (1580), London

# CHAPTER 8

# Old age

Three or four hundred years ago age was a less significant category than rank and ability. Precedence, which dictated the order of processions at funerals and, at table, both the quality and quantity of food you were allotted, was accorded to rank: the youngest earl took precedence over the oldest baron. Regardless of age, the servant deferred to his master and the single woman to her married sister.

Age was much less clearly defined. Although parishes had been obliged to keep records of baptisms since 1538, a proportion of infants went unbaptised, through their parents' negligence or, increasingly, their principled objection to a ceremony not described in the New Testament. In any case, certificates were not issued. In consequence, while those who believed that the stars and planets influenced human affairs kept a careful note of the precise time at which a birth occurred, many other people, especially those without a formal education, had rather a hazy idea of their own age and those of their friends and relations – the coincidence of a public event, a coronation, a visitation of the plague, a great fire was a helpful benchmark.

There was no concept of a standard age of retirement or of pension rights. Not until the twentieth century was there a national scheme to make regular and predictable deductions from the earnings of those in work to provide for those in need. And, as the habit of bracketing the frail old with younger disabled people and small children suggests, mental and physical fitness were important factors in determining an individual's role in her or his community.

The course of human life was unpredictable. A sickly baby could survive to robust old age: Thomas Hobbes (1588–1679) was born prematurely in 1588, the year of the Armada. According to his acquaintance John Aubrey,

> his mother fell in labour with him upon the fright of the invasion of the Spaniards . . . . In his youth he was unhealthy: he took colds, being wet in his feet . . . . From forty or fifty he grew healthier. In his old age he was very bald . . . yet within door he used to study and sit bareheaded, and said he never took cold in his head, but that his greatest trouble was to keep off the flies from pitching on the baldness. Besides his daily walking he did twice or thrice a year play tennis (at about 75 he did it) . . . . In the country for want of a tennis court, he would walk uphill and downhill in the park.

The park was at Chatsworth, the home of his patron, the Earl of Devonshire. Hobbes' chief disability was 'the shaking palsy in his hands' – by his mid-seventies he was unable to write legibly and relied on an amanuensis to get his thoughts on to paper.

A fit young man could be crippled at a stroke: William Blundell, a Lancashire landowner, was born in May 1620. When he was 21, right at the start of the Civil Wars, 'his thigh was broken with a shot in the king's service'. Ever after he was known as 'Halt Will, the Cavalier'. A letter written to his sister-in-law in 1651 contrasted his present condition with what he had been a decade before. He reminded her of 'what a pretty straight young thing, all dashing in scarlet' he was when she last saw him.

> But now, if you chance to hear a thing come thump – thump – up your stairs like a knocker, God bless us, at midnight, look out confidently: a gross body of an ell [45 inches or 115 cm] or more in the waist, with an old peruke [wig] clapped on a bald pate, do you not fear for all that. The thing is no goblin; but the very party we talk on

– himself.

Writing to a cousin in 1677, when he was in his fifties, Blundell signed himself 'the poor old cripple'. He lived into his late seventies, died a few weeks short of his seventy-eighth birthday. Although his letters paint a bleak picture of the persecution and financial hardships endured by a staunchly Catholic family in the troubled times in which he lived, William Blundell was better placed to cope with a loss of physical power than a man or woman whose only means of earning a living was by physical labour in the house, the workshop, the fields or streets of England.

## LIFE EXPECTANCY

As John Smith, Doctor of Medicine, noted in a meditation on old age published in 1666, the Old Testament indicated that God had progressively shortened the human life span: 'The lives of the patriarchs before the Flood were extended to almost a thousand years'. The Bible recorded that Adam was nearly 930 years old when he died, Noah 950, while the proverbial Methuselah, who held the record for longevity, survived until he was 969. Then, Smith tells his readers, 'about the time of the Flood God abbreviates the course of man's life and seems precisely to set it at one hundred and twenty years'. The Psalms associated with Noah's descendant King David suggest seventy or eighty years as the maximum.

There are no dependable figures of life expectancy in seventeenth-century England. The records of burials entered into parish registers provide evidence of the killing power of major epidemics and the influence of failed harvests on the death rate but until 1813 the parish clerks rarely recorded the ages of the deceased and, as a result, patterns of mortality outside these periods of crisis are much harder to discern. However, the custom of identifying the individuals who were baptised, married or buried by reference to their fathers or husbands led researchers interested in the history of birth, death and marriage to devise techniques which, as they put it, enabled them to 'reconstitute' the vital events in the life stories of the, not necessarily typical, individuals and families who stayed put in their home parishes over a long period. Unfortunately only 404 of the 10,000-odd parishes in England have records adequate for this purpose and they do not match the cross-section of communities that the researchers would have chosen for themselves.

The campaigns waged by godly preachers to persuade their hearers and readers that Death stalked the country summoning infants and children, youths and maidens, men and women to meet their maker and the anecdotal evidence of premature death in diaries and letters and published memorial inscriptions tend to confirm the view that, contrary to the assertion of Psalm 90 that 'score years and ten' or even 'four score years' represented the normal span of human life, people in their seventies and eighties were very rarely encountered. As far as we can tell from the analysis of the ages of death of members of the aristocracy and from the exercises in reconstitution that have been carried out, the truth lies somewhere in between these extremes. Lawrence Stone calculated that, of the 243 peers alive in England between 1558 and 1641, 103 died in their fifties and sixties but 33 survived into their seventies and 15 into their eighties. At Colyton in Devon, for example, the ages at death of 227 of the 345 married people who died between 1538 and 1837 have been calculated. The average was 56. Nevertheless, 54 of them survived into their seventies and eighties. And indeed, medical men of the period were prepared to countenance the possibility that their contemporaries might live twice as long.

Thomas Parr, who died in November 1635 at an alleged age of 152, was the best-known ancient Englishman of the seventeenth century. A few months before his death he had been discovered in Shropshire by Thomas Howard (born 1585),the second Earl of Arundel, 'the most accomplished curiosity hunter of his day', and put on show in London. 'Old Parr's picture' found its way into the Ashmolean Museum, the only painted portrait in the collection of natural and artificial rarities made by John Tradescant the elder (died 1638). John Taylor, a prolific versifier, celebrated his life in a doggerel biography, *The Old, Old, Very Old Man*, which, incidentally, records the scepticism of some contemporaries:

> Some may object that they will not believe
> His age can be so much, for none can give
> Account thereof. Time being past so far
> And at his birth there was no register
> The Register was 97 years since
> Given by th'Eighth Henry, the illustrious prince.

The post-mortem on Old Parr was performed by William Harvey (born 1578), the most eminent medical man of the day. Harvey's report, written

in Latin, the language of science, understood by educated men throughout the Western world, was translated into English in the 1840s. Even if we
share the doubts Taylor expressed about Parr's date of birth, Harvey's
report remains a valuable account of the physical state of an 'old, old, very
old man'. 'Thomas Parr, a poor countryman, born ... in the county of Salop,
died on the 14th of November in the year of grace 1635 after having lived
one hundred and fifty two years and nine months and survived nine princes'.

His physical condition was surprisingly good. 'The body was muscular,
the chest hairy and the hair of the forearms still black . The organs of generation were healthy so that it seemed not improbable' that he was sexually active to a ripe age and, specifically,

> that he did public penance under a conviction of incontinence after he had
> passed his hundredth years and his wife, whom he married as a widow in his
> hundred-and-twentieth year, did not deny that he had intercourse with her
> after the manner of other husbands with their wives, not until about twelve
> years back had he ceased to embrace her frequently . . . .
>
> All the internal parts . . . appeared so healthy that, had nothing happened
> to interfere with the old man's habits of life, he might perhaps have escaped
> paying the debt due to nature for more time longer. . . .
>
> The brain was healthy, very firm and hard to the touch, hence shortly before
> his death he heard extremely well, understood all that was said to him, answered
> immediately to questions and had perfect apprehensions of any matter in hand.

However, Harvey tells us, using further information obtained outside
the anatomy theatre, he could not get about unaided and 'was accustomed
to walk about slightly supported between two persons'. His senses had
deteriorated: his memory was 'greatly impaired' and 'he had been blind
for twenty years'. Yet, in Harvey's opinion, it was the foul air of London
and the unaccustomed rich food and strong drink at Arundel's table which
killed him.

Under the heading *Boulimia Centenaria*, another notable medic, Sir Thomas
Browne (born 1605), described

> a woman now living in Yarmouth named Elizabeth Mitchell, an hundred and
> two years old, a person of four foot and a half high, very lean, very poor, and
> living in a mean room without ordinary accommodation [inadequately fur-
> nished]. Her youngest son is forty-five years old. Though she answers well
> enough to ordinary questions, yet she conceives her eldest daughter to be her
> mother. But what is remarkable about her is a kind of *boulime* or 'dog appetite'
> [bulimia actually means 'ox appetite']; she greedily eating day and night all
> that her allowance [parish pension], friends and charitable people afford her,
> drinking beer or water, and making little distinction of any food, either of
> broths, flesh, fish, apples, pears, and any coarse food in no small quantity, inso-
> much that the overseers of late have been fain to augment her weekly allowance.

Curiosity hunting was a characteristic activity of men with money, leisure
and intellectual pretensions. Ralph Thoresby (born 1658), the Leeds mer-

chant, antiquary and collector, who published *The Musaeum Thoresbyanum or a Catalogue of the Antiquities and Natural and Artificial Rarities preserved in the Repository of Ralph Thoresby, Gent.* in 1715, added as an appendix descriptions *Of the Unusual Accidents that have attended some persons*; these covered the whole span of the human career from the child which cried 'audibly in its mother's womb' to a long list of people from Leeds and its environs 'such as have enjoyed a constant health even in old age'.

At the age of 91 or 92 Mr Lawrence Benson went out into the countryside in the middle of the day, 'got half an acre of wheat reaped, brought a peck of it home, sent it to the mill, got it grinded and a cake made of it, which the cant [hale and hearty] old man ate the same evening'. It would be easy to assume that Mr Benson did the reaping, grinding and baking himself, given his standing as a gentleman (the 'Mr' gives it away) it is unlikely that this was so: his vigour was reflected in the organisation, not the execution, of these tasks.

In 1714, the very summer that he was working on the text, Thoresby 'saw good old Mrs Plaxton (mother to the . . . rector of Berwick in Elmet) thread a very small needle (which I now have by me) without spectacles, though in her ninetieth year, she reads also written-hand as well as print without them'.

Among clergymen 'good old Mr Moor', Rector of Guiseley held the local record for long service in a parish, 'baptising a child after he came to that benefice, and burying the same person three score years after, being in all sixty-three years rector'. 'Robert Taylor was clerk in the new church at Leeds sixty-one years though he had a child that could run about in the churchyard when it was building'.

An impressive run of men embarked on fatherhood in their riper years and lived to see their descendants in the second and even third generations. For instance, Mr Peter Mason, Senior, of Leeds was 45 when he married yet lived to be a great-grandfather. Mr Thomas Bernard of Leeds was 50 years old when he married, had eighteen children and was 'so brisk that he rid a-hunting when he was above an hundred years of age'. Thoresby also had 'notice of one James Sagar', who, lacking the honorific 'Mr' was evidently a man of humbler rank than the others he describes, 'who married at four score and yet lived to lead his grandchild to church'.

The collection includes more than a dozen other centenarians, among them 'Widow Nordis of the park side of this town [Leeds] . . ."five score and sax", to use her own expression, which my grandmother Sykes, who lived in that neighbourhood computed was truly so, by certain other circumstances' or, as we should say, on the basis of circumstantial evidence. Thoresby's other grandmother contributed an impressive statistic concerning 'Thomas Whitfield of Headingley in this parish [Leeds again] and his wife Elizabeth (who was related to my grandmother Thoresby) who lived in matrimony full eighty years; she was married at eighteen, had fourteen children, died within ten weeks of her husband, aged 98 or 99, they made near 200 betwixt them'. Thoresby himself, when he was Overseer of the Poor, 'Anno 1687 . . . found in one house an old man and his sister who made nine score years betwixt them and, in the same township, Widow Stirk, who was "an hundred all but two years and a piece", to use her own expression'. Thoresby's catalogue leaves his reader with the impression that a hale and hearty nonagenarian was remarkable – as he or she would be in our own time – but by no means extraordinary and certainly within the experience of most people of Leeds and the surrounding villages three hundred years ago.

## THE EFFECTS OF AGEING

His phenomenal, and somewhat dubious, longevity apart, Harvey's description of Old Parr's diminished capacities would have come as no surprise to his readers, whether they were professional medics or amateurs of science. Ageing was associated with sensory impairment and physical infirmity. Shakiness was a sign of old age: Ann, Lady Fanshawe (born 1625), thought it worthy of note that her father 'enjoyed a firm health till about eighty years of age'. After her mother's death in 1640 Lady Fanshawe's father, Sir John Harrison (1589–1669), 'in his old age [his fifties], married again; he lived to see both his children by his second wife married. Normally, in course of time, sight and hearing deteriorated, teeth dropped out, strength waned, movement became more difficult. Many depended on sticks or crutches; the better off could buy magnifying spectacles but there were no effective false teeth or aids to hearing.

John Smith, reflecting on the process of ageing, characterised 'the old man' as 'beset with a troop of diseases'. John Pechey, another university-educated physician, recognised that the old were 'more subject to chronical diseases' than their juniors. 'Gout', for instance,

> chiefly seizes those old men who after they have the best part of their lives tenderly and delicately, indulging themselves freely with splendid banquets, wine and other spirituous liquors, and at length, having by reason of that sloth that always accompanies old age, wholly omitted those exercises of body which young men are accustomed to.

Inevitably, 'gout' killed 'more rich than poor, more wise men than fools', since the better educated were accounted wiser. Of course, medics hastened to point out, with the aid of 'an honest and able physician', 'the retarding and keeping off of old age' might be secured 'for a competent season'.

Thomas Muffett's *Health's Improvement*, which emphasised the influence of diet on well-being at all stages of life including in old age, was first published in 1584; a second edition, 'enlarged and corrected' by Christopher Bennett, came out in 1655. A few years earlier Thomas Venner 'Doctor of Physick in Bathe' published his *Via Recta as Vitam Longam or A Treatise wherein the right way and best manner of living for attaining to a long and healthful life is clearly demonstrated and punctually applied to every age and constitution of the body* in 1650. Venner, naturally, argued for the efficacy of the increasingly fashionable Bath water.

For the weakly of all ages, Muffett recommended milk 'which the youngest child, the weariest old man, and such as sickness has consumed may easily digest'. To Muffett's way of thinking, a milk diet was the equivalent of a blood transfusion: 'If we would define or describe what milk is, it seemeth to be nothing but white blood'. The most digestible milk was breast milk: 'Neither is women's milk best only for young and tender infants but also for men and women of riper years fallen by age and sickness'. Muffett shared the common belief that the temperament of the nurse transmitted itself through her milk to her nursling. He cited the case of Dr Caius (1510–73), a distinguished and highly successful medical practitioner, trained in Italy and nine times elected President of the College of Physicians in London, who used his great wealth to refound Gonville Hall in Cambridge where he had been a student and later a fellow between 1529 and 1539.

> What made Dr Caius in his last illness so peevish and so full of frets at Cambridge when he sucked one woman (whom I spare to name) froward of conditions and of bad diet; and contrariwise so quiet and well when he sucked another of contrary disposition? Verily, the diversity of their milk and conditions, which being contrary to one another, wrought also in him that sucked them contrary effects.

The therapy was still practised in the middle of the eighteenth century. According to a brief *Life* of Sarah, Duchess of Marlborough (1660–1744), which was published in 1745, 'the most stupid and senseless of all the aspersions cast upon her grace . . . is her sucking divers women to death'. The writer vehemently denied that she had ever been wetnursed in old age.

Since intellectual and physical competence were more significant than any chronological boundary, the milestones in the process of ageing were marked by the loss of power rather than by birthdays. The physician John Smith perceived old age as 'a three-fold state'. In the first,

> While it is yet in the beginning . . . men are able to do business and go about their employments. The second is full, mature or ripe age when men begin to leave off their employments and betake themselves into retiredness, when God hath no more work for them and they have no more strength for him. Or lastly, extreme, sickly, decrepit overgrown old age.

Smith's model tallies with real-life experience: the evidence we have suggests that by the time they were in their eighties most survivors were 'worn out by age'.

## SOCIAL ROLES

In a society in which memory remained an important means of record-keeping, intellectually able old people represented a living archive. When there was a need to confirm local boundaries, customs and practices, the testimony of the aged was sought out. In one Oxfordshire village in 1643, after an epidemic there was an anxiety that 'there scarce remained alive any upholding the customs and privileges of the parish'. Among the commonest cases were those involving tithes, the local taxes due to the church

on crops and so forth arising immediately from the ground, as grain of all sorts, hay, wood, fruits or herbs . . . . Things immediately nourished by the ground, as colts, calves, lambs, chickens, milk, cheese, eggs . . . . Products of any kinds of labour or industry [which amount to] the tenth part of the clear gain after charges deducted.

The sale of monastic lands by the Crown in the 1540s after the dissolution of the monasteries provoked many disputes between the new landowners, who inherited their predecessors' rights to tithes and their tithe-paying tenants. The parties to a case brought in 1598, relating to pasture rights on the fells in the parish of Kirkby Malhamdale in Yorkshire, called on a string of very old men to testify: Nicholas Walton was, or claimed to be, 77, Roger Carr 88, Richard Knowles 80, John Lawson 88, Ralph Buck 80, Owstan Airton 79, Roger Buck 76 and William Lambart 90. In 1667 Henry Jenkins, who died in 1670 and sometimes claimed that he was born in 1501, called on to testify in a dispute between the Vicar of Catterick and one of his parishioners, gave his age as 157.

Because of the law's suspicion of their sex, women were less often called upon to act as witnesses. The dispute over the tithes of hay and corn on land formerly owned by the community of nuns at Moxby Priory in Yorkshire, heard in 1586, almost exactly half a century after the sisters and their servants were evicted, is an exception. Joan Cockell, a 70-year-old widow, who had been 'butler at the monastery or nunnery', recalled that she had gone 'yearly in haytime forth with the prioress and nuns there to see the haymakers of such hay as growed in the grounds belonging to the . . . nunnery and see the hay yearly mown made into cocks'. Elizabeth Burnett, 'spinster aged 73 . . . a nun there herself about five or six years before the said dissolution . . . she herself did yearly for the most part in hay time help to straw and cock the hay'. Margaret Thornaby, now wife of a local farmer, Roger Newstead, aged 72, stated that she

was a professed nun there and for divers years before dwelt and continued in the monastery for nine years together next and immediately before the dissolution and suppression all which time she saith that she amongst other young nuns helped to do such necessary business as was to be done about the same and especially she saith yearly during the time aforesaid helped in haytime to make the hay.

As long as they remained fit enough to participate, their function as a communal memory bank aside, men and women in their sixties, seventies, eighties and perhaps beyond, continued to pursue the calling which they had followed from their youth.

Landed proprietors, the models for the rest of the property-owning ranks, very rarely relinquished control of their estates. The heir waited on his predecessor's death to come into his own: as the cynical John Weever commented, 'The weeping of an heir is laughing under a visage or disguise'. Nor did they normally withdraw from public life while they were intellectually competent. Denzil Holles (1599–1680), a leader of the opposition to Charles I and, in old age, at odds with Charles II, was still active in politics at the end of the 1670s. The French ambassador writing two months before Holles' death, described him as 'the man of all England' to whom other politicians gave 'the most consideration.... Although he does not often go to Parliament, he is consulted by many people and his advice has great weight'.

Unless they were overtaken by infirmity or backed the wrong side in one of the contests which racked English political society in the sixteenth and seventeenth centuries, paid servants of the state remained in office until they died. Beneficed clergymen of the Church of England, the vicars, rectors and their superiors, enjoyed the freehold of their livings. Of course, their tenure was sometimes interrupted as a result of religious and political upheavals – Charles I's minister Archbishop Laud was in his late sixties and fully engaged in the affairs of Church and state when his career was cut short by his imprisonment in the Tower of London; he died on the scaffold in 1645. Edward Foss' *Sketches of [the] Lives of The Judges of England* (1864) include many who lived and practised to three score years and ten and beyond. James Dyer (born circa 1512), who headed the Court of Common Pleas from 1559 to his death in 1582, was 'an ornament to the bench', unusually resistant to the temptations which seduced many a lawyer.

> To put by bribes his hands were ever closed,
> His process just, he took the poor man's part;
> He ruled by law and listened not to art.

John Popham, who was born in or about 1531, presided at the trial of the Gunpowder plotters in 1606. In 1628, at the age of 78, Edward Coke, out of sympathy with the policies of the new King, Charles I, retired from public affairs but, as Foss notes, 'he occupied the five remaining years of his life in ... preparing for the press' his *Institutes*, four monumental volumes of legal commentary.

It is, however, clear that some judges' careers were artificially prolonged to protect their income after their service had effectively come to an end. Judge Walmesley died in 1612, aged 75, and still in office, but, as his monument in Blackburn revealed,

> When as old age creeping on apace
> Made him unable to supply his place,
> Yet he continued with the king's permission
> A Judge until his death still in commission;
> And still received by his special grace
> His fee as full as when he serv'd the place.

Among property holders, old women were inevitably less conspicuous than old men. A very few had public careers. Female reproductive biology meant that none was able to delight or dismay her kin by bearing a child in her sixties or seventies. Nevertheless, women of this age mothered orphaned grandchildren and great-grandchildren. Widows especially exercised power and influence on their families and estates, some simply as a charge on the family's purse, others as important players in dynastic affairs. Bridget, born Hussey, formerly Moryson, the childless widow of Henry Manners, second Earl of Rutland, who died in 1563, survived him by very nearly four decades, all that time, even after her marriage with the Earl of Bedford (died 1583) and third widowing, drawing an income from the Manners estates. Elizabeth of Hardwick (born circa 1527), three times married and widowed, in turn Mistress Barley, Lady St Loe, Countess of Shrewsbury, but better known as 'Building Bess', was 70 when, in 1597, she moved into the flamboyant New Hall, 'more glass than wall', she had constructed at Hardwick and which she had had emblazoned with her initials 'ES' – for Elizabeth Shrewsbury. Much of interior remained to be finished and, as the historian of Hardwick's building observed, she 'must have lived for several years in a house encumbered by builders' mess' – John the painter was still busy in 1601.

Sarah Jenyns (1660–1744), who married John Churchill, the first Duke of Marlborough, though progressively disabled by 'the gout', which eventually reduced her to the helpless condition of 'a child bound up in swaddling clothes' was, by her own reckoning, 'a notable grandmother' and great-grandmother; 'better than any physician' at treating the victims of smallpox; an ambitious builder (Vanburgh, architect of Blenheim, the Churchills' Oxfordshire palace, which was named in commemoration of one of the first duke's famous victories against the French, referred to her as 'that B. B. B. B. Old B, the Dutchess of Marlbr.'); a marriage broker; financier and litigant.

A similar pattern can be discerned among smaller property holders. As her son William recorded in his autobiography, Elizabeth Stout, widow of a Lancashire farmer, stepped into her dead husband's shoes after he died in 1680, leaving her 'with six children, the youngest then about four years of age'. She busied herself, 'looking after her servants in the fields and dressing her corn and going to market with the same'. Twenty-eight years later she was

> about 76 years of age and dwelt with [William's] brother Josias as his housekeeper, and was become very infirm and was urgent on him to marry, he not being willing to keep house with a servant. And thereupon, with his mother's consent and approbation, he married Sibill Green, daughter of Thomas Green of Boulton Holmes, a neighbour. My brother Josias was about 48 years of age, and his wife about 30 years of age, and my mother seemed well satisfied with the marriage. But when the young wife came to housekeeping, my mother thought to have some direction in that, more than the young wife (who had been her father's housekeeper) would allow; which made their mother uneasy.

After a painful year of cohabitation the matriarch removed to her bachelor son William's house where she remained until she 'expired . . . in the eighty-fourth year of her age' in 1716. 'In her last four years she was often seized with falling fits [which] made her insensible for about a quarter of an hour' but 'she continued to spin till within four months of her death'.

Old women had roles to play in the world beyond their households. Their accumulated skills were valued. Thomas Hobbes, who published his last book when he was 87, 'was wont to say that he had rather have the advice or take physic from an experienced old woman that had been at many sick persons' bedsides than from the learnedest but unexperienced physician'.

Leading craftsmen worked on into old age. Inigo Jones (born 1573) staged masques for James I, Charles I and their queens; his architectural commissions for the royal family included the Banqueting House in Whitehall (that splendid chamber from which Charles I stepped on to the scaffold in 1649) and the Queen's House at Greenwich. He went on designing houses into the late 1640s. In 1648 he advised the Earl of Pembroke on the renovation of Wilton after a fire 'but being then very old' (he was 75), and unwilling to travel down to Wiltshire, he 'could not be there in person' to supervise the builders. Grinling Gibbons (1648–1721), the most celebrated wood carver in English history, was working shortly before his death. Practitioners of such stature, who could call on pupils, apprentices and servants to assist them are clearly comparable with the most eminent of today's architects, sculptors and potters, who rarely retire while they are able to work to their own satisfaction and that of their patrons.

However, in the sixteenth and seventeenth centuries the ordinary craftsmen, who would in general today have retired from waged work by the time they were 65, went on working until they were no longer capable. One of the principal functions of craft guilds and other fraternities was to provide for those who, through infirmity or other misfortune, found themselves 'fallen to a sudden poverty' with 'an honest living as long as life did last'. Charitable and municipal records indicate that among the labouring poor, both men and women were expected to support themselves while they could.

## AGED PAUPERS

Before the break with Rome, the needy benefited from the Church's teaching that good deeds paved the road to heaven. The Church of England maintained that good works were a by-product of faith rather than a passport to salvation. Poor neighbours were remembered in wills and those who attended funerals were rewarded with gifts of food, money or clothing. Doles of bread were provided in many parishes but begging was first regulated and then banned. The bigger towns, where the problems posed by the poor were more acute, pioneered schemes to support the helpless and deserving.

At Ipswich only the helpless and very poor were eligible for housing and pensions under the terms of Mr Tooley's bequest. 'Great Tooley', as he was known, died in 1551 but 'Mrs Tooley did impugn her husband's will' and pursued his executors through the courts 'four years and more'. It took even longer to realise his wishes. Tooley's bequest provided five poor couples, either married or pairs of men or women brought together by the trustees, with 'lodgings, a small cash pension, stocks of firewood . . . a bed, a mattress, a bolster, two blankets, three pairs of sheets and a covering'. The number of inmates grew as the town authorities adopted Tooley's model as a means of providing for those who could not survive independently, nevertheless, there was competition for assistance and the needy old often had to wait for dead men's beds. To take a sample of cases from 1588 and 1589: Helen Hadnam was blind; Elizabeth Adryan was 'an old, aged and impotent wench' who had been a 'dweller' in Ipswich 'by the space of 70 years'; Martin Topcliffe was 'an ancient, honest man', disabled, 'having been visited by the handiwork of God'; Martin Harwarde, 'a poor man without wife', was 'placed in the room of Father Loft, deceased, in the almshouses of Mr Tooley's foundation'.

Morning and evening, the foundationers who were able were required to return thanks at the church of St Mary Quay

> for that it pleased the Holy Spirit to move and stir the heart of Henry Tooley deceased, late merchant of this town, to will and give lands and possessions sufficient for a necessary release [relief] of us thy poor servants and to the performance of other deeds of charity about this town.

The badges and uniforms Tooley's pensioners wore reminded those who saw them processing to the church of their benefactor's wealth and charity. Inmates who missed a service risked having their pensions docked; persistent absentees were evicted. The same penalty faced those who refused to work or indulged in 'dicing, drinking or in any other unlawful game or exercise'.

The notes of a survey of the borough's poor 'dwelling abroad in the town' made in 1597 record the allowances allocated to the old to top up their earnings. The 'wants' of Father Herley, a 70-year-old labourer, were identified as clothes, bedding and working tools – a mattock and a shovel. Warner's wife, also 70, who knitted, needed the tools of the textile trade, including a spinning wheel, and 'teaching' – an indication both that the spinning wheel was a new device and that the city fathers of Tudor England took the line that the poor were never too old to learn new skills. 'Discipline' was what 70-year-old George Smith and his wife, a 63-year-old, 'wanted'.

By 1601 a national system had been put in place: when the needs of the poor outran the charitable funds available in their home parish, a rate was levied on their better-off neighbours. The Elizabethan or the Old Poor Law, as it was known from the 1830s, worked well enough in places where there was a reasonable balance between ratepayers and pensioners but, in some of the largest towns, even before the end of the sixteenth century, residential areas had begun to develop a distinctive local character. With the richest and poorest households concentrated in different parishes, the parochial system of poor relief could not be sustained.

The governors of the Bristol Corporation, which was set up at the end of the seventeenth century to address the problems of poverty in the city, anticipated the policies of the New Poor Law enacted in 1834. A workhouse was established to accommodate the poor who could not get by on their own, especially orphaned children and old people 'who had no friends to help them'. The longevity of these very vulnerable people is impressive: in three months twelve men and women in their sixties, nine in their seventies, a dozen in their eighties and two in their nineties were admitted. Like Tooley's foundationers, the inmates of the Mint Workhouse were expected to pull their weight. Four of the old women, who had the task of combing the children's hair for vermin were kitted out with special overalls to protect them from infestation. Other old women minded the youngest children, did the laundry and the mending, knitted stockings and made lace to sell. Old tailors made the paupers' uniforms, other old men did the plumbing and acted as gatekeepers. The governors of the Bristol workhouse 'found it difficult to bend' the inmates 'down to good orders but by degrees' they 'brought them under government', forcing them to wear badges to proclaim their dependency, to buckle down to their 'labours', which, as the governors acknowledged, might amount 'to little' yet served their purpose in keeping the paupers from 'idleness', and to the compulsory diet of twice-daily prayers and two church parades on Sundays.

These references to 'discipline' and 'good orders' are clues to the shared mentality of the ratepayers, managers and recipients of poor relief. The independent householder, however old, however poor, had some dignity and standing in the community. The pensioner or inmate of an almshouse was required to defer to the authority of his benefactor or his benefactor's proxies. Dependence was a bitter pill to swallow. Close supervision might be appropriate and indeed 'very necessary' for the 'vagrants and sturdy beggars that have no habitation and that will not work unless they are held to it as galley slaves are tied to their oars . . . but for such poor people as have habitations of their own and are known in the places where they live' submission to such a regime was, at any age, a humiliating admission of personal failure.

## FURTHER READING

Laslett, Peter (1977) 'The History of Ageing and the Aged' in *Family Life and Illicit Love*, Cambridge

Pelling, Margaret (1991) 'Old Age, Poverty and Disability in Early Modern Norwich: Work, Remarriage and Other Expedients' in *Life, Death and the Elderly*, Margaret Pelling and Richard Smith (eds), London

Thomas, Keith (1976) 'Age and Authority in Early Modern England', *Proceedings of the British Academy*, pp. 205–48

# PART TWO

## Dossier of illustrative texts

# CONTENTS

# INTRODUCTION

This collection is made up of texts where were in the public domain between 1560 and 1720. Most were printed but, for example, parish registers and wills were handwritten; memorial inscriptions were, normally, cut into some durable material such as stone or metal.

Although some of the 'exhibits' deal with entirely mundane topics like bookkeeping, there is a strong sense of interaction between the natural and supernatural worlds in many of the texts I have reproduced. There were sceptics, of course, but most of them had the good sense to keep their doubts to themselves – Alexander Agnew, a Dumfriesshire man who said he knew no god but salt, and oatmeal and water, was executed for blasphemy by the English army of occupation in 1658.

## WRITERS AND READERS

The words in the dossier are overwhelmingly those set down by men educated at grammar schools and the two universities of Oxford and Cambridge. Assured and articulate, they wrote in the course of their professional duties, out of religious conviction or to make money. It could be argued that of all the documents I have included, wills take us closest to the beliefs and intentions of ordinary men and women; some of them had very few possessions to dispose of – and a good many of them could not write for themselves. Some wills, nuncupative wills as they are called, were memorised by the witnesses and committed to paper later on – a reminder that memories were better trained three or four hundred years ago than they are today.

There are good reasons to believe that many more people could read than write. However, like writing, the skill and habit of reading were probably acquired by a minority of English men and fewer still women; most households contained no books at all. Nevertheless, some at least of the texts I have included were familiar to non-readers. The Bible, the Book of Common Prayer and the Homilies were continuously 'broadcast' in churches; Gouge's *Of Domesticall Duties*, Baxter's *The Poor Man's Family Book* and Bunyan's *Pilgrim's Progress* are, in a sense, extended sermons in print. Sometimes an echo of a heard text comes across in a will. William Griggs, a farmer from Orwell in Cambridgeshire, made his will in 1649. Compare his statement that 'nothing is more certain than death, yet there is nothing more uncertain than the time of the coming thereof' (Margaret Spufford, *Contrasting Communities. English Villagers in the Sixteenth and Seventeenth Centuries*, Cambridge University Press, 1974, p. 321) with the words of the Homily on Repentance and True Reconciliation with God (see p. 159). *Poor Robin's Almanack*, William Hicks' *Oxford Jests* and Abel Boyer's *Wise and Ingenious Companion* retell the kinds of joke which might have been swopped on a building site or over a drink in the alehouse, including an early example of a 'good news, bad news' story.

As far as possible I have worked from texts printed in the period: the square brackets give the date of the original publication, the round brackets the date of the edition I have used. Almost always, in the interests of readability, I have modernised spelling and punctuation.

## THE ORDER OF THE EXHIBITS

The order of what I have called the 'exhibits' is, as the Introduction explains, inevitably arbitrary. The index will help you to find your way to the material relevant to the particular topic you are engaged with.

# EXHIBIT 1

# The biblical account of Creation

## SOURCE

**The Holy Bible containing the Old Testament and the New, newly translated out of the original tongues and with the former translations diligently compared and revised by his Majesty's [James I's] special command. Appointed to be read in churches. Printed by Thomas Buck and Roger Daniel, printers to the University of Cambridge, 1637 (1611)**

The images of Adam, Eve, the serpent and the apple were embroidered and painted on to dishes but the story of the Creation was of more than decorative significance in seventeenth-century England: Eve's role justified the subordination of women. The relationships between God and mankind and between men and women informed every stage of the human career from the cradle to the grave.

## Genesis, 2.7–9, 21–5

7And the Lord God formed man of the dust of the ground and breathed into his nostrils the breath of life and man became a living soul. 8And the Lord God planted a garden Eastward in Eden and there he put the man whom he had formed. 9And out of the ground made the Lord God to grow every tree that is pleasant to the sight, and good for food: the tree of life also in the midst of the garden and the tree of the knowledge of good and evil . . . .

21And the Lord God caused a deep sleep to fall upon Adam, and he slept, and he took one of his ribs, and closed up the flesh in stead thereof. 22And the rib, which the Lord God had taken from the man made he a woman, and brought her unto the man. 23And Adam said, this is now bone of my bones and flesh of my flesh: she shall be called Woman, because she was taken out of man. 24Therefore shall a man leave his father and his mother, and shall cleave unto his wife: and they shall be one flesh. 25And they were both naked, the man and the woman, and were not ashamed.

## Genesis, 3.6–7

God forbade Adam to eat the fruit of the tree of the knowledge of good and evil but, led on by the serpent,

6the woman saw that the tree was good for food, and that it was pleasant to the eyes, and a tree to be desired to make one wise; she took the fruit thereof, and did eat, and gave also unto her husband with her and he did eat. 7And the eyes of both of them were opened and they knew that they were naked; and they sewed fig leaves together, and made themselves aprons.

## Genesis, 12–13, 16–21

Charged by God with disobedience,

12the man said, 'The woman, whom thou gavest to be with me, she gave me of the tree, and I did eat'. 13And the woman said, 'The serpent beguiled me, and I did eat'. . . .

16Unto the woman he said . . . 'In sorrow thou shalt bring forth children and thy desire shall be to thy husband, and he shall rule over thee'. 17And unto Adam he said, 'Because thou hast harkened unto the voice of thy wife, and hast eaten of the tree of which I commanded thee, saying, "Thou shalt not eat of it", cursed is the ground for thy sake; in sorrow shalt thou eat all the days of thy life. 18Thorns also and thistles shall it bring forth to thee: and thou shalt eat the herb of the field. 19In the sweat of thy face shalt thou eat bread, till thou return to unto the ground; for out of it wast thou taken; for dust thou art and unto dust shalt thou return'. 20And Adam called his wife's name Eve, because she was the mother of all living . 21Unto Adam also and to his wife did the Lord God make coats of skins and clothed them.

# EXHIBIT 2

# Baptism

## SOURCE

### The Book of Common Prayer, 1662

Infant baptism was a requirement of the state and Church of England. Some godly objectors pointed out that infant baptism does not have the authority of the New Testament.

## The private baptism of children in houses

The curates of every parish shall often admonish the people that they defer not the Baptism of their children longer than the first or second Sunday next after their birth, or other holyday falling between, unless upon a great and reasonable cause, so to be approved by the curate.

And also they shall warn them that without like great cause and necessity they procure not their children to be baptized at home in their houses. But when the need shall compel them so to do, then Baptism shall be administered in this fashion:

. . . the child being named by some one that is present, the minister shall pour water upon it, saying these words: N, I baptize thee in the Name of the Father, and of the Son, and of the Holy Ghost. Amen.

Then all kneeling down, the Minister shall give thanks unto God, and say: We yield thee hearty thanks, most merciful Father, that it has pleased thee to regenerate this infant with thy Holy Spirit, to receive *him* [italicised in the original] for thine own child by adoption, and to incorporate *him* into thy holy Church. And we humbly beseech thee to grant that, as *he* is now made partaker of the death of thy Son, so *he* may be also of his resurrection. And that finally with the residue of thy Saints *he* may inherit thine everlasting kingdom, through the same thy Son, Jesus Christ our Lord.

And let them not doubt but that the child so baptized is lawfully and sufficiently baptized and ought not to be baptized again.

# EXHIBIT 3

# The churching of women

## SOURCE

### The Book of Common Prayer, 1662

The first Prayer Book published for use in the Church of England after the break with Rome called this ceremony by its traditional name, 'The Purification of Women', a title taken over from the Jewish service from which it derived (Luke 2.22). In 1552 the title was altered to 'The Thanksgiving of Women after Childbirth, commonly called The Churching of Women'. This title was retained when the fourth edition was published in 1662, following the Restoration of King and Church.

The prescribed prayer, which is given here in the 1662 version, changed little from edition to edition but, in 1662, new psalms were introduced to replace Psalm 121 which begins 'I have lifted up mine eyes to the hills from whence cometh my help' and portrays God as protector of his people. Psalm 116 puts stress on the risks and sufferings the newly delivered woman had gone through: 'The snares of death compassed me round about and the pains of hell gat hold upon me'. The alternative, Psalm 127, concentrates on children as 'the fruit of the womb, an heritage and gift that cometh of the Lord. Like as arrows in the hand of the giant, even so are the young children. Happy is the man that hath his quiverful of them'.

The mention of 'decent [appropriate] apparel', a reference to the wearing of a veil, was another innovation of the 1662 Prayer Book though, in fact, women who refused to wear veils because they objected to ceremonies without biblical precedent had been prosecuted as much as half a century earlier.

> The woman, at the usual time after her delivery, shall come into the Church decently apparelled, and there shall kneel down at some convenient place, as hath been accustomed . . . . And then the Priest shall say: 'For as much as it hath pleased Almighty God of his goodness to give you safe deliverance, and hath preserved you in the great danger of childbirth, you shall give hearty thanks to God'.

After the psalm and the Lord's Prayer, the priest led the congregation in this prayer:

> O Almighty God, we give thee humble thanks for that thou hast vouchsafed to deliver this woman thy servant from the great pain and peril of childbirth. Grant, we beseech thee, most merciful Father, that she through thy help may both faithfully live and walk according to thy will, in this life present; and also may be a partaker of everlasting glory in the life to come; through Jesus Christ our Lord.

## Psalm 121

1I will lift up mine eyes unto the hills from whence cometh my help.
2My help cometh even from the Lord who hath made heaven and earth.
3He will not suffer thy foot to be moved and he that keepeth thee will not sleep.
4Behold he that keepeth Israel shall neither slumber nor sleep.
5The Lord himself is thy keeper: the Lord is thy defence upon thy right hand.
6So that the sun shall not burn thee by day neither the moon by night.
7The Lord shall preserve thee from all evil yea, it is even that he shall keep thy soul.
8The Lord shall preserve thy going out and thy coming in from this time forth for evermore.

## Psalm 127

1Except the Lord build the house: their labour is but lost that build it.
2Except the Lord keep the city: the watchman waketh but in vain.
3It is but lost labour that ye haste to rise up early, and so late take rest, and eat the bread of carefulness: for so he giveth his beloved sleep.
4Lo, children and the fruit of the womb are an heritage and gift that cometh of the Lord.
5Like arrows in the hand of the giant: even so are the young children.

<sup>6</sup>Happy is the man that hath his quiver full of them: they shall not be ashamed when they speak with their enemies at the gate.

# EXHIBIT 4

# The Homilies

## SOURCE

**Certain Sermons or Homilies Appointed to be read in Churches in the time of the Late Queen Elizabeth of famous memory and now thought fit to be reprinted by the authority of the King's Most Excellent Majesty [James I] [1562/3, 1623] (Oxford, 1822)**

The homilies were a collection of standard, government-approved sermons.

[p. 6] Her Majesty commandeth and straitly chargeth all parsons, vicars, curates, and all others having spiritual cure, every Sunday and holyday in the year ... to read and declare to their parishioners plainly and distinctly one of the said [33] homilies, in such order as they stand in the book, except there be a sermon. . . .

## An exhortation against the fear of death

[pp. 91–2] We see three causes why worldly men fear death. One, because they shall lose thereby their worldly honours, riches, possessions, and all their hearts' desires; another, because of the painful diseases and bitter pangs, which commonly men suffer either before or at the time of death; but the chief cause, above all other, is the dread of the miserable state of eternal damnation both of body and soul, which they fear shall follow, after their departing from the worldly pleasure of this present life.

For the Christian

Death shall be . . . no death at all, but a very deliverance from death, from all pains, cares, and sorrows, miseries and wretchedness of this world, and the very entry into rest, and a beginning of everlasting joy, a tasting of heavenly pleasures, so great that neither tongue is able to express, neither eye to see, nor ear to hear them, no, nor any earthly man's heart to conceive them.

Harmony and what we might call 'fitness for purpose' characterised the created order. Knowing one's place and keeping to it were primary obligations for the members of human societies: the household, the parish or the city, the state.

## An exhortation concerning good order and obedience to rulers and magistrates

[pp. 104–5] Almighty God hath created and appointed all things heaven, earth and waters, in a most excellent and perfect order. In heaven he hath appointed distinct and several orders of archangels and angels. In earth he hath assigned and appointed kings, princes, with other governors under them, all in good and necessary order. The water above is kept, and raineth down in due time and season. The sun, moon, stars, rainbow, thunder, lightning, clouds, and all birds of the air do keep their order. The earth, trees, seeds, plants, herbs, corn, grass and all manner of beasts, keep themselves in order. All the parts of the whole year, as winter, summer, months, nights and days continue in their order. All kinds of fishes in the sea, rivers, and waters, with all fountains, springs, yea, the seas themselves, keep their comely course and order. And man himself also hath all his parts both within and without, as soul, heart, mind, memory, understanding, reason, speech, with all and singular corporal members of his body, in a profitable, necessary and pleasant order. Every degree of people in their vocation, calling and office, hath appointed to them their duty and order. Some are in high degree, some in low, some kings and princes, some inferiors and subjects, priests and laymen, masters and servants, fathers and children, husbands and wives, rich and poor. And every one have need of other so that in all things is lauded and praised the goodly order of God, without which no house, no city, no commonwealth can continue and endure, or last. For where there is no right order, there reigneth all abuse, carnal liberty, enormity, sin, and babylonical confusion. Take away kings, princes, rulers, magistrates, judges and such estates of God's order, no man shall ride or go by the highway unrobbed, no man shall sleep in his own house or bed unkilled, no man shall keep his wife, children and possessions in quietness, all things shall be common. And there needs must follow all mischief and utter destruction both of souls, bodies, goods and commonwealths.

## Against whoredom and adultery

The Flood, from which only Noah, his immediate family and his cargo of animals were spared, was an instance of the punishment which had been meted out when mankind deviated from the godly path. Sexual misconduct was perceived as profoundly disruptive.

[p. 127] To show how greatly he abhorreth adultery, whoredom, fornication and all uncleanness, [God] made all the fountains of the deep earth to burst out and the sluices of heaven to be opened so that the rain came down upon the earth by the space of forty days and forty nights, and by this means destroyed the whole world and mankind, eight persons only excepted.

Neither marriage nor motherhood was glamorised.

## The state of matrimony

[p. 463] How few matrimonies be there without chidings, brawlings, tauntings, repentings, bitter cursings and fightings. Which things whosoever doth commit, they do not consider that it is at the instigation of the ghostly enemy [Satan], who taketh great delight therein.

[p. 467] Truth it is that [women] must specially feel the grief and pains of their matrimony, in that they relinquish the liberty of their own rule, in the pain of their travailing, in the bringing up of their children. In which offices they be in great perils, and be grieved with great afflictions, which they might be without if they lived out of matrimony.

## Repentance and of true reconciliation unto God

[p. 503] The uncertainty and brittleness of our lives . . . is such that we cannot assure ourselves that we shall live one hour, or one half quarter of it. Which by experience we do find daily to be true, in them that be now merry and lusty, and sometimes feasting and banqueting with their friends, do fall suddenly dead in the streets, and other whiles under the board [table] when they are at meat . . . . But as we are most certain that we shall die, so we are most uncertain when we shall die. For our life doth lie in the hand of God, who will take it away when it pleaseth him.

# Exhibit 5

# *The Pilgrim's Progress*

## Sources

**John Bunyan, *The Pilgrim's Progress, from this world to that which is to come, delivered under the similtude of a dream wherein is discovered the manner of his setting out; his dangerous journey and safe arrival at the desired country* (2nd Edition, 1678)**
**John Bunyan, *Grace Abounding to the Chief of Sinners* (1666)**

From the official sermon, represented by the Homilies, we pass to the unofficial teaching of one of the most influential writers in the history of religion in England. To the authorities of his own time, however, John Bunyan was a dangerous subversive: he endured long spells of imprisonment.

John Bunyan was born in Elstow in Bedfordshire in 1628. His autobiography, *Grace Abounding to the Chief of Sinners* (1666), sketches his background:

> [pp. 1–2] In this my relation of the merciful working of God upon my soul, it
> will not be amiss if in the first place I do in a few words give you a hint of my
> pedigree and manner of bringing up.... For my descent then, it was, as is well
> known by many, of a low and inconsiderable generation; my father's house
> being of that rank that is meanest and most despised of all the families in the
> land.
>
> But yet, notwithstanding the meanness and inconsiderableness of my par-
> ents, it pleased God to put into their heart to put me to school, to learn both
> to read and to write, the which I also attained, according to the rate of other
> poor men's children.

John Bunyan was in fact a tinker and a tinker's son, a mender, that is, of
pots and pans. His writings are pungent with images which call to mind
the sorrows and joys and mundane circumstances of life among 'the incon-
siderable':

> I did liken myself . . . unto the case of some child that was fallen into a mill-
> pit; who, though it could make some shift to scrabble and sprawl in the water,
> yet because it could find neither hold for hand nor foot, therefore at last it must
> die in that condition [*Grace Abounding*, 1666, p. 52].

> Some cry out against sin even as the mother cries out against her child in her
> lap when she calleth it 'Slut' and 'Naughty girl', and then falls to hugging and
> kissing it [*Pilgrim's Progress*, 1678 (2nd edition), pp. 135–6].

> Then he took him by the hand and led him into a very large parlour that was
> full of dust because never swept . . . . Now when [the man] began to sweep,
> the dust began so abundantly to fly about that Christian had almost therewith
> been choked. Then said the Interpreter to a damsel that stood by, 'Bring hith-
> er the water and sprinkle the room'. Which, when she had done, was swept
> and cleansed with pleasure [*Pilgrim's Progress*, 1678, p. 39].

But, as the first words of *Grace Abounding* indicate, his essential concern
was his inner self, and not with life on earth but life everlasting.

> [p. 1] From a child I had but few equals . . . both for cursing, swearing, lying
> and blaspheming the holy name of God. Yea so settled and rooted was I in
> these things that they became as a second nature to me. The which . . . did so
> offend the Lord that, even in my childhood, he did scare and affright me with
> fearful dreams and did terrify me with dreadful visions. For often, after I had
> spent this and the other day in sin, I have in my bed been greatly afflicted,
> while asleep, with the apprehensions of devils and wicked spirits who . . .
> laboured to draw me away with them.

> [p. 4] A while after, these terrible dreams did leave me, which also I soon for-
> got for my pleasures did quickly cut off the remembrance of them, as if they

had never been, wherefore with more greediness . . . I did . . . let loose the reins to my lusts and delighted in all transgression against the law of God so that, until I came to the state of marriage, I was the very ringleader of all the youth that kept me company into all manner of vice and ungodliness . . . . My mercy was to light upon a wife whose father was counted godly. This woman and I, though we came together as poor as poor might be (not having so much as a dish or spoon betwixt us both), yet this she had for her part: *The Plain Man's Pathway to Heaven* and *The Practice of Piety*, which her father had left her when he died.

Bunyan's road to grace was long and tortuous but, eventually:

[pp. 74–5] As I was sitting by the fire, I suddenly felt this word to sound in my heart: 'I must go to Jesus'. At this my former darkness and atheism fled away and the blessed things of heaven were set within my view. . . . Then with joy I told my wife: 'O now I know, I know!' But that night was a good night to me, I never had but few better . . . . I could scarce lie in my bed for joy and peace and triumph through Christ.

Bunyan's chief monument, *The Pilgrim's Progress*, became and remained a best seller in the English-speaking world (F. M. Harrison: *Editions of The Pilgrim's Progress, The Library*, 4th series XXII, 1942, pp. 73–81).

As they journeyed, Pilgrim, and Faithful and Hopeful, the godly companions he met on his way, were sustained by the prospect of reaching the Celestial City. An

[pp. 10–11] endless kingdom to be inhabited, and everlasting life to be given us that we may inhabit that kingdom for ever. . . .There are Crowns of Glory to be given us and garments that will make us shine like the sun in the firmament of heaven. . . . There shall be no more crying or sorrow for he that is the owner of the place will wipe all tears from our eyes.

There we shall be with seraphims, and cherubims, creatures that will dazzle your eyes to look on them. There also shall you meet with thousands and ten thousands that have gone before us to that place. None of them are hurtful, but loving, and holy; every one walking in the sight of God and standing in his presence with acceptance for ever. In a word, there, there, we shall see the elders with their golden crowns. There we shall see the holy virgins with their golden harps. There we shall see men that by the world were cut in pieces, burned in flames, eaten of beasts, drowned in the seas for the love that they bare to the Lord of the place, all well, and clothed with immortality as with a garment.

[p. 112] *Faithful:* When I came to the foot of the Hill called Difficulty I met with a very aged man who asked me what I was and whither bound. I told him that I was a pilgrim going to the Celestial City. Then said the old man: 'Thou lookest like an honest fellow. Wilt thou be content to dwell with me for the wages that I shall give thee?' Then I asked him his name and where he dwelt. He said his name was Adam the first.

The first, Old Testament, Adam, ejected from the Garden of Eden for disobedience, was often contrasted with the second, New Testament, 'Adam', that is Christ, who died to wash away the sins of humankind.

> 'And I dwell in the Town of Deceit'. I asked him then what was his work and what the wages that he would give. He told me that his work was many delights and his wages that I should be his heir at last. I further asked him what house he kept and what other servants he had. So he told me that his house was maintained with all the dainties in the world and that his servants were those of his own begetting. Then I asked if he had any children. He said that he had but three daughters: the lusts of the flesh, the lusts of the eyes and the pride of life and that I should marry them; if I would. Then I asked how long time he would have me live with him. And he told me as long as he lived himself.

> [p. 229] *Hopeful:* I delighted much in rioting, revelling, drinking, swearing, lying, uncleanness, Sabbath-breaking and what not, that tended to destroy the soul. But I found at last, by hearing and considering of things that are divine, which indeed I heard of you, as also of beloved Faithful that was put to death for his faith and good living in Vanity Fair, that the end of these things is death. And that for these things' sake the wrath of God cometh upon the children of disobedience.

> [p. 231] *Christian:* What was it brought your sins to mind?
> *Hopeful:* Many things, as,

> 1  If I did but meet a good man in the streets; or,
> 2  If I have heard any read in the Bible; or,
> 3  If mine head did begin to ache; or,
> 4  If I were told that some of my neighbours were sick; or,
> 5  If I heard the bell toll for some that were dead; or
> 6  If I thought of dying myself; or,
> 7  If I heard that sudden death happened to others.
> 8  But especially when I thought of myself that I must come quickly to judgement.

Although their way was hazardous and hard, at the end of their journey Christian and Hopeful were received into the Celestial City which

> [pp. 274–5] shone like the sun, the streets also were paved with gold, and in them walked many men with crowns on their heads, palms in their hands and golden harps to sing praises withall.

But reaching the gate of the city was not a guarantee of admission, as Ignorance, another traveller, discovered:

> Now while I was gazing upon all these things, I turned my head to look back and saw Ignorance come up to the river side but he soon got over . . . for it happened that there was then in the place one Vain-hope, a ferryman, that with his boat helped him over. So he, as the other I saw, did ascend the hill to

come up to the gate, only he came alone, neither did any man meet him with the least encouragement. When he was come up to the gate, he looked up at the writing that was above and then began to knock, supposing that entrance would have been quickly administered to him. But he was asked by the men that looked over the top of the gate: 'Whence came you and what would you have?' . . . Then they asked him for his certificate that they might go in and show it to the king. So he fumbled in his bosom for one and found none. Then said they, 'Have you none?' But the man answered never a word. So they told the king but he would not come down to see him but commanded the two shining ones that conducted Christian and Hopeful to the City to go out and take Ignorance and bind him hand and foot and have him away . . . . Then I saw that there was a way to Hell even from the Gates of Heaven as well as from the City of Destruction. So I awoke and behold it was a dream.

# EXHIBIT 6

# The parish register

## SOURCE

**The Register of Baptisms, Marriages and Burials for Conington, Cambridgeshire, Cambridgeshire Record Office**

The rituals which marked and celebrated the crucial stages of the human career – baptism, marriage and burial – were recorded in registers kept in parish churches. As the inscription on the opening page of this Cambridgeshire Register explains:

> This book was made on the first day of October Anno Domini [in the year of our Lord] 1538 and in the 30th year of the reign of our Sovreign Lord Henry the eighth of that name, King of England and France, Lord of Ireland, Defender of the Faith and in earth its Supreme Head, immediately under God of this Church of England and Ireland by the commandment of our said sovreign lord and his viceregent in all spiritual things Thomas Cromwell . . . [to record] how many and what persons had been christened, married and buried weekly within the said parish of Conington in Cambridgeshire and the name of every such person.

If the curate or his deputy failed to comply with these instructions they were to be fined for each default.

Notes of baptisms, marriages and burials have been used to reconstruct the patterns of birth, marriage and death in England for the three centuries from 1538. The resulting picture is the product of a remarkable collaboration between 230 local historians, who transcribed entries recording 3.7 million events, and the members of the Cambridge Group for the History of Population and Social Structures, who based their calculations of these data (A. E. Wrigley and R. S. Schofield, *The Population History of England 1541–1841*, Cambridge [1981], 1989, Introduction). Dorothy McClaren used the baptismal registers of the district of Minehead in Somerset in her study of the impact of breastfeeding on fertility (Dorothy McClaren 'Marital Fertility and Lactation' in *Women in English Society 1500–1800*, Mary Prior (ed.), London, 1985, pp. 22–53).

Conington lies about nine miles north-west of Cambridge on the borders of Cambridgeshire and Huntingdonshire. There were twenty-six households in the parish in 1563 and twenty-seven in 1728 (*The Victoria County History of Cambridge*, Volume IX, A. P. M. Wright and C. P. Lewis (eds), Institute of Historical Research, 1989, p. 281). No doubt the small size of the community led to the practice of recording baptisms, marriages and burials in a single volume. The Register is unusual, not only in combining the records of baptisms, marriages and burials, it also gives the dates of birth for two of the infants who were baptised and the occupations or status of a number of those who were buried – and of one of the set of parents who brought their child to be christened. The extracts represent the double page spread recording ceremonies from 12 August 1706 to 7 May 1710.

[1706] Temple Cole the son of Simon and Elleanar his wife was born August 12. Baptized September 3rd.
Mary Warren the daughter of George and Jane his wife was born August 17. Baptized September 22.

[1707] Jeremiah King the parish clerk was buried April 12.
Richard Muriel the son of William and Elizabeth his wife was baptized July 20th.
Mary Smith the daughter of Henry and Rose his wife was baptized October 19th.
George Kidson of Elsworth [Cambridgeshire] and Mary King of this parish were married November 27.
William Tyler labourer and thatcher was buried March 23rd.
[signed] John Bird, Curate.

[1708] John Merrill the son of William Merrill labourer was buried February 3rd.
Ann the daughter of James Boston and Eliza his wife was baptized March the 6th.
Jane the daughter of Thomas Colton and Margaret his wife was baptized March the 10th.
Mary Gray widow was buried March the 10th.

[1709] John the son of Jasper Parker and Mary his wife, travellers, was baptized April the 3rd.

Ann Boston was buried April the 4th.

Edward Grayhan of Fenstanton [Cambridgeshire] and Elizabeth Osborn of this parish were married June the 10th.

Elizabeth the daughter of Charles Smith and Mary his wife was baptized July the 12th.

John Johnson labourer was buried September the first.

The Widow Taylor was buried September the 28th.

Robert Gillet and Mary Smith were married October the 6th.

Thomas Elderton labourer was buried October the 18th.

Elizabeth White was buried October the 26th.

Jane the daughter of George Warren and Jane his wife was baptized January the 22nd.

Thomas the son of Thomas Colton and Margaret his wife was baptized February the 28th.

Simon Barret singleman was buried March the 5th.

Susan Sabin singlewoman was buried March the 7th.

[1710] Henry Adams and Catherine Pearson were married April the 11th.

Moses the son of William Hart and Elizabeth his wife was baptized April the 23rd.

James the son of James Boston and Elizabeth his wife was baptized May the 7th.

[signed] Thomas Rutterforth, Curate.

Thomas Ellwood, a Quaker who rejected the ceremonies of the Church of England, was baptised at Crowell in Oxfordshire on 15 October 1639. He recognised his christening as indirect and unsatisfactory evidence of his date of birth – a useful reminder that parish registers record ceremonies associated with births and deaths rather than the events themselves. As he wrote:

> To begin therefore with mine own beginning, I was born in the year of our Lord 1639, about the beginning of the eighth month (so far as I have been able to inform myself) for the Parish Register, which relates to the time (not of birth but) of Baptism (as they call it) is not to be relied on [*The History of the Life of Thomas Ellwood Written by his Own Hand*, S. Graveson (ed.), [1714], London, 1906 p. 2].

# EXHIBIT 7

# Wills

## SOURCES

The will of Richard Goodyear, 1622, Cambridgeshire County Record Office
The will of Samuel Pepys, 1701, 1703, Henry Wheatley, *Pepysiana* (London, 1899)

Willmaking was a solemn business usually undertaken in the belief that death was near. Testators seem to have been inclined to rely on phrases suggested by their scribe (he was often better educated and of higher status), nevertheless, the last will and testament provides an insight into the values and preoccupations of unconspicuous men and women: wills were among the prime sources for Margaret Spufford's enquiry into the beliefs and inheritance customs of Cambridgeshire villagers in the sixteenth and seventeenth centuries (*Contrasting Communities*, Cambridge, 1974). Her subjects included William Brasier of Willingham who made his will in 1589. Like a good many other men, he foresaw the possibility that his wife and son might not be able to 'agree together in the house' after his death and made arrangements to provide for his wife in that event. In the West Country Sir Edward Skory used his will to record his hostility to his wife, the widow of George Lutterell of East Quantoxhead in Somerset, whom he had married in 1629. He left '20s to Giles Baker, my servant, who hath lived under the tyranny of my wife, to the danger of his life during the space of two years'. To 'Dame Silvestra Skory, my wife, whom I heartily forgive all her attempts against me', he left 'a prayer book called The Practice of Piety, desiring that she better love and affect the same than hitherto she hath done'. In spite of this unfavourable reference, Dame Silvestra found a third husband (*Proceedings of the Somerset Archaeological and Natural History Society*, O. L. Dick (ed.), London, 1946, pp. 31–2).

As the following extract from John Aubrey's brief life of Thomas Hobbes demonstrates, wills do not tell the whole story about the material legacies passed on from one generation to the next: by the time a father, or other concerned relative, died, the older children had often been provided for by means of what historians call 'lifetime bequests'.

## A true copy of Mr Hobbes' will

There be five grandchildren of my Brother Edmund Hobbes, to the eldest whereof, whose name is Thomas Hobbes, I have heretofore given a piece of land, which may, and doth I think, content him, and therefore to the other four that are younger, I dispose of the . . . £100 the gift of my Lord of Devonshire, to be divided equally amongst them, as a furtherance to bind them apprentices.

## The will of Richard Goodyear, 1622

The opening passages of the will of Richard Goodyear, a widower who had married for a second time, describe his provision for his daughter Mary. Later sections detailed bequests to his son Richard (like Mary he was under 21 and therefore a minor) and their stepmother, his 'now wife', Margaret. Subject to her renouncing her formal right to a third of his property, Margaret was declared residuary legatee and executrix, under the supervision of her husband's trusted friend, Michael York. In spite of his desperate condition, Goodyear was able to sign his will; two of his three witnesses – all male – made their marks.

Richard Goodyear's will gives us some hints about the physical organisation of his household and its furnishings – many substantial seventeenth-century farmers slept in the highest status room in their house. Beds and bedding were among the most expensive of their household goods. Durable items made of wood, stout fabric or metal were handed down from parent to child and from master to servant. Thrifty farmers maintained an immunity from the seductive power of fashion into the twentieth century.

The implication that Richard Goodyear planned to use the sheet he reserved from his wife's chest of childbed linen as his shroud is an extraordinary revelation of the links he made, perhaps unconsciously, between the meanings of birth and death.

> In the name of God, Amen. The two and twentieth day of May in the year of our Lord one thousand six hundred and twenty-two, I Richard Goodyear of Tydd St Giles in the Isle of Ely and County of Cambridge, yeoman, being sick and weak of body but of sound and perfect mind and memory, thanks be given to God, do make this my last will and testament in manner and form following:
>
> First I bequeath my soul into the hands of Almighty God that gave it and my body to be buried in the churchyard of Tydd aforesaid at the discretion of my executrix [the original reads 'execut', the word appears in full later in the document]. And as for that portion of worldly goods wherewith God has blessed me I give them as followeth:
>
> [First] I give unto Mary Goodyear my daughter one acre of arable ground lying in the South Field next to the land of Robert Cooper on the east, and my own land on the west and the land of Henry Coney Esquire on the south and upon Greatbrodgate on the north to her and to her heirs for ever. Item I give unto her also my bedstead in the hall whereon I now lie with the featherbed thereunto belonging and one bolster and three pillows and one coverlet and a christening sheet and a towel and all the other childbed linen which was her

mother's but one sheet for myself; and I give her the chest where they lie . . .
I give her also one little square table in the hall and one of the best candle-
sticks with two of the best pewter platters . . . I give her one mortar and
pestle and one brass pot . . . I give unto her also my barn to be sold by Michael
York at the best price and the money to be put forth by him to the best use till
she shall accomplish the age of one and twenty.

## The will of Samuel Pepys, 1701, 1703

To his contemporaries, Samuel Pepys (born 1633) was known as a highly
successful civil servant whose loyalty to James II, probably founded in their
common interest in the Navy, led to the termination of his public career
after the Glorious Revolution which brought William and Mary to the throne
in 1688. Today he is primarily remembered for his diary which covers the
1660s. Pepys was childless. His wife Elizabeth died in 1669; although he
never remarried, in his will he made 'the most full and lasting acknowledgement of my esteem, respect and gratitude to the excellent lady Mistress
Mary Skinner for the many important effects of her steady friendship and
assistances during the whole course of my life within the last thirty-three
years' and provided her with an income for life.

Pepys' original preference for 'seniority of age and priority of birth' in
determining his heir is striking because it runs against the grain of temperamental sympathy: his younger nephew John Jackson was much clos-
er to him in ability and tastes; he followed in his uncle's footsteps to
Magdalene College, Cambridge, and later acted as his secretary. After his
uncle's death he married a kinswoman of Pepys' close friend and former
colleague Will Hewer.

### *Henry Wheatley:* Pepysiana *(London, 1899)*

In a will dated 2 August 1701, Samuel Pepys left the bulk of his property

> [p. 252] To my wellbeloved nephew Samuel Jackson [born 1669] of Brampton
> . . . gentleman, eldest son of my late sister Paulina, deceased . . . and after his
> decease then to and for the use and behoof [benefit] of the first son of his body
> lawfully begotten and of the heirs male of the body of such first son lawfully
> issuing and for default of such issue to the use of the second, third, fourth,
> fifth, sixth, seventh and all and every other son and sons of the body of the
> said Samuel Jackson severally and successively and in remainder one after
> another as they and every one of them shall be in seniority of age and priori-
> ty of birth and of the several and respective heirs male of the body and bod-
> ies of all and every such son and sons lawfully issuing, the elder of the said
> sons and heirs male of his body issuing being always to take before and to be
> preferred to the younger.

In a codicil (qualifying clause), added in 1703, Pepys recorded that, [p. 260] since the time of my signing and declaring my said will . . . my said nephew Samuel Jackson has thought fit to dispose himself in marriage against my positive advice and injunctions and to his own irreparable prejudice and dishonour, I do think myself obliged to express the resentments due to such an act of disrespect and imprudence . . . . But forasmuch as no degree of provocation has been able wholly to extinguish my affections towards the said Samuel Jackson,

he made him a much reduced bequest of an income of £40 a year. John Jackson [born 1673] replaced his brother as Pepys' principal heir. Pepys' library was perhaps the possession closest to his heart

[p. 265] The Scheme . . . relating to the completion and settlement of my Library

1st That a general review be taken of my said Library compared with its catalogue and all outlying books [books on loan to friends] immediately looked up and put into their places.

[p. 266] [After specified additions] 5thly That this being done my said Library be closed and from thenceforward no additions made thereto.

6thly That the whole number and bulk of my books being so ascertained one or more new presses be provided for the convenient containing them so as to be neither too much crowded or stand too loose.

For the further settlement and preservation of my said Library after the death of my nephew John Jackson, I do hereby declare that, could I be sure of a constant succession of heirs from my said nephew qualified like himself for the use of such a Library, I should not entertain the thought of its ever being alienated from them. But, this uncertainty considered, with the infinite pains and time and cost employed in my collecting, methodising and reducing the same to the state wherein it now is, I cannot but be greatly solicitous that all possible provision be made for its unalterable preservation and perpetual security against the ordinary fate of such collections falling into the hands of an incompetent heir and thereby being sold, disrupted or embezzled.

[pp. 267–8] the following particulars I declare my present thoughts and prevaling inclinations in the matter . . . .

1st That after the death of my said nephew my said Library be placed and forever settled in one of our universities and rather in that of Cambridge than Oxford.

2ndly And rather in a private college there than in a public library.

3rdly And in the colleges of Trinity or Magdalene preferable to all others.

4thly And of these two, caeteris paribus [other things being equal], rather in the latter for the sake of my own and nephew's education therein. . . .

8thly That my said Library be continued in its present form and no other books mixed therewith save that my nephew may add to them of his own collecting in distinct presses.

9thly That the said room and books so placed and adjusted be called by the name Bibliotheca Pepysiana [Pepysian Library].

10thly That this said Bibliotheca Pepysiana be under the sole power and custody of the Master of the College for the time being who shall neither convey or suffer to be conveyed by others any of the said books from thence to any other place except to his own Lodge in the said college nor there have more than ten of them at a time and that of those also a strict entry be made and account kept of the time of their having been taken out and returned in a book to be provided and remain in the said Library for that only purpose.

[pp. 267–8] 12thly And that for a yet further security . . . the two said colleges of Trinity and Magdalene have a reciprocal check upon one another. And that the college which shall be in present possession of the said Library be subject to an Annual Visitation from the other and to the forfeiture thereof to the possession and use of the other upon conviction of any breach of their said covenants.

The Pepyses' old college, Magdalene, enjoys the distinction of housing the Bibliothecha Pepysiana. The prototypes of the presses in which the collection is housed were made in 1666, to Pepys' own design, by Thomas Sympson master joiner of the naval dockyards on the Thames. The library is open to visitors.

# EXHIBIT 8

# Inventories

## SOURCES

**The inventory of the goods and chattels of John Ashwell of Wisbech, 1687**
**The inventory of the goods and chattles of John Voyce, the elder, of Ely, 1689**

Inventories, compiled by local lay people, neighbours or colleagues of the deceased, record their goods and chattels. Inventories give *an impression* of the contents and layout of dwellings but they must be treated with caution, for example, because they exclude things which were there but did but belong to the subject of the inventory. Farmers inventories reflect the seasonal rhythms of their year.

# The inventory of the goods and chattels of John Ashwell of Wisbech, 1687

A true and present Inventory of the goods and Chattells of John Ashwell of Wisbech within the Isle of Ely and County of Cambridge Tobaccopipemaker Taken and prized by John Rogby, William Fox and John Riches this Thirtieth day of June Annoque Domini 1687 as Followeth.

|  | £ s d |
|---|---|
| Imprimis his purse & Apparell | 00 13 4 |

**In the Hall**

| | |
|---|---|
| Item 1 bedstead, 1 little fetherbed, 2 boulsters, 1 pillow, 2 old blankets, 1 rug and curtaines & valens | 01 00 00 |
| Item 1 little table, 2 buffit stooles, 1 settle, 2 lether chares, 4 rush-bottomed chares, 1 little fir-cupboard, [made of pine] | |
| 6 pewter flagons & 2 pints, 1 gill [¼ pint] pott, two candlesticks & one seeing glass | 00 19 00 |
| Item one old warming-pan, 1 chude, 1 gridiron, 1 iron candlestice [stick] against the chimny, 1 box iron, 1 earthen bason | 00 02 6 |

**In the Parlour**

| | |
|---|---|
| Item 1 chest, 1 old table, 1 buffit stoole, 1 firr-box, 2 old chares & 1 old coffer & 1 candlestick & some od things | 00 06 6 |
| Item 3 old sheets & 5 old napkins | 00 03 6 |

**In the Kitchen**

| | |
|---|---|
| Item 1 Table, 1 old buffet stoole, 4 old chares, 1 pair of fireirons, 1 pair of tongs, 1 fireshovel, one paire of speit [spits], 1 iron pott & pott-hookes & 1 running hooke | 00 10 6 |
| Item 1 old pewter platters 14, 1 wicker baskett, 1 paire of bellowes, 2 old little kettles & 2 pailes, 1 old boule, 1 duzen trenchers [wooden boards on which food was cut up or served], 1 dish & 1 small tray 1 keeler [shallow tub] & 2 tubbs & some other od things | 00 11 10 |

**In the Chamber**

| | |
|---|---|
| Item two old trundle bedsteads with the old furniture upon them & one signe | 00 04 0 |
| | 04 11 2 |

[side 2]

**In the Seller**

| | | |
|---|---|---|
| Item fower hogseads of strong beare | | 04 00 0 |
| 11 hogshead casskes full and empty & 3 | | |
| tubbs & stillages [stands for the casks] | | 00 19 0 |
| Item one pigg [a little wooden pail with | | |
| one long stave for a handle] | | 00 04 0 |
| | | 05 03 0 |
| | on the other side | 04 11 2 |
| | Total sume | 09 14 2 |

John Rogby
Wm Fox
John + Riches
his marke

**Things forgotten**

| | | |
|---|---|---|
| Item one old screen & two old brass moules | | |
| for tobacco pipes | | 00 10 0 |
| | | li s d |
| | The Total sume is | 10 04 2 |

John Rogby
Wm Fox
John + Riches
his marke

# The inventory of John Voyce's goods and chattles, 1689

Inventory of all and singular the Goods and Chattels of John Voyce the elder late of Ely within the Isle of Ely and County of Cambridge, Draper, taken and Appraysed by us Joseph Johnson and Nicholas Chambers this seaven and twentieth day of January in the second yeare of the Raigne of our Soveraigne Lord and Lady, William and Mary, by the grace of God of England, Scotland, France and Ireland, King and Queen and Defendors of the Faith etc. Annoque Domini 1690.

| | £ s d |
|---|---|
| Imprimis his Apparell and money in his purse at | 020 0 0 |

**In the shopp**

| | |
|---|---|
| Item the halfe part & Moyetye [half] of the Goods in the | |
| shop & Browne Chamber as Partner with his | |
| sonne James Voyce and the Debte in the Booke | |
| good and Bad at | 400 0 0 |

**In his Lodging Roome**

One Feather Bedd, two Bollsters, two Pillows, two
Blanketts, one Rugg, Bedsted and Curtaines and
Vallence, One Trundle Bedd [a low bed which could be
rolled out of the way often under a bigger bedstead
during the day] and Bedding, One
Hanging Presse, One Chest of Drawers, two Chests,
two Boxes, one trunke and foure Chayres at        008  0  0

**In the best Chamber**

One Featherbedd and Bedstedd, Two Bollsters, Two
Pillows, two Blanketts, One Rugg, Curtaines and
Vallance at        009  0  0
Item One looking Glasse, One pair of Red
Curtaines and Vallence, Six Chayres, foure Stooles,
One Chest of Drawers, one little Table, one Glasse
Case, Andirons, fire shovell, Tongs, Bellows,
Candlestick, one stand and two Trunkes at        008  0  0
Two Tanckards, Eleaven spoones, one Cupp,
and two small silvers Tasters [small shallow wine cups]    016  0  0
Item twenty paire of sheetes, six dozen of Napkins,
tenne Table Cloaths, tenne paire of Pillowbeers,
twenty Towells and some other Wearing Lynnen     016  0  0
                                                                      477  0  0

[side 2]

**In the Browne Chamber**

Six Turkey Worke Chayres, One Turky Worke Carper,
Six Turkey Worke Cushions, Tenne Leather Chayres,
Two Stooles, one Couch, One Livery Cubboard,
[sideboard] One Table, One Looking Glasse,
one Cushion, Andirons, fire-shovell and Tongs at   [?] 010  0  0

**In the best Garrett**

One Featherbedd and Beddsted, one Bollster, one
Pillow, Two Blanketts, One Rugg, Curtaines,
Vallence, one Chayre, two Stooles and one Table at    005  0  0

**In the Middle Garrett**

One Featherbedd, one Bollster, one Pillow, two
Blanketts, one Rugg, One Curtaine, one Table,
one Cloaths Presse, two Chayres and one other
Bedstedd at        002 10  0

**In the farther Garrett**

| | | | |
|---|---|---|---|
| Two Tables, two Cofers and some other Lumber at | 001 | 0 | 0 |

**In the Hall**

| | | | |
|---|---|---|---|
| One Great Wallnutt Tree Table, One little Oake Table, one Oake Dresser, one other table, three joynt stools,Tenne Chayres, one Skreene, one Cubboard and some other Lumber | 002 | 10 | 0 |
| Pewter, brasse, one Grate, one Jack [a device, often clockwork, for turning a spit], Fire shovell, Tongs and Iron at | 008 | 0 | 0 |

**In the Buttery**

| | | | |
|---|---|---|---|
| One Hoggshead [a very big barrel which would hold around 50 gallons], foure Kilderkyns [smaller barrels holding 16–18 gallons], one powdering [salting] Tubb, one kneading Trough, shelves & other Lumber | 001 | 6 | 8 |

**In the Brewhouse**

| | | | |
|---|---|---|---|
| Brewing vessells, copper Tubbs and other Lumber at | 002 | 0 | 0 |

**In the Stable and Barne**

| | | | |
|---|---|---|---|
| One Gelding, one saddle, Briddle and some Hay at | 010 | 0 | 0 |
| In Bills, Bonds and other Writing & with other Debts good and badd | 250 | 0 | 0 |
| Goods and Lumber omitted and not before valued | 002 | 0 | 0 |
| | 294 | 6 | 8 |
| The other side | 477 | 0 | 0 |
| In the whole | 771 | 6 | 8 |

Appraysed and taken by us
Nicho[las] Chambers
Joseph John Son

# EXHIBIT 9

# Apprenticeship indentures

## SOURCES

The apprenticeship indentures of James Alexander of Bishop's Wickham, Essex, 1627, Essex County Record Office: Chelmsford Branch
The apprenticeship indentures of Martha Love of Littleport, Cambridgeshire, 1695, Cambridgeshire County Record Office

For many, leaving home marked the transition from childhood to youth. During this stage in the human career masters took on the responsibility for training and discipline. The contracts exchanged between the parents and guardians of prospective apprentices and their future masters provide the clearest statements of the formal terms of the arrangement. The documents were called indentures because the contract was written out twice on the same sheet of parchment which was then cut jaggedly to provide each party with a certificated copy.

## The apprenticeship indentures of James Alexander of Bishop's Wickham, Essex, 1627, Essex County Record Office: Chelmsford Branch

James, the son of a gentleman, was apprenticed to a haberdasher in Maldon.

Originally dealers in caps and other headgear, haberdashers diversified to trade in 'a thousand small wares' ranging from essentials such as needles, threads, tapes and dress fastenings to the little luxuries that quite humble people could aspire to – brooches, beads and combs, the sort of trinket that young men would give the women they were courting. (Hoole's *Vocabularium*, designed to teach boys Latin offers two words for haberdasher to make the distinction [p. 61].) As Margaret Spufford demonstrates in *The Great Reclothing of Rural England. Petty Chapmen and their Wares in the Seventeenth Century* (London, 1984), haberdashers provided pedlars with much of their stock.

> This indenture, made the twentieth-eighth day of July in the third year of the reign of our Sovreign Lord Charles by the grace of God of England, Scotland, France and Ireland King, Defender of the Faith etc. between Jacob Malden of Maldon in the County of Essex, haberdasher, of the one part and James Alexander, the son of John Alexander the elder of Bishop's Wickham in the said county, gentleman, of the other part, witnesseth that the said James Alexander, of his own mind and voluntary will, with the assent and consent

of his said father, bindeth himself apprentice unto the aforesaid Jacob Malden unto the trade, craft and occupation of haberdasher and to learn such mysteries therein and of all such other trades, crafts and occupations as the said Jacob Malden now presently doth use and with him to dwell, tarry and abide from the first day of January last past, from which time he hath served and dwelt with the said Jacob, unto the full end and term of seven years from thence next following and fully to be complete and ended. By and during all which said term of years the said James Alexander covenanteth and granteth by these present to and with the said Jacob Malden that he the said James Alexander shall and will him the said Jacob Malden as his master faithfully and truly serve in all his affairs and business, his secrets to keep, his commandments lawful and honest everywhere to do; no fornication within the house of his master or without he shall commit or do; hurt unto his said master he shall none do, nor consent to be done of any other person or persons but to his power shall let or hinder it or give his master warning thereof; taverns or alehouses of custom shall he not haunt unless it be about his master's business there to be done; all dice, cards or any other unlawful game he shall not play nor use. The goods of his said master inordinately he shall not waste nor them to anybody lend without the licence of his said master. Matrimony with any woman during the said term he shall not contract nor espouse nor for his said service neither by day nor night he shall not absent or prolong himself [in the sense of taking an excessive time to do errands] but as a true servant ought to do he shall behave himself both in word and deed. And the said Jacob Malden covenanteth and granteth by these present the said James Alexander in his trade, craft and occupation of a haberdasher and in all other trades, crafts and occupations which now presently he useth, after the best manner that he may or can as much as the capacity of the said James Alexander will take or conceive, to teach and inform, or cause to be taught and informed, and in all due and useful manner to chastise [this does not necessarily mean 'beat', chastise also means 'train', 'correct in an authoritative way'] him; finding unto his said apprentice sufficient meat, drink, linen, woollen, hose, shoes and all other things necessary or belonging to an apprentice of such a trade, craft or occupation to be found and allowed. And the said Jacob Malden covenanteth and granteth likewise by these present to give and deliver or cause to be given and delivered unto the said James Alexander, at his own costs and charges at the end of the said term, double apparel [two sets of clothing] for his body meet and convenient, as well in woollen as in linen, the one for the holy days/holidays ['holydays' in the original – at this time that spelling of the word carried the double meaning], the other for the working days, and also [blank] pair of shoes at his departure. In witness whereof the parties abovenamed to these present indentures interchangeably have set their hands and seals the day and year first above written and in the year of our Lord 1627. [signed] James Alexander.

Jacob Malden would have endorsed the copy of the agreement handed over to James.

## The apprenticeship indentures of Martha Love of Littleport, Cambridgeshire, 1695, Cambridgeshire County Record Office

Martha was an orphan placed in a household where she could be trained to be of use. In practice the contract between her guardians, the parish officers responsible for the relief of the needy, and her employers offered her little protection against exploitation or indeed anything short of gross cruelty.

> This indenture was made the nineteenth day of April in the seventh year of the reign of our most gracious Sovreign Lord William by the grace of God of England, Scotland, France and Ireland King, Defender of the Faith etc. Anno Domini 1695. Witness that William Licence and Robert Crabb, Overseers of the Poor in the parish of Littleport in the Isle of Ely and the County of Cambridge, and William Wilkinson and John Waddelow, churchwardens of the same parish, and with the consent of Roger Jenyns Esquire and Francis Ferne, clerk, two of his Majesty's Justices of the Peace for the said Isle [Jeyns, born 1663, bought an estate in Bottisham in 1700; Ferne (born circa 1648) was rector of Downham], have by these presents placed and bound Martha Love, being a poor fatherless child, as an apprentice with John Smyth of Littleport aforesaid, innholder, and Ann, his wife, as an apprentice, with them, the said John Smith and Ann, his wife, to dwell from the day of the date of these presents until she, the said Martha Love, shall come to the age of one and twenty years or be married, whichever shall first happen, accordng to the statute in that case made and provided by, and during all which time and terms the said Martha Love shall the said John Smyth and Ann his wife well and faithfully serve in all said lawful business as the said John Smyth and Ann his wife shall put her, the said Martha Love, unto, according to her power, wit and ability, and honestly and obediently in all things shall behave herself towards her said master and dame and their family. And the said John Smyth and Ann his wife, for their part, promiseth, covenanteth and agreeth that they, the said John and Ann, the aforesaid Martha Love, their apprentice, in the art and skill of housewifery the best manner that they can or may shall teach and inform or cause to be taught and informed as much as thereunto belongeth or they, the said John Smyth and Ann his wife, knoweth. And also, during all the said term to find unto their said apprentice meat, drink, linen, woollen, hose, shoes, washing and all other things useful or meet for an apprentice. In witness whereof the parties aforesaid to these present indentures their hands and seals interchangeably have put the day and year above written.
>
> The mark and seal of John Smyth.

The other half of the indentures would, again, have been endorsed by the other parties to the agreement.

# Exhibit 10

# The crime of petty treason

## Source

### Sir Matthew Hale, *Pleas to the Crown* (London, 1682)

The wilful killing of husband by wife or employer by servant was legally defined as a crime more serious than murder: the charge was petty treason.

Matthew Hale (born 1609) studied law at Lincoln's Inn, having served as a judge under Oliver Cromwell, he was appointed Chief Justice in 1671. He presided at the trial, in 1665, of two Suffolk women accused of witchcraft, extracts from what is said to be an eyewitness account of the case appear later in the dossier (p. 201f.). Hale was regarded as a notable legal authority.

Petty Treason is the charge
1  Where a servant kills his master

This extends to some other categories:

1  Servant kills his mistress.
2  Servant kills his master's wife.
3  Where a servant, upon malice taken during his service, kills his master after departure from his service.
2  Wife killing her husband.

If the wife and a stranger kill the husband, petty treason in the wife, murder in the stranger . . . . The judgement in Petty Treason for a man to be hanged and drawn. A woman to be burned.

# EXHIBIT 11

# Advice to the country housewife of the sixteenth century

## SOURCE

*The Points of Huswiferie United to the Comfort of Husbandrie,* set forth by Thomas Tusser, Gentleman (London, 1580)

Thomas Tusser, the youngest son of an obscure country gentleman, was born in Essex in the mid-1520s. His musical talents earned him a privileged education, first as a chorister at St Paul's Cathedral, later at Eton and the University of Cambridge. For ten years he was a professional musician, then he married and took to farming. Tusser published *Good Pointes of Husbandrie* in 1557; the edition of 1570 was the first to include advice for farmers' wives. *The Five Hundred points of Good Husbandry,* as the work came to be known, was 'a Tudor best-seller'; there were six editions between 1573 and 1580. These unmodernised extracts are taken from the edition of 1580, the last published in the author's lifetime.

> When husband is absent, let huswife be chiefe,
> and look to their labour that eateth hir biefe. . . .
>
> Where husband and huswife be both out of place,
> there servants doo loiter, and reason their cace.
> The huswife so named (of keeping the house),
> must tend on hir profit, as cat on the mouse . . . [159].
>
> New bread is a waster, but mouldie is wurse,
> what that way dog catcheth, that loseth the purse [167].
>
> Though scouring be needfull, yet scouring too mutch,
> is pride without profit, and robbeth thine hutch.
> Keep kettles from knocks, set tubs out of Sun,
> for mending is costlie, and crackt is soone dun [169].
>
> Give servant no dainties but give him ynough. . . .
> Poor seggons halfe starved worke faintly and dull,
> and lubbers doo loiter, their bellies too full [171].
>
> Enough is a plentie, too much is a pride. . . [172].
>
> Good semsters be sowing of fine pretie knackes,
> good huswifes be mending and peecing their sackes.

Though making and mending be huswifely waies,
yet mending in time is the huswife to praies. . . .

Though Ladies may rend and buie new ery day,
good huswifes must mend and buie new as they may.

Save fether of all thing, the softer to lie . . . [173].

Provide for thy tallow, ere frost commeth in,
and make thine owne candle, ere winter begin [174].

Remember those children whose parents be poore,
which hunger, yet dare not crave at thy doore . . . [176].

Good huswives provides, ere sicknes doo come,
of sundrie good things in hir house to have some.
Good Aqua composita, Vineger tart,
Rose water and treakle to comfort the hart.

Cold herbes in hir garden for agues that burne,
that over strong heat to good temper may turne. . . .

Get water of Fumentorie, Liver to coole,
and others the like, or els lie like a foole [179].

Good huswives take paine, and doo count it good luck,
to make their owne brest their own child to give suck [180].

# EXHIBIT 12

# The duties of husbands and wives, parents and children, masters and servants

## SOURCE

### William Gouge, *Of Domesticall Duties* (London, 1622)

The work consisted of eight 'treatises', listed on the title page as follows:

I    An Exposition of that part of Scripture out of which Domesticall Duties are raised.

William Gouge (born 1578) was educated at Eton and King's College, Cambridge. Family connections with the university were strong, his mother's sisters were married to the Masters of Emmanuel and St John's. In 1608 Gouge took up a post in the London parish of St Anne's, Blackfriars. There was no church and he raised over £1,500 to build one. As 'the watchman of [their] souls', he dedicated *Of Domesticall Duties* to his parishioners. It is a hefty volume – 693 pages plus three lines recording 'Some faults escaped thus to be corrected' (most seventeenth-century books ended with a note of errata). Gouge explained the scale of his work:

> It is the variety of many, not the prolixity of few points which has made this book to swell to that bigness which it hath. The first Treatise (which is the fourth part of the book) containeth a Commentary on that part of Scripture out of which Domesticall Duties are raised . . . . The other Treatises, wherein the Duties themselves are handled, are every of them much shorter than the first.

Gouge was an experienced family man; he and his wife had seven sons and six daughters. And his manual apparently filled a need; very soon after *Of Domesticall Duties* was published it was purchased by the recently married Nehemiah Wallington (born 1598), who owned a woodworking business. As a new householder, 'feeling the weight of so many souls', Wallington planned to use the text as a guide 'so that everyone of us may learn and know our duties and honour God everyone in his place where God has set them' (Paul Seaver, *Wallington's World. A Puritan Artisan in Seventeenth-century London*, Stanford, 1985, p. 79).

Gouge maintained that the right observance of 'domesticall duties' was fundamental to the health of society. As he observed in The Epistle Dedicatory,

> [p. 2] Oh if the head and several members of a family would be persuaded every one of them to be conscionable in performing their own particular duties, what a sweet society and happy harmony would there be in houses? What excellent seminaries would families be to Church and Commonwealth? Necessary it is that good order be first set in families for, as they were before other polities, so they are somewhat the more necessary and good members of a family are likely to make good members of Church and Commonwealth.

## The Second Treatise, Part I: A RIGHT CONJUNCTION OF MAN AND WIFE

[p. 180] Ripeness of years is absolutely necessary for consummating a just and lawful marriage: wherefore as God at first made Adam of full age, so when he sought out a wife for him, he made her of full age too: he made her a woman, not a child.

[pp. 181–3] Impotent persons . . . ought not to seek after marriage . . . for by those signs of impotency God showeth that he calleth them to live single . . . . [However] there is great difference betwixt impotency and barrenness . . . . For though procreation of children be one end of marriage, yet it is not the only end, and so inviolable is the marriage bond that though it be made for children's sake, yet for want of children it may not be broken.

*Of the things which are absolutely necessary to make a person fit for marriage*

[pp. 185–6]

1  One of the same kind. . . . Contrary to this is the detestable sin of buggery with beasts.
2  One of the contrary sex. . . . Contrary are those unnatural commixtions of parties of the same sex.
3  One beyond those degrees of consanguinity and affinity which are forbidden by the law of God. . . . Contrary is incest.
4  One that is free: nor married, nor betrothed to another . . . . So firm is the contract as the law calleth a betrothed maid 'a wife'. . . . Contrary is bigamy and polygamy.

Other qualifications, while not prerequisites for a legal union were regarded as necessary to ensure a harmonious life-long partnership

[pp. 188–9] That matrimonial society may prove comfortable, it is requisite that there should be some equality betwixt the parties that are married in Age, Estate, Condition, Piety. . . . For Age . . . this equality is not over strictly to be taken, as if the married couple were to be just of the same age . . . it is very meet that the husband should be somewhat elder than his wife because he is an head, a governor, a protector of his wife. The Scripture noteth many husbands to be elder than their wives. . . . To my remembrance an approved example of an husband younger than his wife cannot be given out of Scripture.

*Of equality in estate and condition betwixt those that are to be married together*

[pp. 189–90] Great portions make many women proud, dainty, lavish, idle and careless; a man were much better, even for the help of his outward estate, to marry a prudent, sober, thrifty, careful, diligent wife, though with a small portion than such a one. A proud back, a dainty tooth and a lavish hand will soon consume a great portion.

[p. 200] Many good and weighty reasons may be alleged to show how requisite it is that a contract should go before marriage. For it addeth to the honour of the marriage that it should be deliberately and advisedly, step after step, by one degree after another consummated and made up. . . . It is a means of knitting the hearts of the two parties to be married more firmly and inviolably together before they come together.

As Gouge says elsewhere (p. 197), 'Mutual love and good liking of each other is as glue'.

[p. 202] It is a means to stir up the parties which are to be married more carefully and diligently to provide all things fit for their dwelling together and well ordering their household beforehand that they may be not to seek for necessaries when they should use them. For being contracted they know that it cannot be long ere they must come to dwell together.

## *Of the ends of marriage . . .*

[pp. 209–10]

1 That the world might be increased: and not simply increased but with a legitmate brood, and distinct families, which are the seminaries of cities and commonwealths.
2 That men might avoid fornication.
3 That man and wife might be a mutual help one to another.

## *Of the privileges of marriage . . .*

1 By it men and women are made husbands and wives.
2 It is the only lawful means to make them fathers and mothers.
3 It is the ordinary means to make them masters and mistresses. All of these are great dignities.

## The Second Treatise, Part II: OF COMMON MUTUAL DUTIES BETWIXT MAN AND WIFE

### *Of Adultery . . .*

[p. 219] I deny not but that more inconveniences may follow upon the woman's default than upon the man's: as greater infamy before men, worse disturbance of the family, more mistaking of legitmate for illegitimate children, with the like. The man cannot so well know which be his own children, as the woman; he may take base children to be his own, and so cast the inheritance upon them; and suspect his own to be basely born, and so deprive them of their patrimony. . . .Yet in regard of the breach of wedlock, and transgression against God, the sin of either party is alike.

[p. 220] I find no sin throughout the whole Scripture so notoriously in several colours thereof set forth, as it is.

[It is a sin] against one's neighbour, as the party with whom the sin is committed (for this sin cannot be committed singly by one alone); the husband and wife of each party (who cannot rest contented with any satisfaction); the children born in adultery (whom they brand with an indelible character of infamy and deprive of many privileges that otherwise they might enjoy); the alliance and friends of each party (to whom the grief and disgrace of this foul sin reacheth); the whole family pertaining to either of them (for this is as fire in a house); the town, the city and the nation where such unclean birds roost (for all they lie open to the vengeance of God for this sin).

## *Of remedies against adultery . . .*

[p. 221] A diligent keeping of the heart (that lustful thoughts proceed not from thence); of the eyes (that they wander not on the beauty or properness of any one's person, or on lascivious pictures, or any like allurements); of the ears (that they harken not to any enticements of others); of the tongue (that it utter not unchaste and corrupt communication); of the lips (that they delight not in wanton kisses); of the hands (that they use no wanton dalliance); of the feet (that they carry thee not to the place where adultery may be committed); of thy company (that thou be not defiled with others' wantonness and uncleanness); of thy diet (that it be not immoderate) of thine apparel (that it be not garish and lascivious); of thy time (that it be not vainly and idly spent).

One of the best remedies that can be prescribed to married persons . . . is that husband and wife mutually delight in each other.

[p. 230] Discord betwixt man and wife in a house is as contention betwixt master and pilot in a ship.

## The Third Treatise: OF WIVES' PARTICULAR DUTIES

[p. 271] Though the man is as the head, yet is the woman as the heart, which is the most excellent part of the body next the head, far more excellent than any other member under the head, and almost equal to the head in many respects, and as necessary as the head.

[p. 272] What if a man of mean place be married to a woman of eminent place, or a servant be married to his mistress, or an aged woman to a youth, must such a wife acknowledge such a husband her superior?

Yea, verily, for in giving herself to be his wife, and taking him to be her husband, she advanceth him above herself and subjecteth herself unto him.

[p.273] But what if a man of lewd and beastly condition, as a drunkard, a glutton, a profane swaggerer, an impious swearer, and blasphemer, be married to a wife, a sober, religious matron, must she account him her superior, and worthy of an husband's honour?

. . . Surely she must.

Couples should behave decorously,

[p. 283] if a stranger . . . espy any matrimonial familiarity betwixt you [man and wife], what can he judge it to be but lightness and wantoness? . . . [Pet names are undignified. Gouge provides us with a list.] Sweet, Sweeting, Sweetheart, Love, Joy, Dear, etc.; . . . Duck, Chick, Pigsnie, etc. and husbands' Christian names which if they be contracted, as John, Thomas, William, Henry (as many use to contract them thus: Jack, Tom, Will, Hal) they are much more unseemly – servants are usually so called.

## The Fourth Treatise: OF HUSBANDS' PARTICULAR DUTIES

[p. 388] A husband's gesture ought to be so familiar and amiable towards his wife as others may discern him to be her husband . . . [but] some are never well but when they have their wives in their laps, ever colling [hugging], kissing and dallying with them, they care not in what company; thus they show more lightnness, fondness and dotage than true kindness and love, which forgetteth not an husband-like gravity, sobriety, modesty and decency.

Much greater liberty is granted to man and wife when they are alone than in company. Besides there are many other ways to show kindness than by lightness and wantonness.

[pp. 390–1] May not . . . an husband beat his wife? Can it be thought reasonable that she who is the man's perpetual bedfellow, who hath power over his body, who is a joint parent of the children, a joint governor of the family, should be beaten by his hands? What if the children or servants should know of it? (as they must needs – for how can such a thing be done in the house and they of the house know it not?) Can they respect her as a mother, or a mistress who is under correction as well as they?

On the contrary, as the stronger partner, a husband should take tender care of his wife.

[p. 394] For precious things, whereof we make high account, the weaker they be, the more tenderly, and charily are they handled, as china dishes, and crystal glasses. And of all parts of the body, the eye is most tenderly handled. Now, what persons are more dear and precious than a wife? Yet withal she is a weak vessel: therefore she is much to be borne withall.

## *Of an husband's provident care for his wife about childbearing*

[pp. 399–400] Her weakness is joined with much pain: the pain of a woman in travail [childbirth] is the greatest pain that ordinarily is endured by any for the time. None know it so well as they that feel it and many husbands, because they are not subject to it, think but lightly of it. But, if we duly weigh that the Holy Ghost, when he would set forth the extremity of any pains and pangs, resembleth them to the pains of a woman in travail, we may well gather that of all they are the greatest, which is further manifested by the screeches and outcries which not only weak and faint-hearted women utter in the time of their travail but also are forced from the strongest and stoutest women that be, and that though beforehand they resolve to the contrary.

## *Of an husband's maintaining his wife against children of a former venter [by a previous wife]*

[pp. 409–10] If she be the wrongdoer, he may by no means bolster her up against his children, and so make their wrong the greater. Yet so far ought he to respect his wife as, by all the fair means he can, to labour to pacify her mind and turn her heart towards them. And, if he observe her heart to be clean alienated from them, then to put them forth to be brought up in some other place, and so to take away from her the object of her displeasure, that he and she may live more quietly together. For, if a man must forsake father and mother, he must also forsake children and cleave to his wife.

## The Sixth Treatise: THE DUTIES OF PARENTS

## *Of a mother's care over her child while it is in her womb*

[p. 505] The first part of a child's infancy is while it remaineth in the mother's womb. . . . A mother then must have a tender care over herself when she is with child for, the child being lodged in her and receiving nourishment from her (as plants from the earth), her wellbeing tendeth much to the good and safety of the child.

[p. 506] Husbands also in this case must be very tender over their wives and helpful to them in all things needful, both in regard to that duty which they owe to their wives, and also of that they owe to their children . . . .

They who through violence of passion, whether of grief or anger, or through violent motion of the body, as by dancing, striving, running, galloping on horseback, or the like or through distemper of body, by eating things hurtful, by eating too much, by too much abstinence, by too much bashfulness in concealing their desire and longings (as we speak) cause any abortion or miscarriage, fall into the offence contrary to the forenamed duty. . . .

But they who purposely take things to make away their children in their womb are in far higher degree guilty of blood, yea even of wilful murder. For that which hath received a soul formed in it by God, if it be unjustly cast away, shall be revenged.

## *Of mothers giving suck to their own children*

[p. 508] Many strong arguments there be to press it upon the consciences of mothers and to show that (so far as they are able) they are bound to give suck to their own children. Some are taken from God's word and some from the light of nature. God's word doth in many places, by just consequence, imply that it is a bounden duty; in other places it doth expressly commend it by the practice of holy women; and again in other places it taketh it for a granted truth, and ruled case, not to be denied.

[p. 518] If husbands were willing that their wives should perform this duty, and would persuade and encourage them thereto, and afford them what helps they could, where one mother now nurseth her child, twenty would do it.

## *Two things are required of parents, in regard of the temporal good of their children*

[p.526]

1 To nourish them well.
2 To nurture them well.

Children must be well [fed/taught] . . . .

Recreation . . . in young children especially, is needful for their health. In that Zachary (Chapter 8 v. 5) told the Jews, and that in the way of blessing, that boys and girls should play in the streets, he implieth that it is a lawful and meet [appropriate] thing, which parents should permit unto their children. But yet the time, and measure, and kind of recreation must be well ordered.

[p. 548] The means of helping forward the good work of nurture are especially two:

1 Frequent admonition.
2 Due correction.

## *Of correcting children*

[p. 552] The latter and more proper kind of correction, which is by stripes and blows, is also a means appointed by God to help the good nurture and education of children. It is the last remedy which a parent can use; a remedy which may do good when nothing else can.

[p. 553] Correction is as physic to purge out much corruption which lurketh in children, and as a salve to heal many wounds and sores made by their folly . . . . In regard of the inward operation of this physic, correction is further said to preserve a child from death . . . and that not only from temporal death (as many children are thus preserved from the magistrate's sword) but also from eternal death.

[p. 555] . . . for well using this biting corrosive of correction, parents must have respect to the matter for which they do correct and to their manner of correcting.

That they be sure there is a fault committed . . . so there be just cause of correcting.

That the fault be made known to the child corrected and he apparently convinced thereof.

[pp. 556–7] Due order must be kept. Correction by word must go before correction by the rod.

Due respect must be had to the party corrected: if he be young and tender, the lighter correction must be used . . . . Due respect must be had to the fault.

Parents are responsible for 'providing fit callings for their children' (p. 558) and 'fit marriages for them'.

[p. 565] An especial outward means whereby parents may be the better enabled to provide fit callings and marriages for their children is beforehand to lay up some stock or competent portion for their children.

## Of neglecting to make a will

[pp. 571–2] The mischiefs that follow these neglects are many, as:

1 Discredit to the party deceased.
2 Contentions among his surviving children.
3 Wasting a great part, if not the whole of his estate, in suits of law.
4 Defeating many creditors of their due debt.

[pp. 575–7] Parents ought to have an impartial respect for all their children . . . . [Nevertheless it is] just . . . that the eldest son should have a greater patrimony than any of the rest . . . . For . . . God hath appointed it . . . . Our law giveth the whole inheritance of freeholds to the eldest son . . . in civil and temporal matters this rule is true, we live by the law. . . . Houses and families are by this means upheld and continued from age to age. How needful it is for the establishment of a commonwealth that families should thus be continued is evident . . . by experience to all such as have but half an eye to see wherein the stability of a commonwealth consisteth.

[However], parents ought to be . . . provident for their other children, in training them up to callings, or laying up portions, or settling other estates upon them beside the main inheritance, or in taking order that competent portions be raised out of the inheritance of the eldest son in case God take them away before they have otherwise provided for their children.

## Of the duties of fathers- and mothers-in-law [step-parents]

[pp. 580–2] If the world's proverb holds true (Love me, love my dog), how much more true is this Christian rule: Love me and love my child . . . . Contrary is the carriage of most fathers- and mothers-in-law, especially of those who are married to husbands or to wives that had children before marriage . . . the fault taxed here is so common . . . . Let widowers or widows that have children seriously think of it beforehand and be the more circumspect in taking a second or a third husband or wife.

## Of the duty who are instead of parents to orphans

[p. 583] Those who are instead of parents are those who in blood and kindred are next to parents: as grandfathers, grandmothers, uncles, aunts, elder brothers or sisters, their husbands or wives, and cousins.

The duties which were prescribed to natural parents appertain to them . . . . Their duty is to see these orphans well educated, well placed in some good calling, well married and (if the orphans be left destitute of means) well provided for.

# Exhibit 13

# The arguments for maternal breastfeeding

## Source

**Elizabeth Clinton, Countess of Lincoln, *The Countess of Lincolne's Nursery* (Oxford, 1628)**

Maternal nursing was one of William Gouge's many injunctions to the married couples of Jacobean London. The Countess of Lincoln devoted a whole pamphlet to promoting the practice. Elizabeth Knyvett, one of the granddaughters of the celebrated clothier Stumpe of Malmesbury, was married in the mid-1580s; she had eighteen children. Her book is dedicated to Bridget, wife of her third son Theophilus who inherited the earldom from his father in 1618. Few women of the Countess' rank would have breastfed in the 1620s or indeed for many decades after. As the tone of her pamphlet makes clear, her arguments were derived from the sermons and writings of godly ministers. The nursing mother's inspiration was the Blessed Virgin: 'as her womb bare our blessed Saviour', so her 'paps gave him suck' (p. 5).

> [p. 8] God . . . hath ordained that they should nurse their own children: for by his secret operation, the mother's affection is so knit by nature's law to her tender babe, as she finds no power to deny to suckle it, no not when she is in hazard to lose her own life, by attending on it, for in such a case it is not said, let the mother fly and leave her infant to the peril, as if she were dispensed with: but only it is said, 'Woe to her', as if she were to be pitied, that for nature to her child, she must be unnatural to herself: now if any them being at liberty, and in peace, with all plenty, shall deny to give suck to their own children, they go against nature; and show that God hath not done so much for them as to work any good, no not in their nature, but left them more savage than the dragons, and as cruel to their little ones as the ostriches.

In *Of Domesticall Duties*, Gouge (p. 507) remarked that, 'It is noted as a point of unnaturalness in the ostrich to leave her eggs in the earth and in the dust in which respect she is said to be hardened against her young ones as though they were not hers'.

[p.14] But there are some women that object fear, saying that they are so weak and so tender that they are afraid to venture to give their children suck, lest they endanger their health thereby. Of these I demand why then they did venture to marry and so to bear children and, if they say they did not choose and they thought not that marriage would impair their health, I answer that for the same reason they should set themselves to nurse their own children because they should not choose but do what God would have them to do and they should believe that this work will be for their health also seeing it is ordinary with God to give good stomach, health and strength to almost all mothers that take this pains with their children.

[pp. 14–16] Now if any reading these few lines return against me that it may be I myself have given my own children suck and therefore am bolder and more busy to meddle in urging this point, to the end to insult over and make them to be blamed that have not done it, I answer that, whether I have or have not performed this my bounden duty, I will not deny to tell my own practice. I know and acknowledge that I should have done it and, having not done it, it was not from want of will in myself but partly because I was overruled by another's authority, and partly deceived by some's ill counsel, and partly because I had not so well considered of my duty in this motherly office as since I did, when it was too late for me to put it in execution. Wherefore, being pricked in heart for my undutifulness, this way I study to redeem my peace: first, by repentance towards God, humbly and often craving his pardon for this my offence; secondly, by studying how to show double love to my children to make them amends for neglect of this part of love to them, when they should have hung on my breasts, and have been nourished in mine own bosom; thirdly, by doing my endeavour to prevent many Christian mothers from sinning in the same kind against our most loving and gracious God.

[pp. 18–19] Therefore, be no longer at the trouble and at the care to hire others to do your own work. Be not so unnatural as to thrust away your own children. Be not so hardy as to venture a tender babe to a less tender heart. Be not accessory to that disorder of causing a poorer woman to banish her own infant for the entertainment of a richer woman's child, as it were, bidding her unlove her own to love yours. We have followed Eve in transgression, let us follow her in obedience. When God laid the sorrows of conception, of breeding, of bringing forth, and of bringing up her children upon her, and so upon us in her loins, did she reply any word against? No a word. So I pray you all mine own daughters and others that are still child-bearing, reply not against the duty of suckling them when God hath sent you them.

# Exhibit 14

# Advice to the seventeenth-century housewife

## Source

**Gervase Markham, *A Way to Get Wealth, containing the principal vocations or callings in which every good husband or housewife may lawfully employ themselves* (London [1623], 1631)**

Gervase Markham (born circa 1568) was the third son of a Nottinghamshire landowner. Information about his life is sparse but there is evidence to suggest that he was a student at King's College, Cambridge, in the 1580s. He began to write after his father's imprisonment for debt in 1595. Poetry and horsemanship were the twin arts on which he hoped to launch a career in the service of a noble patron, unfortunately, his lord, the Earl of Essex, was executed for rebellion in 1601.

Markham produced a series of books designed to exploit the evidently insatiable appetite for instruction on the breeding and management of horses. By July 1617 he had five in print and another on the stocks. The Stationers Company, which sought to control the book market in the publishers' interest, extracted the following undertaking from him: 'I, Gervase Markham of London, gentleman, do promise hereafter never to write any more book or books to be printed of the disease or cures of any cattle or horse, ox, cow, sheep, swine, goats etc.'.

The edition of *A Way to Get Wealth* from which these extracts come includes 'a short table expounding all the hard words in this book'. It is in fact a list of unfamiliar plants and substances, including turmeric, 'a yellow sample, of strong savour, to be bought at the 'pothecaries', and ivory, 'the shavings of the elephant's tooth'.

The first book, 'Cheap and Good Husbandry' is devoted to 'the well-ordering of all beasts and fowls and for the general cure of their diseases'; the third book is 'The English Housewife containing all the virtuous knowledges and actions, both of mind and body, which ought to be in any complete housewife of any degree or calling soever'. It is striking that, unlike Book One, which is a technical manual, Book Three combines instruction in housewifely skills with injunctions about wifely conduct.

[pp. 1–2] Having already in a summary briefness passed through those outward parts of husbandry which belong unto the perfect husbandman, who is the father and master of the family . . . it is now meet that we descend in as orderly a method as we can, to the office of our English housewife.

Let our English housewife be a godly, constant and religious woman, learning from the worthy preacher and her husband those good examples which she shall with all careful diligence see exercised amongst her servants.

[p.3 ] Next unto this sanctity and holiness of life it is meet that our English housewife be a woman of great modesty and temperance . . . in her behaviour and carriage towards her husband wherein she shall shun all violence of rage, passion and humour, coveting less to direct than to be directed, appearing ever unto him pleasant, amiable and delightful . . . recalling in her mind that evil and uncomely language is deformed though uttered even to servants, but most monstrous and ugly when it appears before the presence of a husband.

[p.4] Let . . . the housewife's garments be comely and strong . . . altogether without toyish garnishes or the gloss of light colours, and . . . far from the vanity of new and fantastic fashions. . . . Let her diet be wholesome and cleanly, prepared at due hours, and cooked with care and diligence, let it be rather to satisfy nature than our affections, and apter to kill hunger than revive our appetites, let it proceed more from the provision of her own yard than the furniture of the markets, and let it rather be esteemed for the familiar acquaintance she hath with it than for the strangeness and rarity it bringeth from other countries.

Our English housewife must be of chaste thought, stout courage, patient, untired, watchful, diligent, witty, pleasant, constant in friendship, full of good neighbourhood, wise in discourse, but not frequent therein, sharp and quick of speech but not bitter or talkative, secret in her affairs, comfortable in her counsels and generally skilful in the worthy knowledges which do belong to her vocation.

Her first priority is 'the preservation and care of the family touching their health and soundness of body'; next in importance is cookery:

[p. 62] She that it utterly ignorant of therein . . . can . . . but perform half her [marriage] vow for she may love and obey but she cannot cherish, serve and keep him with that true duty which is ever expected.

# Exhibit 15

# Advice to the head of a modest seventeenth-century household

## Source

**Richard Baxter,** *The Poor Man's Family Book ... With a request to landlords and rich men to give their tenants and poor neighbours either this or another fitter book* **(London, 1674)**

Richard Baxter (born 1615), largely self-educated, was perhaps the most influential nonconformist divine in England in the second half of the seventeenth century. He broke with the Anglican Church because he was unable to reconcile himself to the use, without biblical sanction, of the priest's surplice (robe) and the sign of the cross in baptism; he was also opposed to the 'promiscuous giving of the Lord's Supper to drunkards, swearers and all who had not been excommunicated [formally excluded from membership of the church]'. But, although highly critical of the practice of the Church of England, Baxter was a political conservative who spoke against the execution of Charles I 'at the risk of his life' and welcomed the Restoration. It was for theological reasons, therefore, that he turned down Charles II's offer of a bishopric. *The Poor Man's Family Book* is one of his hundred published works.

[pp. 303–5] Be sure.... 1. To breed your children to a temperate and healthful diet and keep tempting meats, but specially drinks, from before them. 2. Breed them up to constant labour which may never leave mind or body idle, but at the hours of necessary recreation which you allow them. 3. Let their recreations be such as tend more to the health of their bodies than the humouring of a corrupted fancy: keep them from gaming for money, from cards, dice and stage plays, play books and love books and foolish wanton tales and ballads.... 4. Let their apparel be plain, decent and warm, but not gaudy.... 5. Be sure when they grow towards ripeness that you keep them away from opportunity, nearness or familiarity with tempting persons of another sex.... Be sure you engage your children in good company and keep them as much as possible out of bad. ... Keep a special watch upon their tongues, especially against ribaldry and lying. For dangerous corruptions do quickly this way obtain dominion....Teach them to value time.... Labour to make time-wasting odious to them. And set death still before their eyes and ask of them whether they are ready to die.... Let correction be widely used, as they need it; neither so severely as to disaffect them to you, nor so little as to leave them in a course of sin and disobedience.

Let it always be in love, and more for sin against God than any wordly matters. And show them scripture against the sin and for the correction.

## The special duties of the husband

[p. 308] They are: 1. To exercise love and authority together (never separated) to his wife. 2. To be the chief teacher and governor of the family and the provider for its maintenance. 3. To excel the wife in knowledge and patience, and to be her teacher and guide in the matters of God, and to be the chief in bearing infirmities and trials. 4. To keep up the wife's authority and honour in the family over inferiors.

## The special duties of the wives

[pp. 308–9] 1. To excel in love. 2. To be obedient to their husbands and examples therein to the rest of the family. 3. Submissively to learn of their husbands (that can teach them) and not to be self-conceited, teaching, talkative or imperious. 4. To subdue their passions, deny their own fancies and wills, and not to tempt their husbands to satisfy their humours and vain desires in pride, excess, revenge or any evil, nor to rob God and the poor by a proud and wasteful humour (as the wives of gentlemen ordinarily do). 5. To govern their tongues, that their words may be few and sober; and to abhor a running and a scolding tongue. 6. To be contented in every condition, and not to torment their husbands and themselves with impatient murmurings. 7. To avoid the childish vanity of gaudy apparel, and following vain fashions of the prouder sort. And to abhor their vice that waste precious time in curious and tedious dressings, gossipings, visits and feasts. 8. To help on the maintenance of the family by frugality and by their proper care and labour. 9. Not to dispose of their husband's estate without his consent, either explicit or implicit. Above all, to be constant helpers of the holy education of their children. . . . And so they may become chief instruments of the reformation and welfare of churches and kingdoms and of the world.

## Directions for a safe and comfortable death

[pp. 360–1] The flesh that must be daily pleased, and nothing is too good for it, must be an ugly, black and stinking carcass, many years rotting out of sight and smell lest it should annoy the living and mar their mirth before it can come to be dry and less abominable dust, and equal with the common earth.

[p. 363] Our diseases and pains of the body forewarn us. Our weariness in our labours tells us that we have a body that must break at last. Our grey hairs tell us, as the golden leaves on the trees in autumn, that our fall is at hand. Our children tell us that others are rising up in our steads while we are going off the stage.

[p. 364] Every clock that striketh, every watch that moveth, every hour glass that runneth, hath a voice to call to senseless sinners: See and hear O Man or

Woman how thy time passeth away. How quickly will thy last hour come! . . .
Your days are numbered! It is determined how many more breaths you must
breathe and how many times your pulse must beat! Your last pulse and your
last breath is near at hand.

## On your deathbed

[pp. 416–17] If your disease allow you an expressing strength, magnify God's
goodness . . . make others to see that there is a reality in the comforts of faith
and hope . . . . Your tongues are given you to praise the Lord; they have but a
little while more to speak, let their last work be done to his glory, as strength
will bear . . . . And turn your last words to God himself in prayer and praises
beginning the work which you must do in Heaven. Imitate your dying Lord,
Luke 23.46 [Father into thy hands I commend my spirit] And his first martyr,
Acts 7.59 [Lord Jesus receive my spirit].

# EXHIBIT 16

# A gallery of good children

## SOURCE

**James Janeway, Minister of the Gospel,** *A Token for Children Being an
Exact Account of the Conversion, Holy and Exemplary Lives and Joyful
Deaths of Several Young Children* **(Suffer little children to come unto me,
and forbid them not: for of such is the Kingdom of God: Mark 10.14)
(First published in the 1670s)**

Janeway died unmarried in March 1674 'in the thirty-eighth year of his
age'. The son of a Hertfordshire curate, he was educated at Oxford. In the
mid-1660s he became a popular nonconformist preacher in London. His
*Token for Children* was frequently reprinted and continued to be read into
the nineteenth century.

## The Preface

Whither do you think those children go when they die that will not do what
they are bid but pay the truant and lie and speak naughty words and break
the Sabbath? Whither do such children go, do you think? Why, I will tell you,
they which lie must go to their father the Devil into everlasting burning. They

which never pray, God will pour out his wrath upon them, and when they beg and pray in Hell Fire, God will not forgive them but there they must be forever. And are you willing to go to Hell to be burned with the Devil and his Angels? Would you be in the same condition with naughty [wicked] children? O Hell is a terrible place that's a thousand times worse than a whipping. . . .

Well now, what will you do? Will you read this book a little because your good mother will make you do it, and because it is a new little book, but as soon as ever you have done, run away to play and never think of it?

How do you know but that you may be the next child that may die? And where are you then if you be not God's child?

## Example VII

[p. 56] Of a notorious wicked child, who was taken up from begging and admirably converted; with an account of his holy life and joyful death when he was nine years old.

A very poor child of the parish of Newington Butts came begging to the door of a dear Christian friend of mine in a very lamentable case, so filthy and nasty that he would even have turned one's stomach to look on him.

[pp. 57–8] There seemed to be very little hopes of doing any good upon this child for he was a very monster of wickedness and a thousand times more miserable and vile by his sin than by his poverty. He was running to Hell as soon as he could go and was old in naughtiness [wickedness] when he was young in years . . . [but the good Christian was determined] to do all that possibly he could to pluck this firebrand out of the fire.

[p. 59] An amazing change was seen in the child, in a few weeks' he was soon convinced of the evil of his ways; no more news now of his calling of names, swearing or cursing; no more taking of the Lord's name in vain. Now he is civil and respectful and such a strange alteration was wrought in the child that all the parish that rung of his villainy before was now ready to talk of his reformation.

[pp. 65–6] The child grew exceedingly in knowledge, experiences, patience, humility and self-abhorrency, and he thought he could never speak bad enough of himself; the name he would call himself by was – a Toad.

[p. 68] The Wednesday before he died the child lay as it were in a trance for about half an hour, in which time he saw a vision of angels. When he was out of his trance he was in a little pet and asked his nurse why she did not let him go. 'Go whither, child?' she said. 'Why along with those brave gentlemen', said he. 'But they told me they would come and fetch me away for all [in spite of] you upon Friday next'. And he doubled [repeated] his words many times, 'Upon Friday next those brave gentlemen will come for me.' And upon that day the child died joyfully.

[pp. 71–2] And on Friday morning he sweetly went to rest, using that very expression. 'Into thy hands, Lord, I commit my spirit'. He died punctually at that time which he spoke of and in which he expected those Angels to come to him. He was not much above nine years old when he died.

This narrative I had from a judicious holy man unrelated to him who was an eye and ear-witness to all these things.

Another of Janeway's examples, John Harvy, a merchant's son, born 1654, died in 'that dreadful year sixty-five' (p. 77), the year of the plague.

## Example XIII

[p. 69] One day seeing one of his near relations come into his father's house distempered with drink, as he thought, he quickly went very seriously to him and wept over him that he should so offend God and hazard his soul and begged of him to spend his time better than in drinking and gaming and this he did without any instruction from his parents but from his own inward principle of grace.

[p. 70] Once hearing a boy speak very profanely, and that after two or three admonitions . . . he was so transported with zeal that he could not forebear falling upon him to beat him . . . . This is observed not to vindicate the act but to take notice of his zeal.

[p. 78] He would put his brother and sister upon their duties and observe then whether they performed it or no and when he saw any neglect he would soon warn them; if he saw any of then take a spoon into their hands before they craved a blessing [said grace], he said 'That is just like a hog indeed'.

His sister was afraid of darkness and would sometimes cry upon this account. He told her she must fear God more and she need then be afraid of nothing.

# EXHIBIT 17

# Advice on educating sons (designed for the upper ranks of society)

## SOURCE

**John Locke, *Some Thoughts Concerning Education* (London, 1693)**

Locke (born 1632) was educated at Westminster School and Oxford. He stayed at the University, teaching and studying medicine, until he became a member of the household of Anthony Ashley Cooper, first Earl of

Shaftesbury, an opponent of the Stuart regime, in the 1660s. As a result of this connection, he spent much of the 1680s in exile in Holland. The *Observer's* notice of David Wootton's edition of his *Political Writings* (12 September 1993) provides a useful brief assessment of Locke as a political actor:

> the decisive philosopher of political liberalism, arguing for limited govern-
> ment, against the divine right of kings, in favour of toleration, defining inalien-
> able rights, all of which influenced the founding fathers of the United States.
> [But as Wootton shows] . . . Locke was a considerably more complicated, ambigu-
> ous figure, sinuously moving through a political environment in which exile,
> torture and execution were a common response to provocative speculation.

He is frequently credited with the transformation of parental attitudes among the ranks of the cultivated country gentlemen and professionals. As these extracts suggest, he is not the advocate of permissive parenting that he is sometimes assumed to be. The secular tone of his *Thoughts Concerning Education* is, however, striking.

> [p. 35] Parents, by humouring and cockering them when little, corrupt the
> principles of Nature in their children, and wonder afterwards to taste the bit-
> ter waters, when they themselves have poisoned the fountain. For when their
> children are grown up, and these ill habits with them, when they are too big
> to be dandled, and their parents can no longer make use of them as play-things,
> then they complain that the brats are untoward and perverse; then they are
> offended to see them wilfull, and are troubled with those ill humours which
> they themselves inspired and cherished in them.

> [p. 37] For if the child must have grapes or sugar plums when he has a mind
> to them, rather than make the poor baby cry or be out of humour, why, when
> he is grown up must he not be satisfied too, if his desires carry him to wine or
> women? These are objects as suitable to the longing of one of more years as
> what he cried for when little was to the inclinations of a child.

> [p. 38] If they were never suffered to obtain their desire by the impatience they
> expressed for it, they would no more cry for other things than they do for the
> moon.

> [p. 55] Esteem and disgrace are, of all others, the most powerful incentives to
> the mind, when it is brought to relish them. If you can once get into children
> a love of credit and an apprehension of shame and disgrace, you have put into
> them the true principle, which will constantly work, and incline them to the
> right.

> [p. 66] Pray remember, children are not to be taught by rules, which will be
> always slipping out of their memories. What you think necessary for them to
> do, settle in them by an indispensable practice, as often as the occasion returns;
> and if it be possible, make occasions. This will beget habits in them, which
> being once established, operate of themselves easily and naturally without the
> assistance of memory.

[p. 116] Dominion . . . is the first original of most vicious habits that are ordinary and natural. This love of power and dominion shows itself very early . . . . We see children (as soon almost as they are born, I am sure long before they can speak) cry, grow peevish, sullen and out of humour for nothing but their wills.

[p. 117] Another thing wherein they show their love of dominion is their desire to have things to be theirs; they would have propriety and possession.

[p. 120] Children who live together often strive for mastery.

[p. 123] Crying is a fault that should not be tolerated in children, not only for the unpleasant and unbecoming noise it fills the house with, but for more considerable reasons . . . . Their crying is of two sorts either stubborn and domineering or querulous and whining.

[p. 134] Curiosity in children . . . is but an appetite after knowledge, and therefore ought to be encouraged in them, not only as a good sign but as the great instrument Nature has provided to remove that ignorance they were born with . . . . Answer all his questions and explain matters he desires to know.

[pp. 175–6] When he can talk, 'tis time he should begin to read . . . but . . . a great care is to be taken that it never be made as a business to him nor he look on it as a task.

[pp. 177–8] There may be dice and play-things with letters on them to teach children the alphabet by playing – and twenty other ways may be found, suitable to their tempers, to make this kind of learning a sport to them.

[p. 184] As soon as he begins to spell as many pictures of animals should be got him as can be found with the printed names to them, which at the same time will invite him to read and afford him matter of enquiry and knowledge.

[pp. 189–90] When he can read English well, it will be seasonable to enter him in writing. And here the first thing that should be taught him is to hold his pen right . . . the way to teach him to write without much trouble is to get a plate [en]graved with characters of such a hand as you like best – but you must remember to have them a pretty deal bigger than he should ordinarily write, for everyone naturally comes by degrees to write a less hand than he at first was taught but never a bigger. Such a plate being graved, let several sheets of good writing paper be printed off with red ink, which he has nothing to do but go over with a good pen filled with black ink, which will quickly bring his hand to the formation of those characters, being at first showed where to begin and how to form every letter.

This was not a novel suggestion. In his *School Pastime*, published in 1669, John Newton had advocated the use of a similar text printed 'in red as well as in black', 'a child tracing them over with ink will in a short time produce so great a proficiency that I dare say no man shall ever repent of the charge that this will put him to'.

# Exhibit 18

# The mercenary aspect of choosing a bride

## Source

*THE LEVELLERS. A dialogue between two young ladies concerning matrimony, proposing an Act for the enforcement of marriage, for equality of matches, a taxing of single persons; with the danger of celibacy to the Nation. Dedicated to a Member of Parliament* (1703)

This satirical piece, which would have shocked the godly writers of conduct books quoted earlier, was an item in the 'collection of scarce, curious and entertaining pamphlets and tracts' from the Earl of Oxford's library which were published as the *Harleian Miscellany* (Volume V, London, 1745).

The parties to the conversation, both orphans in fruitless search of a match, are – as the extracts below explain – Sophia, the daughter of a landed gentleman who ruined himself by political misjudgement, and Politica, the daughter of a tradesman, who mistakenly endowed her with all the accomplishments of a fine lady.

> [p. 419] Though we have a common proverb in England that matches are made in heaven, I can truly say, as the country wench did, 'They are a long time in coming down'. I have waited for one a great while to no purpose. My money will not grow to the height of a husband though I water it with tears and air it with sighs.

> [p. 420] *Politica*: You know my father was a tradesman and lived very well by his traffic; and, I being beautiful, he thought Nature had already given me part of my portion [dowry], and that therefore he would add a liberal education that I might be a complete gentlewoman. Away he sent me to the boarding school there I learned to dance and sing, to play upon the bass viol, virginals, spinet and guitar. I learned to make wax work, japan [enamel], paint upon glass, to raise pies, make sweetmeats, sauces, and every thing that was genteel and fashionable. My father died and left me accomplished, as you find me. And me with £300 portion, and with all this I am not able to buy an husband . . . an honest tradesman that wants a portion of £300 has more occasion of a wife that understands cookery and housewifery than one that understands singing and making of sweetmeats.

Sophia's father had rebelled against the Catholic King James II,

> in that enterprise he lost his life and estate, and so I lost my portion and have

nothing to subsist on but the charity of my good aunt. I can marry nothing but a gentleman, and very few, if any of them, are inclined to marry the poor remains of an honourable and virtuous family.

---

## EXHIBIT 19

# Witchcraft beliefs and witchcraft trials

### SOURCES

Henry Holland, *A Treatise against Witchcraft, or A Dialogue wherein the greatest doubts concerning that sin are briefly answered; a satanical operation in the witchcraft of all times is truly proved; the most precious preservatives against such evils are showed. Very needful to be known of all men but chiefly of the masters and fathers of families that they may learn the best means to purge their houses of all unclean spirits, and wisely to avoid the dreadful impieties and great dangers which come by such abominations* (Cambridge, 1590)

William Perkins, *A Discourse of the Damned Art of Witchcraft, so far forth as it is revealed in the Scriptures and manifest by true experience* (Cambridge, 1608)

*A Trial of Witches, at the Assizes held at Bury St Edmund's for the County of Suffolk 17 Charles II* [Charles' reign officially began with the death of his father which we now date to January 1649. However, until 1752, when England came into line with Scotland and 'almost all other nations of Europe', the English year officially began 25 March] *1665. Before Sir Matthew Hale Knight then Lord Chief Baron of His Majesty's Court of Exchequer. Taken by a Person then attending the Court* (London: printed for William Shrewsbery, at the Bible, in Duck-lane, 1682)
*A Full and Impartial Account of the Discovery of Sorcery and Witchcraft practised by Jane Wenham of Walkerne in Hertfordshire . . . The proceedings against her from her being first apprehended till she was committed to gaol by Sir Henry Chauncy. Also her trial at the Assizes at Hertford before Mr Justice Powell where she was found gulty of felony and witchcraft and received sentence of death for the same* March 4 1711–12. 'Thou shalt not suffer a witch to live'. (London, 1712)

Although witchcraft was a capital offence in England from 1563, the country escaped the panics which led to witch-hunts in some French and German regions, in Scotland and in the English settlements in Massachusetts.

The witch was believed to use supernatural means to harm those who got on the wrong side of her. Most English 'witches' were poor, old women, unable to return favour for favour and, therefore, excluded from the neighbourly system of good turns. Their sense of grievance translated itself into ill-wishing and the result was that they were often condemned out of their own mouths.

## Henry Holland, *A Treatise against Witchcraft*

Holland, who died in 1604, was educated at Magdalene College, Cambridge. At the time that his *Treatise* was published he was Vicar of St Bride's in London. Holland dedicated his *Treatise* to the Earl of Essex.

> The Scriptures of God (right Honourable) in sundry places do most evidently teach us that there are two spiritual kingdoms in this world which have continual hatred and bloody wars without hope of truce for ever. The Lord and king of one is our Lord Jesus; the tyrannical usurper of the other is Satan. Again, this also we are clearly taught that all men living, without exception, are either true subjects of the one or slaves unto the other. For, albeit the neuters of the world dream that they may indifferently view the scars and wounds of other men, and never approach near those bloody skirmishes, yet the truth is they are foully deceived for the great Lord and king hath said with his own mouth: 'He that is not with me is against me'.

## William Perkins, *A Discourse of the Damned Art of Witchcraft*

William Perkins was born in Warwickshire in 1558. Educated at Cambridge, he stayed on and became a popular preacher with town and gown. He was a prolific and influential writer whose work was translated not only into Latin but also into minority languages like Welsh and Irish.

> [pp. 3–4] Witchcraft is a wicked art, serving for the working of wonders by the assistance of the Devil, so far forth as God shall in justice permit.

> [p. 19] The Devil is . . . an ancient spirit whose skill hath been confirmed by experience of the course of nature for the space of almost six thousand years [i.e. since God created the heavens and earth]. Hence he hath attained to the knowledge of many secrets and, by long observation of the effects, is able to discern and judge of hidden causes in nature which man in likelihood cannot come unto by ordinary means.

> [p. 200] The discovery of a witch is a matter judicial, as is also the discovery of a thief and a murderer and belongeth not to every man but is to be done judicially by the magistrate according to the form and order of law.

[pp. 255–6] As the killing witch must die, the healing and harmless witch must die . . . though he kill not, only for the covenant he made with Satan. For this must always be remembered, as a conclusion, that by witches we understand not only those which kill and torment but all diviners, all wizards – commonly called wise men and wise women . . . and in the same number we reckon all good witches, which do not hurt but good, which do not spoil and destroy but save and deliver. . . . By the laws of England, the thief is executed for stealing and we think it just and profitable. But it were a thousand times better for the land if all witches, but specially the blessing witch, might suffer death. For the thief by his stealing and the hurtful enchanter by charming bring hindrance and hurt to the bodies and goods of men but these are the right hand of the Devil by which he taketh and destroyeth the souls of men.

[p. 257] Death therefore is the just and deserved portion of the good witch.

## A Trial of Witches, at the Assizes held at Bury St Edmund's

This is reprinted in *Cobbett's Complete Collection of State Trials and Proceedings for High Treason and other Crimes and Misdemeanours from the Earliest Period to the Present Time. Volume VI comprising the Period from the Thirteenth Year of the Reign of King Charles the second, AD 1661, to the Thirtieth Year of the Said Reign, AD 1678* (London, 1810, columns 687–702) and accuses Rose Cullender and Amy Duny, widows, of 'Leystoff' in Suffolk of betwitching seven children ranging in age from a baby in arms – the only boy – to 18.

[column 688] As concerning William Durent, being an infant, his mother Dorothy Durent, sworn and examined, deposed in open court, that about the 10th of March, nono Caroli Secundi [in the tenth year of the reign of Charles II], she having a special occasion to go from home, and having none in her house to take care of her said child (it then sucking) desired Amy Duny, her neighbour, to look to her child during her absence, for which she promised her to give her a penny; but the said Dorothy Durent desired the said Amy not to suckle her child, and laid a great charge upon her not to do it. Upon which it was asked by the court, why did she give that direction, she being an old woman and not capable of giving suck? It was answered by the said Dorothy Durent that she knew very well that she did not give suck, but that for some years before she had gone under the reputation of a witch, which was one cause made her give the caution. Another was that it was customary with old women that, if they did look after a sucking child, and nothing would please it but the breast, they did use to please the child, to give it the breast, and it did please the child, but it sucked nothing but wind, which did the child hurt.

When Dorothy returned and discovered that Amy had suckled her child, a shouting match ensued.

That very night [Dorothy's] son fell into strange fits of swounding . . . and so continued for divers weeks. And the said examinant farther said that, she being exceedingly troubled at her child's distemper, did go to a certain person named

Dr Jacob, who lived at Yarmouth, who had the reputation in the country [district] to help children that were bewitched; who advised her to hang up the child's blanket in the chimney corner all day, and at night, when she put the child to bed, to put it into the said blanket, and, if she found any thing in it, she should not be afraid, but to throw it into the fire. And this deponent did according to his direction, and it night, when she took down the blanket with an intent to put her child therein [column 689], there fell out of the same a great toad, which ran up and down the hearth, and she, having a young youth only with her in the house, desired him to catch the toad and throw it into the fire, which the youth did accordingly and held it there with the tongs; and as soon as it was in the fire it made a great and horrible noise, and after a space there was a flashing in the fire like gunpowder, making a noise like the discharge of a pistol, and thereupon the toad was no more seen nor heard . . . .

And the next day there came a young woman, a kinswoman of the said Amy, and a neighbour of this deponent, and told this deponent that her aunt (meaning the said Amy) was in a most lamentable condition, having her face all scorched with fire, and that she was sitting alone in her house in her smock without any fire [when she was injured]. And thereupon this deponent went into the house of the said Amy Duny to see her and found her in the same condition as was related to her; for her face, her legs and thighs, which this deponent saw, seemed very much scorched and burnt with fire . . . [Dorothy] asked the said Amy how she came into that sad condition and the said Amy replied that she might thank her [Dorothy] for it, for that she, this deponent, was the cause thereof, but that she should live to see some of her children dead, and she walk upon crutches. And this deponent farther saith that, after the burning of the said toad, her child recovered and was well again and was living at the time of the assizes.

But her daughter Elizabeth had since died and she had herself been struck lame.

There was one thing very remarkable, that after she had gone upon crutches for upwards of three years . . . upon the jury's bringing in their verdict by which the said Amy Duny was found guilty, to the great admiration [astonishment] of all persons, the said Dorothy Durent was restored to the use of her limbs and went home without making use of her crutches.

[column 692] [As for other alleged victims], Elizabeth and Deborah Pacy, the first of the age of eleven, the other of the age of nine years or thereabout . . . their fits were various, sometimes they would be lame on one side of their bodies, sometimes on the other; sometimes a soreness over their whole bodies, so as they could endure none to touch them; at other times they would be restored to perfect use of their limbs and deprived of their hearing; at other times of their sight; at other times of their speech; sometimes by the space of one day, sometimes for two; and once they were wholly deprived of their speech for eight days together, and then restored to their speech again. At other times they would fall into swoonings, and, upon recovery to their speech, they would cough extremely and bring up much phlegm and, with the same, crooked pins and, one time, a two-penny nail with a very broad head, which pins (amounting to forty or more) together with the two-penny nail, were produced in court . . . . Commonly at the end of every fit they would cast up a pin, and sometimes they would have four or five fits in one day.

[column 691] [Their father] Samuel Pacy, a merchant of Leystoff (a man who carried himself with such soberness during the trial, from whom proceeded no words either of passion or malice, though his children were so afflicted . . . [column 692]) was present when the nail was brought up and also most of the pins.

Like Dorothy Durent, Samuel Pacy called in a medical advisor,

[column 691] Dr Feavour, a doctor of physic . . . saw the child [Deborah] in those fits but could not conjecture, as he . . . affirmed in open court . . . what might be the cause of the child's affliction.

[column 693] . . . his children being thus tormented . . . and finding no hopes of amendment, he sent them to his sister's house, one Margaret Arnold, who lived at Yarmouth, a to make trial whether the change of air might do them any good . . . .

Margaret Arnold, sworn and examined, saith that the said Elizabeth and Deborah Pacy came to her house about the thirtieth of November last, her brother acquainted her that he thought they were bewitched for that they vomited pins. . . . This deponent said that she gave no credit to that which was related to her conceiving possibly the children might use some deceit in putting pins in their mouths themselves. Wherefore this deponent unpinned all their clothes, and left not so much as one pin upon them, but sewed all the clothes they wore instead of pinning them. [Pins were used as fastenings, instead of buttons or hooks and eyes. They were also used to attach one piece of clothing to another – the bib of an apron to the bodice of a dress, for example. These pins were coarser and stronger than dressmakers' pins, more like tie pins or hat pins, in fact.] But this deponent saith that not withstanding all this care and circumspection [vigilance] of hers, the children afterwards raised at several times at least thirty pins in her presence, and had the most fierce and violent fits upon them.

The children would in their fits cry out against Rose Cullender and Amy Duny, affirming that they saw them . . . . At some times the children (only) would see things run up and down the house in the appearance of mice; and one of them suddenly snapped one [of them] with the tongs and threw it into the fire, and it screeched like a rat.

In this case, it was implied that Amy Duny's malice against the Pacys stemmed from the occasion when she went to their house

[column 691] to buy some herrings but, being denied she went away discontented and presently returned again, and was denied, and likewise the third time and was denied, as at first; and at her last going away, she went away grumbling; but what she said was not perfectly understood.

[column 697] Mr Serjeant Keeling [a lawyer present at the hearing] seemed much unsatisfied with [the evidence] and thought it was not sufficient to convict the prisoners for, admitting that the children were in truth bewitched, yet, said he, it can never be applied [made to stick] to the prisoners upon the imagination [opinion] only of the parties afflicted; for if that might be allowed, no person whatsoever can be in safety, for perhaps they might fancy another person, who might be innocent in such matters.

There was also Dr Brown of Norwich [better known as Sir Thomas Browne], a person of great knowledge; who after this evidence was given, and upon view of the three persons in court –

three of the alleged victims (Ann Durent, Susan Chandler and Elizabeth Pacy) had been brought to the assizes; Elizabeth Pacy lay on a 'table in the court', 'upon cushions . . . upon her back, her stomach and belly by the drawing of her breath, would arise to a great height'

– and desired to give his opinion what he did conceive of them: and he was clearly of opinion that the persons were bewitched; and said that in Denmark there had lately been a great discovery of witches, who used the very same way of afflicting persons by conveying pins into them, and crooked as these pins were, with needles and nails. And his opinion was that the devil in such cases did work upon the bodies of men and women . . . to stir up and excite such humours super-abounding in their bodies to a great excess, whereby he did in an extraordinary manner afflict them with such distempers as their bodies were most subject to, as particularly appeared in these children; for he conceived that these swooning fits were natural, and nothing else but that they call the mother [hysteria], but only heightened to a great excess by the subtlety of the devil, cooperating with the malice of these which we term witches.

The possibility that the children were lying was taken seriously:

during the time of the trial there were some experiments made with the persons afflicted, by bringing the [accused] persons to touch them.

[column 698] [As a final experiment,] it was privately desired by the judge that Lord Cornwallis, Sir Edmund Bacon and Mr Serjeant Keeling and some other gentlemen there in court would attend one of the distempered persons in the farther part of the hall, whilst she was in her fits, and then to send for one of the witches to try what would happen, which they did accordingly: and Amy Duny was conveyed from the bar [the rail at which the prisoners stood in court] and brought to the maid. They put an apron before her eyes and then one other person [not the witch] touched her hand which produced the same effect as the touch of the witch did in court. Whereupon the gentlemen returned, openly protesting that they did believe the whole transaction was a mere imposture [fraud].

This put the court and all persons into a stand [brought proceedings to a halt]. But at length [eventually] Mr Pacy did declare that possibly the maid might be deceived by a suspicion that the witch touched her when she did not

. . . . This saying of Mr Pacy was afterwards found to be true afterwards when his daughter was fully recovered (as she afterwards was).

This experiment . . . was rather a confirmation that the parties were really bewitched than otherwise for, say they, it is not possible that any should counterfeit such distempers . . . much less children; and for so long time, and yet undiscovered by their parents and relations. For no man can suppose that they should all conspire together (being out of several families, and, as they affirm, no way related one to the other and scarce of familiar acquaintance) to do an act of this nature whereby no benefit or advantage could redound to any of the parties but a guilty conscience for perjuring themselves in taking the lives of two poor simple women away.

After all the evidence had been heard, the accused women were asked

[column 700] what they had to say for themselves. They replied nothing material to anything that was proved against them. Whereupon the judge, giving his direction to the jury, told them that he would not repeat the evidence unto them, lest by doing so he should wrong the evidence on one side or the other. Only this he acquainted them that they had two things to enquire after: First, whether or no these children were bewitched. Secondly, whether the prisoners at the bar were guilty of it. That there were such creatures as witches he made no doubt at all. For first, the scriptures had affirmed so much. Secondly, the wisdom of all nations had provided laws against such persons.

[column 701] With this short direction, the jury departed from the bar and within the space of half an hour returned and brought them both in guilty upon the several indictments which were thirteen in number.

This was upon Thursday in the afternoon, March 13 1665. The next morning the three children, with their parents, came to the Lord Chief Baron Hales's lodging, who all of them spake perfectly and were in as good health as ever they were; only Susan Chandler, by reason of her very much affliction, did look very thin and wan. And their friends were asked what time they were restored thus to their [column 702] speech and health. And Mr Pacy did affirm that, within less than half an hour after the witches were convicted they were all of them restored.

After, they were all of them brought down to the court, but Ann Durent was so fearful to behold them that she desired she might not see them [the 'witches']. The other two continued in the court and affirmed, in the face of the country and before the witches themselves, what before had been deposed by their friends and relations; the prisoners not much contradicting them. In conclusion, the judge and all the court were fully satisfied with the verdict and thereupon gave judgement against the witches that they should be hanged.

They were much urged to confess, but they would not.

That morning we departed for Cambridge but no reprieve was granted and they were executed on Monday the 17th of March following. But they confessed nothing.

## Francis Bragge, *A Full and Impartial Account of the Discovery of Sorcery and Witchcraft practised by Jane Wenham*

Jane Wenham was the last person to be convicted of witchcraft in England. Starving poor before her arrest, she benefited from her notoriety in the long run, attracting patrons who maintained her until her death in 1730.

Although the charges were almost literally laughed out of court, the part played by reputation and circumstantial evidence, the pattern of favours asked and denied were characteristic of the accusations made by unsophisticated complainants when belief in witches was conventional among magistrates and academics.

> [pp. 1–2] One John Chapman, a farmer at Walkern, had long entertained a suspicion that the strange deaths of many of his and the neighbours' horses and cattle were occasioned by the witchcrafts of this woman and thought that he himself had suffered by them to the value of £200 in a short time but, not being able to prove anything upon her, he did not inform against her but waited till time should present a favourable opportunity of convicting her. And soon after an accident fell out, which, in its consequences, brought on this prosecution. I shall relate it in the very words of the information of Matthew Gilston, servant to the abovesaid John Chapman, taken on the 14th day of February 1711–12 [1712] before Sir Henry Chauncy.
>
> Matthew Gilston of the parish of Walkern, says upon oath that on New Year's Day last past, he carrying straw upon a fork from Mr Gardiner's barn, met Jane Wenham who asked him for some straw, which he refused to give her; then she said she would take some, and accordingly took some away from this informant.
>
> And farther this informant saith that on the 29th of January last, when this informant was threshing in the barn of his master John Chapman, an old woman in a riding-hood or cloak, he knows not which, came to the barn door and asked him for a pennyworth of straw, he told her he would give her none, and she went away muttering.
>
> And this informant saith that, after the woman was gone, he was not able to work but ran out of the barn as far as a place called Munders Hill (which is above three miles from Walkern) and asked at a house there for a pennyworth of straw and, they refusing to give him any, he went farther to some dung heaps and took some straw from thence, and pulled off his shirt and brought it home in his shirt. He knows not what moved him to this but he says he was forced to do it, he knows not how. Thus far this informant.
>
> It was also further observed by some persons, who met this Matthew Gilston running on his fool's errand that he went at a very great pace and when he came to a river he did not go over a bridge on his way but directly through the water.
>
> [p. 14] Thomas Adams Junior of Walkern maketh oath that about three weeks or a month before Christmas last he met Jane Wenham in his turnip field with a few of his turnips which she was carrying away, and upon his threatening

her, she threw them down. He, this informant, told her that she might keep them for she should pay dear for them. Then she was very submissive and begged pardon, saying that she had no victuals all that day and had no money to buy any. Afterwards they parted and he saw her not after. But on Christmas Day morning one of his best sheep died without any signs of illness found upon the body after it was opened. And nine or ten days after died another sheep in an unaccountable manner and shortly after two more sheep died also, none of them having any marks of a disease upon 'em but being sound in all their parts, as his shepherd informs him. He also saith that his shepherd tells him that one other sheep was taken strangely, skipping and standing upon its head, but in half an hour was well and continues so. And another sheep was likewise ill two or three days but is now well again. And Jane Wenham, having the common fame of a witch, he does believe that, if they were bewitched, she did bewitch them.

Some accusations related to events several years earlier. Susan Aylott testified that:

[pp. 13–14] About twelve years ago . . . Jane Wenham came to this informant's house and looked upon a child that was in her lap and stroked it and said, 'Susan, you have a curious child. You and I had some words but I hope we are friends'. And asked this informant to lend her a glass to carry some vinegar from the shop. This informant lent Jane Wenham a glass, who went away. And this informant was afraid for her child remembering she [Wenham] was thought to have bewitched Richard Harvey's wife [who died].

This informant farther saith that on Sunday following she was at her brother Jeremy Harvey's house with her child and that her child was taken in a grievous condition, stark distracted, and so died the Thursday following. And this informant saith she thinks that Jane Wenham bewitched her child; and saith also that Jane Wenham has had the reputation of a witch for several years before.

The reason why Jane Wenham should bewitch Harvey's wife (as we have since been informed by Thomas Harvey, her son) was as follows: This Jane Wenham's husband had desired Richard Harvey to speak to the town crier at Hertford to cry down his wife lest any person should trust her to his damage and Richard Harvey had accordingly done it.

Anne Thorne, the most seriously afflicted of Jane Wenham's alleged victims, was troubled with a succession of 'fits . . . the noise of scratchings and the appearances of cats', pins and enchanted feathers. Confronted with an accumulation of indirect evidence, Chauncy sought conclusive proof:

[p.11] Sir Henry ordered four women to search Jane Wenham's body, directing them to enquire diligently whether she had any teats or other extraordinary and unusual marks about her by which the Devil in any shape might suck her body. After about an hour's search and consultation they returned and affirmed that they found no such teats or marks on her body.

# Exhibit 20

# Almanacs

## Sources

*Mercurius Anglicanus,* 1695
*John Taylor's Almanac* for 1696
*The London Almanack,* 1696
*An Almanack for the Year of Christ 1699*
*Poor Robin's Almanack*

The essential components of an almanac were the tables of astronomical and astrological events for the year in question. Printed tables were widely available by the 1470s, to these were added predictions, other advice and factual information – a list of fairs became a standard item in English almanacs of the 1560s. A century later the annual sale of almanacs totalled something like 400,000 copies. At that time almanacs had perhaps the widest currency of any printed books, the Bible excepted (Bernard Capp, *Astrology and the Popular Press. English Almanacs 1500–1800,* London, 1979, p. 23). They can be used as political barometers – welcoming the Revolution which put his Protestant son-in-law William of Orange on the throne in place of the Catholic James II, John Whalley commented that 'one drop of Orange juice works greater effects than a whole barrel of holy water' (*Mercurius Britannicus,* 1691; Capp, p. 97). Almanacs were small, often, the size of their descendants, today's pocket diaries – indeed, from the 1560s blank sheets were provided so that the owner could record 'things that passeth from time to time (worthy of memory to be registered)' (Capp, p. 30).

The small collection once owned by John Moore (born 1646), Bishop of Ely, and now in the University Library in Cambridge, gives an indication of the range of supplementary material which an almanac might contain. University-educated men like Moore were fluent in the astrological code but readers included unlearned men and women. John Taylor's *Almanack* for 1696, addressed to the inhabitants of Norwich and Norfolk, offered a plain man's Introduction to 'the names and marks that we know the planets by . . . the names and characters [symbols] of the twelve signs' and, 'that my directions may be plain and methodical . . . a complete and plenary example of the month of January'. The chapman, a pedlar, a travelling salesman dealing in such portable goods as haberdashery and popular reading material, had his own almanac. The edition of 1695 claimed to include:

> all the post roads with their several branches and distances. The marts, fairs
> and markets in England and Wales are alphabetically disposed in every month
> so that the place where and the days of which any of them are kept is imme-

diately found out. To which is added a Table of Accounts, already cast up for the buying and selling of any commodity, by number, weight or measure, from one farthing [there were 960 farthings in £1] to £10 and of any quantity from one to ten thousand. With a sundial and other tables and things useful for all travellers, traders or chapmen whatsoever.

*An Almanack for the Year of Christ 1699*, published at Oxford, was a fore-runner of the university diaries with which today's students may be familiar. It listed the Colleges and Halls at Oxford and at Cambridge, together with the names of the Heads of Houses and the Professors – at Cambridge 'the Mathematical Professor' was Dr Isaac Newton.

William Salmon used his *London Almanack* to promote his pharmaceutical products and to campaign against shopkeepers like John Hollier who attempted to counterfeit his

Family Pills and Family Powder. Both . . . fitted to the cure of the same diseases, but the pills work more gently; the powder more strongly, yet both very safely and may be given to old or young, whether man, woman or child, being given in a fit dose. The design of having both pills and powder is that they who cannot swallow the pills may take the powder and they who cannot take the powder may make use of the pills, they being universal purgers . . . [1696].

For some curious reason, publishing and the production of quack medicine went hand in hand. John Newbery (born 1713), the most famous publisher of children's books in eighteenth-century England, who brought out his first volume for children, *A Little Pretty Pocket Book*, in 1744, had an interest in Dr James's Powder and other preparations for the home doctor. Goody Two Shoes, the heroine of one of his later books, was orphaned when her father 'was seized with a violent fit of fever in a place where Dr James's Fever Powder was not to be had'.

Salmon also provided 'Physical Recipes' for each month. In September 1696 he offered two prescriptions 'to stop vomiting':

Take a spoonful of juice of lemons, to which put half a dram of salt of tartar and mix them with 4 ounces of mint water for a dose.
*or*
Another for the same,
Take white port wine, 6oz; strong tincture of clove, half a spoonful; mix them for a dose. It will stop vomiting presently [instantly].

Many predictions were vague enough to guarantee their fulfilment. George Parker, compiler of *Mercurius Anglicanus*, anticipated that in November 1695,

honour is now or near this time conferred upon a very deserving person, either clergyman or lawyer or some patriots graciously rewarded with preferment. Mercury is fallen retrograde and Mars hath entered the Virgin, being near the Lion's tail and there meets with a square of Mercury upon which follows clandestine whisperings, very pernicious to states and kingdoms, as also to private families.

*Poor Robin's Almanack* guyed the genre:

> And thus astrologers do write and say:
> The moon doth oe'r man's body bear such sway
> But not withstanding all their chitter chatter,
> Believe't or not believe't, tis no great matter.

In his 'Brief Chronology' of unmemorable things in 1696 'Robin' noted that eight years had passed 'since the apprentice, finding his mistress had locked the cupboard door, nailed up the door of the house of office [privy], saying that, if they could not have the use of one, they should not have any use for the other'. His 'Observations' for May that year included the statement that 'some wits will be so atheistical as to believe that there is no other Heaven but a tavern, not Hell but an empty pocket' while, for December, the stars foretold 'frequent conjunctions of ribs of beef, legs of mutton and loins of veal celebrated near the watery triplicity of plum porridge'.

To the reader of the present day, among the most interesting of John Moore's almanacs are those which he used for memoranda of his own. His jottings include the births of his children and other memorable events; addresses and appointments; notes of the prices of books purchased and receipt from his bookseller when he settled his account; prescriptions for medicines, some with priced ingredients; suggestions for ecclesiastical appointments (1681: 'John Davis M.A. recommended by the Bishop of Peterborough for a living in North Wales').

# EXHIBIT 21

# Jest books

## SOURCES

**William Hicks, *Oxford Jests Refined and Enlarged. Being a Collection of Witty Jests, Merry Tales and Pleasant Jokes collected and composed by Capt. W. Hicks, Native of Oxford.* 14th edition (no date)**
**Abel Boyer, *The Wise and Ingenious Companion* (London, 1741)**

## William Hicks, *Oxford Jests*

Hicks was a poor boy who began his working life in an Oxford inn. Anthony Wood noted the publication of the second edition of *Oxford Jests* in November 1669: 'From this book', he observed, example was given to others to publish *Cambridge Jests, Westminster Drolley, Windsor Drollery . . . (Life and Times of Anthony Wood, Antiquary of Oxford, 1632–1695, described by himself,* Andrew Clark (ed.), Oxford, 1892, Volume II, p. 176, note 6).

[p. 13] 59. One when the hangman came to put the halter about his neck, desired him not to bring the rope too near his throat. 'For I am', says he, 'so ticklish about that place that I shall hurt myself so with unreasonable laughter that it will go near to throttle me'.

[p. 16] 70. A lord in this kingdom, a great lover of rich Venice glasses, having two presented to him worth £50, by accident his butler broke one of them and he was so furious for it that he called him rogue and rascal and asked him how he did it; and repeated that so often that the fellow told him, 'My Lord, I'll show you how I did it, if you'll have a little patience'. So he took the other glass in his hands and said, 'Thus and thus I broke the other'. And so let the second glass fall, and broke that. The conceit of which made the lord pardon him.

[pp. 20–1] 90. A miller had wooed an abundance of girls and did lie with them; upon which he refused to marry them. But one girl he did solicit very much, but all would not do. Then he married her and told her on the marriage night if she would have let him done as the rest did, he would never have had her, 'By my Troth, I thought so,' she said, 'for I was so served by half a dozen before'.

[p. 35] 146. A country fellow coming to London and looking upon a sign where he did read 'Here are horses to let (1663)', 'Good Lord', says he, 'How do they do for stableroom for so many horses?'

[p. 38] 158. Another came to a lady to be hired and [the lady] told her she was no maid. 'Yes', she says, 'but I am'. 'How can that be when, to my knowledge, you had a child?' 'Well', says she, 'it was but a very little one'.

[p. 50] 202. An Oxford scholar, having been ten days at Cambridge together, it seems they kept him drinking so all night that he never could rise before dinner. And being asked how he liked Cambridge, said, 'I like the place well enough but there are no forenoons in't'.

[p. 62] 242. A Hall in Cambridge is called Catherine Hall and an old lady meeting with a Cambridge man asked him how her nephew behaved himself. 'Truly, Madam', says he, 'he is a great student and holds close to Catherine Hall'. 'I vow', says she, 'I feared as much, for the boy was ever given to wenches from his infancy'.

[p. 78] 295. One hearing a man and his wife chiding furiously together, advised them to agree as man and wife. 'Why so we do', says he, 'for we are like a pair of cards – shuffle one with another all day long, and at night lie close together like good friends'.

[p. 81] 304. A drunken fellow named John Tompson, driving his cart towards Wells in Somersetshire and being fast asleep in his cart, his two horses were stolen away. He awaking said, 'Either I am John Tompson or I am not John

Tompson. If I am John Tompson, then I have lost my two horses; if I be not John Tompson, then I have found a cart'.

[p. 89] 333. A rich bumpkin had a son something simple, yet he would have him made priest. So he, having spoke to the bishop before and desired him to be favourable to him, [the son] being come, the bishop said: 'Noah had three sons, Shem, Ham and Japhet. Now who was Japhet's father?' 'Truly, my lord', says he, 'I never learned that yet'. But coming back again, his father hearing of it, said, 'Has not Cole my dog three whelps, Rig, Trig amd Tribal?' 'Oh father', says he, 'now I have it'. So the next day he went to the bishop again and the bishop asked the former question, 'Who was Japhet's father?' 'Why', says he, 'Cole, my father's dog'.

[pp. 112] 419. In paying of a great subsidy [tax], the rich would not, the poor could not, so the middle sort paid for all.

[pp. 137–8] 500. One who loved himself better than his wife used to make her go to bed first in the wintertime to warm the same until he came. Then he would make her remove and lie in her place and, for this cause, he used commonly to call her his warming pan. She, vexed hereat, resolved to fit him and, accordingly, one night, when he was ready to come, she (Sir reverence) shit in his place. He, going to bed and smelling what was done, 'Wife', said he, 'I think the bed is beshit'. 'No, husband', said she, 'It is only a coal dropped out of your warming pan'.

## Abel Boyer, *The Wise and Ingenious Companion*

Abel Boyer (born 1667) was a French Protestant who sought refuge in England in 1689. Not long afterwards, he was appointed French tutor to the Duke of Gloucester, the son of Princess – later Queen – Anne. Boyer's *The Wise and Ingenious Companion*, printed in parallel in English and French, was, as its title page explained,

> a collection of the wise sayings, noble sentiments, witty repartees, jests and pleasant adventures of illustrious persons both Ancient and Modern; a work not only useful to young scholars who desire to learn French but entertaining and instructive to all English and French readers.

The extracts reproduced here are taken from a copy of the fifth edition, published in London in 1741, which, at some time, passed through the hands of one (or perhaps more than one) W. Calvert. This name is inscribed three times, once, in pencil, in very wobbly block letters, once printed in ink and once fluently written, again in ink.

Boyer provides sound advice to the novice teller of 'jests and stories'.

> First of all, never to usher in jests or stories with formal commendations. Likewise, when we are about to tell them, we must not begin to laugh ourselves, if we intend to make the company laugh: for those who promise us

mirth beforehand are seldom so good as their words, and how silly and ridicu-
lous that man looks who laughs by himself at a cold and threadbare jest whilst
the rest can scarcely force a smile to keep him in countenance. Lastly, we must
avoid telling a jest or story several times over to the same persons, an impertinence [absurdity] which makes the conversation of old people very ungrate-
ful [disagreeable].

His Ancient examples include:

[p. 9] 16. The Emperor Augustus [born 63 BC – the first Roman Emperor],
endeavouring to find the reason of the great likeness which a young Grecian
bore to him, asked whether his Mother was ever at Rome. 'No, sir', answered
the Grecian, 'but my father [w]as many a time'.

[p. 41] 74. Alcibiades [an Athenian general and politician who lived in the fifth
century BC] cut off the tail of his dog, which was extraordinary fine, and of
great value, and, as the people who saw the dog go about the streets without
a tail wondered at the oddness of the thing, he said, 'I have done it with the
design that people's tongues may be busy about that trifle, and not censure
my more important actions'.

[p. 41] 77. One of Agesilaus's [Agesilaus ruled Sparta in the fourth century BC]
friends, having found him playing with his children, and riding on a hobby
horse [a child's toy: a horse's head on a stick], seemed to be surprised at it, but
the king told him, 'Pray tell nobody what thou seest till thou hast children of
thine own'.

[p. 59] 115. One day Socrates (born 469 BC), having for a long time endured his
wife's brawling, went out of his house and sat down before the door to rid
himself of her impertinence. That woman, enraged to find all her scolding was
not able to disturb his tranquillity, flung a chamberpot, full, upon his head.
Those that happened to see it, laughed at poor Socrates; but that philosopher
told them, smiling, 'I thought, indeed, after so much thunder, we should have
some rain'.

[p. 79] 163. An Athenian lady, asking by way of derision, a Lacedemonian
[Spartan] matron what portion [dowry] she had brought her husband,
'Chastity', answered she. [Spartans were famously terse.]

Among the 'Moderns' were

[p. 115] 3. Sir Francis Bacon, another renowned Chancellor of England [Sir
Thomas More was the first cited], received a visit from Queen Elizabeth at a
country house, which he had built before his preferment, near St Albans. 'Why',
said the Queen to him, 'have you built so little a house?' 'Madam', replied the
Chancellor, ''Twas not I made my house too little but your Majesty that made
me too great for my house'. Besides the wit and humour of this answer, it car-
ries with it such an air of modesty and gratitude as ought to recommend it to
our esteem.

[p. 133] 37. The same king [Alphonsus of Aragon, perhaps Alfonso the Magnanimous, born in 1396, is the most likely candidate] used to say, 'To live quiet in marriage, the husband ought to be deaf that he mayn't hear his wife's scolding and impertinence, and the wife blind that she may not see her husband's debauchery'.

[p. 169] 103. A gentleman came into an inn in Chelmsford upon a very cold day and could get no room near the fire; whereupon he call up the ostler [the employee who looked after customers' horses] to fetch a peck [a measure of corn] of oysters and give them to his horse presently [at once]. 'Will your horse eat oysters?' replied the ostler. 'I pray try him', says the gentleman. Immediately the people running to see this wonder, the fire side was cleared, and the gentleman had his choice of seats. The ostler brings the oysters back, and says, 'The horse would not meddle with them'. 'Why then', says the gentleman, 'I must be forced to eat them myself'.

[p. 171] 105. Two friends, who had not seen one another a great while, meeting by chance, one asked the other how he did. He said he was not very well, and was married since he saw him. 'That is good news, indeed', says he.
'Nay, not so much good news neither', replies the other, 'for I have married a shrew'.
'That is bad', said the other.
'Not so bad neither', says he, 'for I had £2,000 with her'.
'That's well again', says the other.
'Not so well, neither, for I laid it out in sheep and they died of the rot'.
'That was hard indeed', says his friend.
'Not so hard neither', says he, 'for I sold the skins for more money than the sheep cost'.
'That made you amends', says the other.
'Not so much amends neither', says he, 'for I laid out my money in a house and it was burned'.
'That was a great loss indeed!'
'Nay, not so great a loss neither, for my wife was burnt in it'.

# EXHIBIT 22

# Penny merriments

## SOURCES

*The Pleasant History of Thomas Hic-ka-thrift*. **Printed by J. M. for W. Thackeray and T. Passinger (no date)**
*The Famous History of Aurelius the Valiant London Apprentice Shewing his Noble Exploits at Home and Abroad, his Love and Great Success*

The penny merriments are 'chap' [cheap] books designed to entertain. They seem to have appealed to a wide range of readers from the just literate to the highly educated and sophisticated. These extracts were transcribed from the collection of penny merriments put together by Samuel Pepys and now housed in the Pepys Library at his old college, Magdalene, in Cambridge.

### *The Pleasant History of Thomas Hic-ka-thrift*

[pp. 1–3] In the reign before William the Conqueror I have read in ancient histories that there dwelt a man in the marsh of the Isle of Ely in the County of Cambridge whose name was Thomas Hic-ka-thrift, a poor man and a day labourer, yet he was a very stout [robust] man, and able to perform two days work instead of one, he having one son and no more children in the world, he called him by his own name Thomas Hic-ka-thrift. This old man put his son to good learning but he would take none, for he was, as we call them . . . none of the wisest sort but something soft . . . God calling this old man his father out of the world, his mother being tender of him . . . maintained him with her hand labour as well as she could, he being slothful and not willing to work to get a penny for his living, but all his delight was to be in the chimney corner, and [he] would eat as much at one time as might very well serve four or five ordinary men – for he was, in length, when he was but ten years old, about eight foot . . . and his hand was like unto a shoulder of mutton.

[p. 7] *'Tom's fame being spread abroad in the country', a brewer wanted to hire him as a drayman:*
But Tom seemed coy and would not be his man until his mother and friends did persuade him and his master entreated him and likewise promised him a new suit of clothes and clothe him from top to toe, and besides he should eat and drink of the best so Tom at last yielded to be his man.

And thus Tom encountered his great adversary, the Giant. Tom's duties took him 'every day to Wisbech which was a very great journey for it was twenty mile by the road way. Tom going so long that wearisome journey and finding that the way that the Giant kept was nearer by half, Tom, having gotten more strength by half than before by being so well kept and drinking so much strong ale as he did' he made up his mind 'to make the nearest way to be a road . . . kill or be killed' (pp. 9–10). 'Intending to take his beer for a prize . . . the Giant he met Tom like a lion' but 'Tom cared not a fart for him'. Faced with the Giant's club, 'Tom bethought himself of a very good weapon for he makes no more ado, but takes his cart and turns it upside down and takes the axle tree [axle] and the wheel for his sword and buckler [shield]' (p. 11). 'He made the Giant reel . . ."What", said Tom, "Are you drunk with my strong beer already?" [p. 12]. Tom, having no more mercy on him than a dog of a bear . . . cut off his head'. In the Giant's cave he found a 'great store of silver and gold' which 'made his heart to leap'.

> [p. 12] Tom took possession of the cave by the consent of the country . . . [then] Tom pulled down the cave and built himself a brave house where the cave stood. All the ground that the giant kept by force and strength, some he gave to the poor for their common and the rest he made pastures of and divided the most part into good ground to maintain him and his old mother Jane Hicka-thrift and . . . then it was no longer Tom but Mr Hickathrift so that he was the chiefest man among them, for the people feared Tom's anger as much as they did the Giant before. So Tom he kept men and maids and lived most bravely, and he made him a park to keep deer in, and by his house which is a town he built a famous church and gave it the name of Saint James's church because he killed the giant on that day.

The chapter headings of *The Famous History Of Aurelius the Valiant London Apprentice* give a flavour of another story in Samuel Pepys' collection.

*Chapter I* An account of his birth, education and earlier valour etc.

*Chapter II* An account of his first adventures and enterprises, where he won the virgin's heart etc.

*Chapter III* How the fair Lucinda fell in love with him and how those she despised for his sake conspired against him.

*Chapter IV* How they attempted to destroy Aurelius but were overcome and left naked in the wood.

*Chapter V* How his father put him apprentice to a merchant and the leave he took of Lucinda.

*Chapter VI* How he gained the love of his master and became enamoured of Dorinda, his fair daughter.

*Chapter VII* How he got leave to go to Turkey and what ensued.

*Chapter VIII* How he arrived in Turkey and of his reception. How he overthrew the Turks and killed a Turkish prince.

*Chapter IX* How he destroyed two lions prepared to devour him and had the king's daughter in marriage.

Finis [The End].

# Exhibit 23

# Reckoning

## Sources

Robert Recorde, *The Grounde of Artes Teaching the Perfecte Worke and Practise of Arithmaticke*, 1582
Edward Hatton, *Arithmetic or the Ground of Arts*, 1699
Robert Chamberlain, *The Accomptant's Guide or Merchant's Book-keeper*, 1679

For all but the very poorest, the ability to count accurately was recognised as a fundamental preparation for the business of getting and spending.

Leonardo of Pisa took credit for introducing 'the art of reckoning in Indian numbers [1–9 – as opposed to the Roman i–ix] to the West'. Although place value [1, 10, 100 – as opposed to i, x, c] enabled the user to work with pen and paper rather than an abacus or counting board, advocates of the new notation encountered resistance from hardheaded men of business – it was so easy to turn 'a zero into a 6 or a 9' that Indian numbers were an open invitation to fraud. Progress was slow.

When Robert Recorde wrote *The Grounde of Artes* (1582), first published in 1541, he found it necessary to introduce the nine 'signifying figures' as follows:

1 2 3 4 5 6 7 8 9

and explain that 'this is their value'

i ii iii iiii v vi vii viii ix

Like many teaching manuals, *The Grounde of Artes* was written as a dialogue between a Master and his Scholar. The section on 'signfying figures' ends with a test:

*Master*: How write you then five?
*Scholar*: By this figure 5.
*Master*: And how six?
*Scholar*: Thus, 6.
*Master*: Write these numbers each by itself as I speak them vii. iiii. iii.
*Scholar*: 7. 4. 3.
*Master*: Now write ye these four other – ii. i. ix. viii.
*Scholar*: Thus, I trow [trust]: 2. 1. 6. 8.
*Master*: Nay, there you miss. Look on mine example again.
*Scholar*: Sir, truth it is I was to blame. I took 6 for 9 but I will be warer [warier] hereafter.

An edition of 1673 reproduced the text figure for figure and almost word for word-though 'I will be warer hereafter' became 'I will beware hereafter'. 'I trow' clearly meant nothing to the editor or his typesetter who rendered it 'It row' (1673, pp. 11–12). The 1673 edition also retained instruction in 'the art of counters' which 'doth not only serve for them that cannot write and read but also for them that can do both but have not at some time their pen or paper ready with them' (p. 179).

Edward Hatton, who edited *Arithmetic or the Ground of Arts*, which came out in 1699, acknowledged 'the esteem and credit the book acquired for near 150 years together' – a sound argument for keeping the title – 'yet at length the style and phrase growing obselete'–a sound argument for investing in his edition – he had brought it up to date. Hatton cut out the dictation exercise and incorporated 'a new treatise of decimal arithmetic'.

Twenty years earlier Robert Chamberlain had brought out *The Accompant's Guide or Merchants' Book-keeper*, which opened with 'an explanation of all the most useful and necessary rules of arithmetic that the meanest capacity thereby may attain to the knowledge thereof'. He fulfilled his prospectus by laying out the theory and practice of book-keeping in the form of a series of sample pages from a merchant's records. He assumed that some of his readers would lack experience of place values and provided them with this, in its original format, elegant aid:

[p. 2]
1 Units 1
12 Tens 10
123 Hundreds 100
1234 Thousands 1000
12345 X Thousand 10000
123456 C Thousand 100000
1234567 Million 1000000
12345678 X Millions 10000000
123456789 C Millions 1000000000

he that will be ready and willing at arithmetic must learn the said table by heart and be able to know at first sight the value of any number of figures according to the places they do stand in.

Having worked an example of The Back Rule of Three to resolve the problem (p. 15) 'If 15 shillings worth of wine will serve . . . 69 men when the tun of wine is worth £12, for how many men will the same 15 shillings worth of wine suffice when the tun is worth £18?' (answer: 46), he concluded that 'I have showed to the reader so much of the Art of Arithmetic as will make him capable of exercising the following method of keeping Merchants' Books of Accompts [p. 50] in a methodical way of keeping merchants' accompts the understanding how to keep the following [p. 9] books is chiefly necessary' – the last and least was 'A Book of Household Expenses'.

## The book of household expenses

[p. 56] The keeping of this book a mean capacity may comprehend, which is commonly left to the youngest apprentice, wherein is daily set down what is expended for housekeeping, setting down every particular thing, with the particular cost, and weekly, monthly or quarterly you transmit the same into your cash book.

# EXHIBIT 24

# Teaching yourself French

## SOURCE

**Abel Boyer, Gent., *The Compleat French Master for Ladies and Gentlemen, being a New method to Learn with ease and delight the French Tongue, as it is now spoken in the Court of France* ... Dedicated to His Royal Highness the Duke of Gloucester (London, 1694)**

Boyer offered guidance on pronunciation, grammar plus a vocabulary together with Twelve Discourses on subjects such as religion, history, mathematics, manners, travels, pleasure, love and friendship and Four Collections of jests and stories, letters, proverbs and songs.

[p. 5] *O* sounds in French as in these English words, ore, over, as *paroles* words, *monopole* monopoly.

But *o* before *m* and *n* sounds like *oo* in these words, soon, moon, as *homme* man, *garcon* boy.

**Dialogue XXXV, 'Between a Gentlewoman and her [Waiting] Woman' (p. 229)** begins:

Who waits?
Did your Ladyship call, Madam?
Bring me my hoods and tippet.
Let me see, hold the glass. Lord! I look wretchedly today.
Why don't you help me?
How awkward you are!
How can I help it?

[p. 230] Is not my head wry [crooked]?
No Madam, it sits very well.

Give me a clean handkerchief.
Go now to the footman and bid him get a chair with a high roof or a very low seat [to accommodate her hairdo].
I run.
Stay mistress Sue, you are so ready to go to the footman.

---

## EXHIBIT 25

# The medical uses of English herbs

### SOURCE

**Nicholas Culpeper, Gent., Student in Physic and Astrology,** *The English Physician Enlarged with three hundred, sixty and nine medicines made of English herbs . . . Being an Astrologo-Physical Discourse of the Vulgar Herbs of this Nation, containing a complete method of Physic whereby a man may preserve his body in health, or cure himself, being sick, for three-pence charge, with such things only as grow in England, they being most fit for English bodies* **[1653] (1656)**

Culpeper (born 1616), the son of Surrey clergyman, was apprenticed to an apothecary in London. He opposed the physicians' claims to a monopoly of practice and subverted it by publishing an English version of their *Pharmacoepia* in 1649 under the title *A Physical Directory or Translation of the London Dispensatory.*

The study of astrology was not seen as incompatible with the practice of Christianity. As Thomas Tryon observed:

'I cannot . . . hold it more unlawful or vain to study astrology, any more than the art of medicine. By astrology . . . I mean not the fraudulent way of telling fortunes etc. by setting figures of the heavens, but the method of God's gov-ernment in nature and the administration of the world – though I deny not but that much may be discovered by a scheme of any person's nativity, when the true time of birth is obtained' [*Some Memoirs of the Life of Mr Thomas Tryon, Late of London, Merchant, written by himself*, 1705, pp. 22–3].

# The medlar

## Description

The tree groweth near the bigness of the quince tree, spreading branches reasonable large, with longer and narrower leaves than either the apple or the quince, and not dented about the edges. At the end of the sprigs stand the flowers made of five white, great-pointed leaves, nicked in the middle with some white threads also; after which cometh the fruit of a brownish-green colour, being ripe, bearing a crown, as it were, on the top, which were the five green leaves; and, being rubbed off or fallen away, the head of the fruit is seen to be somewhat hollow. The fruit is very harsh before it is mellowed, and hath usually five hard kernels within it.

There is another kind hereof differing nothing from the former, but that it hath some thorns on it in several places, which the other hath not; and usually the fruit is small and not so pleasant.

## Time

They grow in this land, and flower in May for the most part, and bear ripe fruit in September and October.

## The medlar was useful in the treatment of

fresh wounds; stone in the kidneys. The fruit is old Saturn's, and sure a better medicine he hardly hath to strengthen the retentive faculty, therefore it stays [pregnant] women's longings – the good old man cannot endure women's minds should run agadding. Also a plaster made of the fruit dried before they be rotten, and other convenient things, and applied to the reins of the back stops miscarriages in women with child. They are very powerful to stay any fluxes of blood or humours in man or woman; the leaves have also the like quality. The fruit eaten by woman with child stayeth their longings after unusual meats and is very effectual for them that are apt to miscarry and be delivered before their time to help that malady and make them joyful mothers. The decoction of them is good to gargle and wash the mouth, throat and teeth; when there is any defluxion of blood, to stay it, or of humours, which causeth pains and swellings. It is a good bath for women to sit over that have their [menstrual] courses flow too abundantly, or for the piles when they bleed too much. If a poultice or plaster be made with dried medlars, beaten and mixed with the juice of red roses, whereunto a few cloves and nutmeg may be added and a little red coral also, and applied to the stomach that is given to casting [throwing up] or loathing of meat, it effectually helpeth. The dried leaves in powder, strewed upon fresh bleeding wounds, restraineth the blood and healeth up the wound quickly. The medlar stones, made into powder and drunk in wine wherein some parsley roots have lien infused all night, or a little boiled, do break the stone on the kidneys, helping to expel it. For the cure of all diseases read my Riverius and Riolanus in English.

## Exhibit 26

# Observations of the natural world in the 1660s

### Source

Robert Hooke, *Micrographia or Some Physiological Descriptions of Minute Bodies Made by Magnifying Glasses with Observations and Inquiries thereupon* (London, Printed by John Martyn and James Allestry, Printers to the Royal Society, and are to be sold at their Shop at the Bell in St Paul's Churchyard, 1665)

The Royal Society, the successor of a club established in 1660 (subscription a shilling a week), followed the precepts of Francis Bacon (1561–1620) who rejected speculation and advocated instead experiment and observation as the proper methods of investigating the natural world. The Society became 'Royal' when Charles II granted it a charter in 1662.

Robert Hooke (born 1635) was the son of a curate on the Isle of Wight. He too was intended for the Church but, as a sickly boy, he was let off his books and spent his time making models and drawing. His 'genius' seeming to lie in the manual arts, he was sent up to London when he was 13 to be apprenticed to the painter Peter Lely but, perhaps because of an allergy to paints, he opted instead to go to Westminster School. Hooke worked his way through Oxford, doing domestic chores in his college and later as a laboratory assistant to the medic Thomas Willis and the chemist Robert Boyle, a younger son of the first Earl of Cork, before becoming Curator of Experiments at the Royal Society. As a salaried employee, he was the Society's dogsbody, at the beck and call of the gentlemen members. His experiments were made on their instructions and presented at their regular meetings on a Wednesday or Thursday afternoon. The research for *Micrographia* was undertaken between March 1663 and March 1664. Hooke's subjects included, in addition to those quoted here, 'the hairs of [his own] head' and 'the mustacheos of a cat'. As his account of the louse makes clear, many of the creatures he observed and described with such respect and wit were among the irritations of everyday life. He was not aware of the role of fleas in transmitting plague and of lice as vectors of typhus.

> [p. xix] It is the great prerogative of Mankind above other creatures that we are not only able to behold the works of Nature, or barely to sustain our lives by them, but we have also the power of considering, comparing, altering, assisting and improving them to various uses.

[pp. xxi–xxii] The first thing to be undertaken in this weighty work is a watch-fulness over the failings and an enlargement of the dominion of the senses. To which end it is requisite, first, that there should be a scrupulous choice and a strict examination of the reality, constancy, and certainty of the particulars that we admit. . . .

The next care to be taken, in respect of the senses, is a supplying of their infirmities with instruments, and, as it were, the adding of artificial organs to the natural. This, in one of them, has been of late years accomplished with prodigious benefit to all sorts of useful knowledge by the invention of optical glasses. By the means of telescopes, there is nothing so far distant but may be represented to our view; and by the help of microscopes there is nothing so small as to escape our enquiry. Hence there is a new visible world discovered to the understanding.

[p. xxiii] The truth is, the science of Nature has already too long made only a work of brain and fancy. It is now high time that it should return to the plain-ness and soundness of observations on material and obvious things.

[pp. xxiv–xxv] Nothing is to be omitted and yet everything to pass a mature deliberation. No intelligence from men of all professions and quarters of the world to be slighted, and yet all to be so severely examined that there remain no room for doubt or instability; much rigour in admitting, much strictness in comparing, much slowness in debating and shyness in determining is to be practised. . . . So many are the links upon which the true philosophy depends, of which, if any one be loose or weak, the whole chain is in danger of being dissolved. It is to begin with the hands and eyes, and to proceed on through the memory, to be continued by the reason; nor is it to stop there but to come about to the hands and eyes again and so, by a continual passage round from one faculty to another, it is to be maintained in life and strength, as much as the body of man is by the circulation of the blood.

[pp. xxv–xxvi] And, as at first mankind fell by tasting of the forbidden tree of knowledge, so we, their posterity, may be in part restored by the same way, not only by beholding and contemplating but by tasting too those fruits of natural knowledge that were never yet forbidden. . . .

'Tis not unlikely but that there may be yet invented several other helps for the eye, as much exceeding those already found as those do the bare eye . . . . And as glasses have highly promoted our seeing, so 'tis not improbable but that there may be found many mechanical inventions to improve our other senses – of hearing smelling, tasting, touching.

[p. xxxiii] And I do not only propose this kind of experimental philosophy as a matter of high rapture and delight of the mind but even as a material and sensible pleasure.

## Figured snow

[p. 91] Exposing a piece of black cloth or a black hat to the falling snow I have often, with great pleasure, observed such an infinite variety of curiously figured snow . . . so that in a very little time I have observed above a hundred several sizes and shapes of these starry flakes.

## Of an ant or pismire

[p. 203] This was a creature more troublesome to be drawn than any of the rest, for I could not, for a good while, think of a way to make it suffer its body to lie quiet in a natural posture. But whilst it was alive, if its feet were fettered in wax or glue, it would so twist and wind its body that I could not any ways get a good view of it. And, if I killed it, its body was so little that I did often spoil the shape of it before I could thoroughly view it. For this is the nature of these minute bodies, that as soon almost as ever their life is destroyed, their parts immediately shrivel and lose their beauty. . . . The dead body of an ant, or other such little creature, does almost instantly shrivel and dry and your object shall be quite another thing before you can half delineate it, which proceeds . . . from the small proportion of body and juices to the usual drying of bodies in the air, especially if warm. For which inconvenience, where I could not otherwise remove it, I thought of this expedient: I took the creature I had designed to delineate and put it into a drop of very well rectified Spirit of Wine, this I found would presently dispatch, as it were, the animal and, being taken out of it and laid on a paper, the Spirit of Wine would immediately fly away and leave the animal dry, in its natural posture or at least in a constitution that it might easily with a pin be placed in what posture you desired to draw it, and the limbs would so remain without either moving or shrivelling. And thus I dealt with this ant which I have here delineated.

## Of a flea

[pp. 210–11] The strength and beauty of this small creature, had it no other relation to man, would deserve description . . . . But, as for the beauty of it, the microscope manifests it to be all over adorned with a curiously polished suit of sable [black] armour, neatly jointed and beset with multitudes of sharp pins, shaped almost like porcupine's quills or bright conical steel bodkins [needles]. . . . It has two . . . biters . . . shaped very like the blades of a pair of round-topped scissors and were opened and shut just after the same manner. With these instruments does this busy little creature bite and pierce the skin and suck the blood out of an animal, leaving the skin inflamed with a small round red spot.

## Of a louse

[p. 211] This creature is so officious that 'twill be known to everyone at one time or other, so busy and so impudent that it will be intruding itself in everyone's company, and so proud and aspiring withall that it fears not to trample on the best and affects nothing so much as a crown; feeds and lives very high and that makes it so saucy as to pull anyone by the ears that comes in its way and will never be quiet until it has drawn blood. It is troubled at nothing so much as at a man that scratches his head, as knowing that man is plotting and contriving some mischief against it and that makes it oftentime skulk into some meaner and lower place and run behind a man's back . . . . Which ill conditions of it having made it better known than trusted, would exempt me from making any further description of it, did not my faithful Mercury, my microscope bring me further information.

---

# EXHIBIT 27

# Memorial inscriptions

## SOURCES

Henry Chauncy, *The Historical Antiquities of Hertfordshire* (London, 1700)
*Monumental Inscriptions and Coats of Arms from Cambridgeshire chiefly as recorded by John Layer about 1632 and William Cole between 1742 and 1782*, W. M. Palmer (ed.) (Cambridge, 1932)

Memorials were a means of self-expression confined to the well off. The status of the men, women and children commemorated here is not untypical.

Chauncy was a lawyer. After a career at the bar, he became a judge. In 1681 he inherited the family estate at Ardeley Bury in Hertfordshire. In 1712 he was a leading player in the events leading up to the trial of Jane Wenham for witchcraft (see Exhibit 17).

These are among his collection of 'Epitaphs and Memorable Inscriptions'. The pages of the folio volume are printed in parallel columns – this accounts for the 'a's and 'b's in the page references.

## Bishop's Stortford

[pp. 167b–168a] An Epitaph on the Death of Thomas Edgecombe, the Son of Richard Edgecombe of Mount Edgecombe, Knight, and Dame Mary his Wife, who died the 22d of May An. 1614.

Edgecombe, an Infant, born of gentile Race;
By this chief Cause, to live, did but begin
By Baptism to be cleansed, and by Grace
From that foul Spot of Original Sin:

Whose happy Soul, with actual Sin, not stain'd
By short Life here, eternal Bliss hath gain'd,
Ye Parents mourn not, fix your Joys herein;
The Promise made to faithful Seed is debt,
As by that sweet Embrace Christ gave was seen;
Ye procreate to Number God's Elect;
Angels and Souls alike pure Essence be,
And new born Babes are pure in next Degree.

# Sawbridgeworth

[p. 178] In the upper end of the church near the chancel a Monument of black and white marble is erected over the seat of the Lady Wiseman; and, in an oval, the effigies of a Knight in Armour and his Lady, cut in stone, holding each other by the Hand, and he having his left hand on his sword, and she a book, under whom it is engraved [in parallel]:

Obiit 7 October 1637
Sacred
To the pretious Memory and Name of Sir Wil-
liam Hewyt, Kt. who by Eliz. his Wife, Daughter of
Richard Wiseman Esq;
Had issue
Mary, Thomas, Elizabeth, Mary, Richard, Anne,
Robert, William, Robert, Margaret, Anne.
He was
A tender Husband to his Wife, a
provident Father to his Children,
A just Master to his Servants.
He stood
A strict Observer of Times past; a fair
Example to Times present; a rare
Memorial to Times future.

He lived
A sincere Member of the Church;
A severe Master of himself,
A faithful Servant to his God.
He died
In the firmness of his Faith,
In the fulness of good Works,
 In the favour of his Jesus.
He rests
Disburthened from the brunt of Sorrow,
Delivered from the bonds of Sin,
Triumphing with the bands of Angels.

Obiit 17 Octoborn 1646
Sacred
To the Name and Memory of Dame Elizabeth
Hewyt, Wife to Sir William Hewyt Kt.
Daughter of Richard Wiseman Esq;
She shewed
A sacred strictness to things Good, a solemn
severity to things Ill, a seasonable inoffensivness to
things Indifferent.
She cared
Prudently to read, punctually to observe, piously
to practise the Gospel of Christ Jesus.

She stood
The espoused maid of Piety, the divorced
Wife of Vanity, a Widow married to her Widowhood.
She lived
The firm Friend of her Friends,
The kind Friend of her Enemies,
The strict Enemy of her Sin.
She died
In the full Faith of her Redemption,
In the fast Hope of her Resurrection,
In a fixt Charity with God and Man.
She rests
Safe from the Sufferings of the separate
Sequestred from the Sorrows of the Sinful,
Settled in the state of the secured.

## Layston

[pp. 130b–131] 'In the South Wall . . .

Near hereunto lyeth interr'd the Body of Mr William Slatholme, Dr of Physick, a Person studious and of exemplary temperance and Sobriety, Charitable to his poor Neighbours, and Courteous to Strangers, Conscientious and wary in his Profession, of whose expert Skill wherein, his Book de Febribus (multum in parvo) [On Fevers (of small size but great merit)] is no small Witness.

At his Feet lye his three Children, viz.

1 John Sennock, an ingenious lovely pious Youth, a hopeful Blossom crop off in the 17th Year of his Age, Anno Dom. 1662.
2 Susanna, an Infant, who died within the Month [the four weeks of her mother's confinement before she resumed normal life].
3 Sarah, a Virgin, beautiful of Countenance, but of a more beautiful Soul, who at 12 Years of Age was so compassionately sensible of her Father's consumptive Sickness that for Grief she died before him; over whose Herse,

himself half dead, crept [a reader of the copy of Chauncy's *Historical Antiquities* now in the Library of the University of Cambridge sensibly changed this to 'wept'] out this Divine Farewel: Adieu, Sweet Lamb! I shall follow Thee with A competent Pace thro' the Gates of Death to Eternity; and soon after he fulfilled his Word, July 24 1665.

In pious Memory of all whom Mrs Anne Slatholme as a loving Wife and tender Mother hath erected this due Memorial.
Thus daily Sighing,
Dear Husband, and sweet Children rest in Peace,
Till I, to live with you again, Decease;
Where all of us together shall enjoy
Such Glory as no Malice can annoy.

Mihi mors Medicina malorum [Death is the prescription for my ills].

William Slatholme, a Cambridge graduate licensed to practise medicine in Hertfordshire, dedicated his Latin text *On Fevers*, published in London in 1657, to Francis Prujean (variant spellings suggested that it was said Pridgeon), President of the Royal College of Physicians from 1650 to 1654 and thereafter Treasurer until 1663. (Slatholme wrote in Latin to make his work accessible to the international scientific community.) Within his life time Slatholme's work was overshadowed by another book with the same name, published in 1659 by the eminent Oxford-trained physician Thomas Willis.

Cambridge University Library has a copy of Slatholme's *On Fevers* inscribed 'Ex dono Senocki Slatholme Aulae Pemborn Cantab [Pembroke Hall, Cambridge]', his father's old college. It came into the university's possession in 1715 along with another 29,000-odd volumes of print, including the almanacs used earlier in the dossier, as the gift of George I, who purchased the library of John Moore, the recently deceased Bishop of Ely to reward the university for welcoming him more enthusiastically than Oxford had, as the evenhanded verse went:

King George, observing with judicious eyes
The state of both the universities
To Oxford sent a troop of horse – and why?
That learned body wanted loyalty.
To Cambridge Books he sent, as well discerning
How much that loyal body wanted leaning.

The late Bishop of Ely, John Moore, and young Slatholme were at Cambridge in the same calendar year and it would be nice to think that the volume went straight into the embryo of the great library as the gift of the author's son. Moore certainly collected medical texts as a young man but the inscription is not in his hand. Of course, it might be in Slatholme's.

On 17 July 1745 William Cole, an antiquary, who collected inscriptions and coats of arms, recorded the monument at Conington in Cambridgeshire to Robert Cotton, carved and signed, 'G. Gibbons fecit', by Grinling Gibbons,

Master Sculptor and Carver of Wood to the Crown. No other example of a signed Gibbons monument is known.

The great collection of manuscripts amassed by Robert's great-grandfather, Sir Robert Bruce Cotton (born 1571), was given to the nation at the beginning of the eighteenth century and became a founding element in the British Museum when it opened in 1753.

[pp. 30–1]

Near this Place

lies interred the Body of Robert Cotton Esqr.

the only Son of Sr Robert Cotton Knt of Hatley St George in the County of Cambridge

great Grandson of Sr Robert Cotton of Connington in the County of Huntingdon Bartt Founder of the Cotton Library.

He died April the 9 day Anno Dom 1697

aged 14 years 3 months and 7 days; makeing good by his Death, this Saying, that Immodicis brevis est Aetas ac rara Senectus:

For he was a youth of very great Hopes, the Vivacity of his Wit was wonderfull;

His Questions and Answers were discerning, nice and pleasant:

With all this he was religious, compassionate and charitable;

Affable with his Companions, meek in his Disposition;

And yet there were visible in him all the Marks of a spritely Courage:

Hee had made a considerable Progress in all the Knowledge that suited with his years. He was so inquistive after Truth that, had Time ripened his Perfections,

He would have shown himself a worthy Offspring

of the Cotton Family, so famed for Learning.

While he remain'd in this World,

He was the Joy of his Parents, and the Delight of all who knew him:

Innocent and beautifull as those Angells with whom he is

now singing the Praises of his Creator,

God blessed for ever.

# Exhibit 28

# The Sondes murder, 1655

## Sources

**Robert Boreman,** *A Mirror of Mercy and Judgement or an exact true Narrative of the Life and Death of Freeman Sondes Esq., Son to Sir George Sondes of Lees Court in Shelwich in Kent, who, being about the age of 19, for Murdering his elder Brother on Tuesday, the 7th of August, was Arraigned [charged] and condemned at Maidstone, executed there on Tuesday the 21st of the same Month 1655 (London, 1655)*
*Sir George Sondes his plain Narrative to the World of all the Passages upon the Death of his two Sons* **(London, 1655)**
**Both reprinted in** *The Harleian Miscellany: A Collection of Scarce, Curious and Entertaining Pamphlets and Tracts,* **Volume X (London, 1813), pp. 23–42, 42–67**

I have included the truly shocking history of Sir George Sondes and his two sons because it seems to me to illuminate a number of the themes introduced in earlier exhibits – and because of its human interest: scandal in high places; family feuds over money and marriage; frustrated love affairs; gambling; jealousy; murder; the wasted life and salutary death of a young man who killed his elder brother, heir to the family fortune, while, it was said, the balance of his mind was disturbed by love and envy and who paid for his passion on the scaffold.

In 1620 George Sondes (born 1599), the son of a Kentish landowner, married Jane, the daughter and heiress of Ralph Freeman, a London clothworker, and, in 1633, Lord Mayor. (The office of Lord Mayor, chief magistrate of the City of London, was one of great 'magnificence, gravity and state'.) Sondes was 'a man of great power and estate' in his home county. He displayed his wealth, pride and cultivation when he 'pulled down the old mansion of Lees Court' and replaced it with a house 'the front of which' was, according to the collective memory of the neighbourhood, 'built after a design by Inigo Jones', whose leading patron was King Charles I. Sondes' marriage was not blest. 'Many' of the children died in infancy; Jane died in childbed in 1637. In Stuart England this was the stuff of ordinary tragedy, much worse was to come. Loyalty to the King cost Sondes dear during the difficult years of the 1640s and 1650s. But the ultimate catastrophe was the murder of his heir George by his younger son Freeman. The narrative and commentary which follow have been taken from the two pamphlets written by the Reverend Mr Robert Boreman, a former Fellow of Trinity College,

Cambridge (with contributions from the Reverend Mr Theophilus Higgons, Rector of Hunton, near Maidstone), the town where Freeman was tried and hanged and by Sir George himself, who, having had 'one son murdered, another executed', went in to print to defend his own reputation and that of the victim.

Robert Boreman describes the murder:

[p. 27] When he [Freeman Sondes] had given his sleeping brother the first deadly blow, on the right side of his head, with the back of a cleaver taken out of the kitchen the Sunday night before he did the fact, he, after the first blow, said he would have given all the world to recall it, and made a stop to see how deep he had wounded him; and finding it to be a mortal wound, (having broken the skull) his brother stretching himself on his bed, and struggling for life, and he gathering from thence that he was in great torment, discovered then, even in that storm of temptation, so much of a relenting spirit, that to put him out of his pain, (at which he confessed to me he was sadly troubled) he did reiterate his blows with a dagger, that he had in his pocket.

[p. 28] When he had thus embrued his hands with his brother's blood he threw the cleaver out of the window into the garden and came, with great confusion and disturbance in his face, into his father's bedchamber, adjoining to his brother's, with the dagger in his pocket, (surely he had no farther intentions of murder, God restraining the malicious power of Satan) and undrawing the curtains, [round the bed] shook his father by the shoulder, who being thus awakened out of his sleep, received from his mouth this heart-breaking message, 'Father, I have killed my brother!' He, being astonished at it, made this reply with much horror. 'What sayest thou? Hast thou, wretch, killed thy brother? Then thou hadst best kill me too'. The son replied, 'No, sir, I have done enough. . . .' The father, Sir George, upon this said, 'Why, then you must look to be hanged', and presently [at once] springing out of his bed, took his son along with him to behold his bleeding brother and called in the servants to seize upon the other.

Boreman attempted to explain what had triggered Freeman Sondes' attack on his sleeping brother:

[p. 25] Now, sir, who but the malicious (who look with a squint eye upon all good intents and actions) will not say that you had towards your son the same bowels [pity or 'heart'] as David had in him towards his Absalom [Absalom slew his brother in revenge for his rape of their sister Tamar and later led an uprising against David].

Who can imagine that he can be guilty of discouraging severity towards his child, to whom he had used too much cockering [pampering] indulgence in his life, and of whom he was so charitably careful and forgiving before his death? . . . An act of disobedience and contempt of command, from one we have admitted to a deep affection is ever entertained with greater dislike, repaid with frowns, neglect and slighting. Thus a command from you, his father, in reference to his elder brother, being not obeyed, forced you to a paternal severity, to threats etc., which were not a sufficient ground to provoke him to that bloody act, unless a melancholy passion (he being deeply in love with a fair gentlewoman) together with a diabolical suggestion had (God's grace for a time deserting him) possessed his heart and carried on his hand to attempt and act so horrid a sin.

Because the murder coincided with the annual session of the Kent assizes the drama rapidly reached its climax. Once or twice a year judges rode ceremoniously out from London to try cases in the shires. Trumpeters greeted them as they crossed the county boundary; church bells peeled as they entered the assize town (in Kent most often Maidstone) escorted by local landowners and armed guards. A sermon marked the opening of proceedings. The assizes were theatrical occasions which the county's gentry could ill-afford to miss. The trial of Freeman Sondes upon a charge of fratricide made the session of August 1655 particularly memorable.

J. A. Sharpe's investigations of the fate of murder suspects in Essex between 1620 and 1640 confirm the exceptional nature of the Sondes case and help to explain the interest it aroused. Of the 261 male accused, 115 were labourers and eighteen gentlemen. In the sixty years covered by Sharpe's study, 'no murderer described as a gentleman was executed'. Sharpe's research suggests that the combination of the guilty plea, the use of blades and the further evidence of premeditation contributed to the capital sentence.

[p. 28] [After his arrest Freeman Sondes was] carried . . . the same day to a house adjoining to his father's where he stayed that night under guard, and from thence, about noon the next day, he was brought to Maidstone (the assizes being there) and delivered to the custody of Mr Foster, the prison-keeper, a civil honest man, who took him to the gaol, where (though it was stenched with the noisome scent of prisoners) he behaved himself with great patience and meekness. That night he was, out of respect to his family, conveyed to the keeper's house, and the next day, being Thursday the 9th of this month, brought to the bar . . . where the indictment was read that charged him upon the two statutes of stabbing and murder, and being asked what he could plead for himself against the charge of killing his brother, he cried, 'Guilty', and showed a great willingness to suffer death for that barbarous fact, as appeared by his mild composed behaviour then at the bar, which struck the judges and justices, and the other gentlemen of the county then present with astonishing amazement.

Having thus pleaded guilty, he was carried to the dungeon in the gaol, where condemned persons are always put, whither divers persons resorted to him, and finding him in that loathsome place, there being nothing but a jakes [a slop bucket] to sit on, asked him if he were not sick, and how he could endure it. He replied that it was more pleasant to him than his father's dining room (which is, I hear, a place of great magnificence).

Freeman petitioned 'for a few days longer to his life';

[p. 29] that in a deeper and more sensible apprehension of his fact, he may more penitently, in remorse and sorrow of conscience, make his peace with God, and reconcile himself to his deservedly and highly offended father, that he may not only die in a more settled peace of conscience, but also testify to the world the sincerity of his petition.

Judge Crook granted him a week's reprieve.

The *cause célèbre* attracted the attention of a number of clergymen. In addition to Mr Boreman and Mr Higgons, Mr Yate, the Rector of Belmire and Mr Gunton, the domestic chaplain of the Duchess of Richmond, were in attendance. In Mr Higgons' opinion, Freeman Sondes' fate was a warning:

[p. 36] to the proud gallants of this age, who mind the outward dress of their body more than the inward dress of their souls . . . that spend whole mornings in decking a rotten carcase and sleep away those hours they should employ in prayers and reading of the holy scriptures.

It was a warning too to 'all stubborn children' and (p. 37) 'to all indulgent parents'. Freeman Sondes made an exemplary end:

He demeaned [expressed] himself in sighs, tears, groans in his bed, in mournful confessions and prayers to God, and in frequent reading of his holy word (especially such psalms and chapters as were commended by several divines).

It is not in the power of man to out-sin mercy. . . . No man can be so wanting to Christian charity as not to entertain a belief or hope of his salvation.

On 13 August Freeman Sondes dictated his confession to his friend Edmund Crisp. Mr Boreman composed 'a prayer for his private devotions, daily used by him'.

On the eve of his son's execution, Sir George wrote a letter, which Boreman quotes:

[p. 24] I hope thou hast some sparks of grace in thee, though deeply buried under a world of rubbish, and I hope all these godly bellows (you mean the breath of the ministers) will blow it away and make thy fire of true repentance and godly sorrow burn clear; and make thee truly say with the Prodigal, 'Father, I have sinned against heaven and against thee and am no more worthy to be called thy son'; then he will embrace thee in the arms of his mercy, he will feast thee in his heavenly mansions, and say unto thee, 'Thou wert lost, but now art found; thou wast dead in sin, but now thou art alive in Christ etc.' Oh, happy sadness, if it will produce this joy! Oh, happy death, if it will procure thee this blessed life! Happy change, to leave a sinful world and a sea of misery, to go to a haven of bliss.

On the day of his hanging, Freeman Sondes

[p. 35] was conveyed, in a mourning habit, on horseback, to the place of execution, many gentlemen attending him, with myself [Mr Boreman] and that reverend divine [Mr Higgons]. When he came to that place [the scaffold], being dismounted from his horse, he stood like a mournful penitent, whilst a discourse for an half hour and more was uttered by me, concerning the heinousness of sin in general, and of his murder in particular, together with the nature of conversion . . . to which was adjoined the freeness of God's [p. 36] mercy in the Lord Jesus to all repentant sinners. This done, with an exhortation to the people to entertain a charitable and Christian persuasion of the truth and sincerity of Mr Sondes's conversion, the penitent standing at my right hand, a prayer was conceived to commend his soul to God. This ended, he (having meekly and humbly submitted himself unto death) went up the ladder. . . . [Finally he said] with a soft voice (for his nature was not to speak either aloud or much) 'God's will be done' and 'Lord, receive my soul'. After which words the executioner did his office; and his body (after it had hung a good while) being cut down, was put into a coach and carried to a church not far from Maidstone . . . where it was interred, expecting a joyful resurrection through the mercies of the Lord Jesus.

Sir George, in his turn, was aware that 'the actions of his life' were being scrutinised on the assumption that 'some notorious sins' would be revealed to explain the 'calamities' which had befallen his family. In his own words: 'my afflictions had been great and many, and that for these twenty years last past'. They included 'the loss of my wife and many children when they were young'; his imprisonment as a royalist and the confiscation of his property by the victorious Parliament; [p. 42] 'and now my only two sons, when they were come to man's estate, and I began to have comfort in them, the youngest so foully to murder the eldest in his bed sleeping and thereby to suffer so ignominious a death at the gallows, his foul offence justly deserving it'.

Sondes looked to the Bible for precedents. He was worse off than Adam. When Adam's son Cain killed his brother Abel (p. 65), 'God the judge did not at that time execute Cain for it, but only banished him from his presence, and suffered him afterwards to grow numerous, and to build cities. Mine are both dead and no remembrance left of them'. Job,

> it is true, lost seven sons and three daughters, all at one time: God's hand was so heavy on him that he became a map of misery. He lost but all the children that he had, and so did I. His children were killed by the fall of a house which the wind blew down; it might seem a casualty: but mine, one murdered in his bed by his brother and the other deservedly hanged for it. A sadder end.

Sondes defended himself against charges that he had failed to maintain the free school at Throwly established by his grandfather, Sir Thomas Sondes; that, as executor, he had not honoured charitable bequests; that he was inhospitable; a bad landlord; a royalist; that he had deprived his half-brothers and -sister of their rightful share of their father's estate; that, after his wife's death, he had lived unchastely; that he had taken too little care of his sons' education; that, when he found out that his son George had secretly married 'a virtuous gentlewoman', he had not only threatened to cut him out of his will but also encouraged him into the worst of company, caring 'not what became of his soul if I could keep his body from her'. It is worth exploring his defences to some of the charges in some detail.

He claimed that he had made more than adequate provision for his half-brothers, 'brothers by a second venter', as he put it. He had released funds to enable the eldest to travel overseas, the second had studied medicine abroad at his expense; the third had gone as a soldier to the Low Countries, Sir George had 'furnished him with money to buy places of preferment as they fell' – by 1655 he was a 'captain or a major'. The others he had apprenticed: one to his own father-in-law; another to a 'Russia merchant', trading in the Baltic; the last to a woollen draper. Their failure to thrive might be attributed to 'their mother being a lunatic'. Their sister had betrayed the family by marrying one of the sequestrators – the men who had seized the Sondes lands as the property of a man hostile to the Parliamentary regime.

> [p. 50] To the charge of my being unmarried and not living so chastely and virtuously as a Christian ought to do, I confess that for almost twenty years I have lived unmarried and I thank heaven I have a healthy able body, and have natural and carnal affections in me, and a love to women and their company and I think he deserves to be unmanned that hath not. I confess I have been more vain and foolish with them than I ought to have been, heaven forgive me. But for committing fornication or adultery with any single or married woman, I protest before heaven (though perhaps few may believe it) I am clear from it. I never had illegitimate issue, nor ever had carnal knowledge of any woman, save of my own wife; nor of her but as was fitting for procreation; seldom or never after I knew her to be with child. Neither was this abstinence in me from any frigidity or disability in nature, for my dispositions that way were (I think) as strong as most men's. Neither was it for want of invites and opportunities to it, of them I had enough. Nothing restrained me but fear of offending heaven; *illa vox terribilis* [that awe-inspiring voice] always sounding in my ears, 'Whoremongers and adulterers God will judge' [Hebrews 13.4]. This hath all along been the bridle to my unlawful desires, and I hope ever shall be.

Defending himself against the charge of neglecting his sons' education, Sir George outlined the curriculum they had followed and then launched into an attack on Freeman's character. After 'very good and careful schools', Sondes sent his sons to 'Sydney College', Sidney Sussex, Cambridge. Thereafter he intended that George should travel on the Continent and Freeman, 'because he had no disposition to travel', should further his education at the London law schools, the Inns of Court.

> [p. 52] But France at that time being in much garboil, I durst not venture him. After that some overtures of matches stayed him; and the eldest not going abroad, the youngest would not be persuaded to go to the Inns of Court, though I much pressed him to it.

Meanwhile, in London, he was footing a hefty bill for classes in the gentlemanly graces – singing, dancing, fencing, mathematics and riding 'the great horse'. To his displeasure, the young men became addicted to gambling on cockfighting and cards.

> [p. 53] My eldest son . . . left both, and was ready to harken to his father's advice . . . but his brother of a contrary, pleasing and courteous to none, but cross-grained to all, as much to his father as to any, and I knew not how to break him of it. I was in hope that years and discretion might in time have made him to leave it; and so possibly it might, had not envy to his brother's virtue and growing goodness, thrust upon him that devilish fact, which caused him most deservedly to be cut off by a shameful death, before he was come to the age of twenty years.

Young George's conduct was not above reproach, however. He had fallen in love with his cousin Anne Delaune. Sir George argued that it was 'unlawful for cousin-germans [first cousins] to marry'. His sister, Ann's mother favoured the match, indeed she suspected that it might have gone too far for second thoughts:

> 'Brother, what if my daughter is with child?' she asked. 'Truly, sister (said I) it is a question very unseasonably put, and I think upon no ground, for I am confident he never lay with her' (which he has often since professed, and that he did not know whether she were man or woman). 'But if she be with child' (said I), 'the bastard must be kept, better so than worse [switching targets], for I tell you, George, if you marry her, you must not look to come within my doors'.

Mrs Delaune refused to give in. She

> carried her daughter up to London and there endeavoured to have them asked at church and cried at market, which, coming to my ear, I prevented and that most fearfully madded her and her party.

> [p. 48] And I verily believe, had it not been for the mother, little dispute had been about it; for, not long before his death, he was heard to say that he would not for £10,000 that he had ben married to his cousin Anne Delaune. 'For I could not have loved her' (said he) 'a month to an end'.

As for the murder (p. 62), Sir George was aware that 'There is much discourse abroad about a doublet, and a falling out between my sons in that business: I will set down the true and plain story of it'.

Earlier in the year of his death, the younger George had gone up to London, carrying with him a grey doublet which his servant had taken of to the tailor to be altered. The tailor recognised it as the work of another shop and, on reflection, George agreed. 'It was too little for me', he said. He had gone off with his brother's doublet by mistake. When George got home asked for his own doublet back, Sondes refused and the brothers fell out. Their father became involved.

> [p. 63] To Freeman, I said, 'These cross and dogged humours of yours, if you continue them, will ruin you. You need not be so dogged to your brother, for

I tell you, if I die, you will be beholding to him . . . and therefore you need not carry yourself so stubbornly and doggedly towards him . . . I tell you, if you mend not your manners, it will be the worse for you'. . . . This was all the reproof I gave him, and to my best remembrance the very words: and I think to such an obstinacy, there being no reason for it, but only his own humour, a father could not say less . . . . And that this wicked wretch should make these words the occasion that provoked him to murder his brother is a most desperate wickedness, and, I believe, a most devilish untruth. God forgive him.

Sir George was a widower: 'In all the time of my troubles, I have not had a wife either to comfort or vex me' – 'Job had a wife . . . that vexed him. She gave him counsel to curse God and die'. Now Sondes 'desired' a wife 'and shall endeavour to get one; God send me a good and fruitful one, who may help to sweeten all my miseries'. His second wife, the daughter of a baronet, gave him two daughters. He married the elder to Baron Duras, a naturalised Englishman, French by birth and very well connected. When Sondes was created Earl of Feversham in 1676, the King conceded that the earldom should descend to Duras and the heirs male of his body. Lady Duras died the same year 'of bleeding', perhaps a miscarriage. Her widower held high posts of honour and power under the last two Stuart kings but he died childless in 1709 and with his death the earldom of Feversham was extinguished. The estates passed to Duras' brother-in-law, the Earl of Rockingham, husband of Sir George's younger daughter. Rockingham's heir Edward predeceased him. None of Edward's three sons fathered a child to inherit. What would believers in an interventionist God have made of this sad fading out of an ancient lineage?

# PART THREE

## Dossier of illustrative images

# CONTENTS

---

# PLATE 1

---

# John Ogilby's *Britannia*, 1675

*Britannia* was the first English road atlas. Volume 1 – no more were published – contained one hundred double-page strip maps. Seventy-three 'principal highways' were measured, using the new standard mile of 1,760 yards – that is the task of the man who is trundling a wheel in the picture; the man on the horse is using a compass to plot changes in direction.

John Ogilby (born 1600) was a Scot who started his working life as a dancing master; he became a theatrical impresario. During the Civil Wars, hard times for actors and producers, he learned first Latin and then Greek and set himself up as a translator and publisher of illustrated volumes of the works of classic authors – Virgil, Aesop and Homer.

The engraving is by Wencelaus Hollar, based on a design by Francis Barlow (born ?1626). Born Vaclav Holar in Bohemia in 1607, Hollar settled in England in the 1630s, he taught Prince Charles, later Charles II, to draw.

*Reproduced by permission of Sotheby's*

The Road from
LONDON TO BARWICK
Tottenham high Cross
MIDDLESEX
Kingsland
London
BRITANNIA
VOL. I
or an
Illustration
of ye Kingdom of
ENGLAND
and dominion of WALES
By a
Geographical & Historical
Discription
of the Principal
ROADS.

---

# PLATE 2

---

# Milestone, Trumpington Road, Cambridge

The investigators who surveyed Cambridge for the Royal Commission on Historical Monuments in the 1950s identified this as one of the 'first true milestones set up in Britain since Roman times'. Dating from 1728, it stands precisely one 1,760-yard mile from the University Church, Great St Mary's, which is, in Cambridge custom, the centre of the universe. Customary miles varied in length. As Robert Plot complained in his *Natural History of Oxfordshire*, published in 1677:

> As for the scale of miles, there being three sorts in Oxfordshire, the greater, lesser and middle miles, as almost everywhere else [the map] is contrived according to the middle sort of them; for these I conceive may be most properly called the true Oxfordshire miles, which upon actual dimens-uration at several places, I found to contain for the most part nine furlongs and a quarter.

There are eight furlongs to a standard mile and 220 yards to a furlong. The milestone was one of a series commissioned by the charity which Dr William Mowse of Trinity Hall (died 1588) established to maintain the highway in and around Cambridge; it bears his arms and those of the college.

Like milestones, signposts were novelties in England three hundred years ago. Celia Fiennes, who visited Lancashire in 1698, commented on, as a novelty, the signposts which had been set up in obedience to the statute of 1697:

> They have one good thing in this country . . . that at all crossways there are posts with hands pointing to each road with the names of the great town or market towns that it leads to (*The Illustrated Journeys of Celia Fiennes, 1685–c. 1712*, Christopher Morris (ed.), London, 1982, p. 164).

*Photograph: Jonathan Griffiths*

---

# PLATE 3

---

# Hobson's Conduit, at the junction of Trumpington Road and Lensfield Road, Cambridge

From 1614 until 1856 Hobson's Conduit, as the fountainhead is known, stood on Market Hill in the middle of the town. Three or four years before it was erected the town and the university joined forces to pipe water from springs in Great Shelford south of Cambridge to the conduit head, where the Jacobean fountain is now, and from there on into the town. The wide gutters in Trumpington Street are another still-visible relic of the project.

The original plan was to flush out the King's Ditch, an open sewer and rubbish dump, which had been dug, as a cheap alternative to a wall, to enclose the medieval town. The decision to provide drinking water soon followed. Up to this time most Cambridge residents had relied on communal and private wells; Trinity College had an independent supply piped in from north of the town.

Thomas Hobson (circa 1544–1631), the carrier who made his fortune transporting goods and people between Cambridge and London, was one of several local men who were 'benefactors of the watercourse and conduit'. A well-known character whose reputation grew after his death, Hobson was the subject of a number of verse epitaphs, one of them written by the poet John Milton, who was an undergraduate and graduate student at Christ's College between 1625 and 1632.

*Photograph: Jonathan Griffiths*

---
## PLATE 4
---

# Market Cross, Bungay, Suffolk, showing the shackles on the whipping post

This eight-sided cross in the classical taste was put up in 1689; the statue of Justice was added in 1754. Whipping and exhibition in the stocks were used as cheap and exemplary punishments for plebeian delinquents throughout the sixteenth and seventeenth centuries. The Reverend William Harrison (born 1534) observed that 'rogues and vagabonds are often stocked and whipped' while the Reverend Timothy Nourse (died 1699) favoured 'a good strong pair of stocks and a whipping post' as a means of dealing with the 'obdurate rogue'. It is estimated that there were sixty whipping posts in London in 1630.

*Photograph: Jonathan Griffiths*

# PLATE 5

# The Effigies
# [portrait, Latin singular] of
# King George by the Grace of God
# King of Great Britain, France
# and Ireland, Defender of the Faith,
# Duke of Brunswick and Luneburg,
# Arch-Treasurer and Elector of the
# Holy Roman Empire

This image comes from a deluxe edition of the Book of Common Prayer published in 1717 and dedicated to George Augustus, 'Prince of Wales, Duke of Cambridge etc.' and 'his illustrious consort', 'Her Royal Highness Princess Wilhelmina-Carolina of Wales' by John Sturt, the distinguished engraver (born 1658) who, for this edition of the Book of Common Prayer, made 188 silver plates including elaborate borders and illustrations at the head of almost every page.

Portraits of the Prince and Princes of Wales face the Effigies of the King (George had divorced his wife Sophia Dorothea in 1694 and had all references to her struck out of services said in Hanover).

The Effigies was an ingenious device to tempt pounds from pockets – this Book of Common Prayer cost thirty shillings – but, more importantly, the badge of supporters of the Protestant Succession. In 1715, the year after George I's entry into London (Plate 20), his distant cousin, James, the Pretender to the throne his father and namesake the Catholic James II of England and VII of Scotland had occupied from 1685 to 1688, led an unsuccessful bid to recover his inheritance. The loyalist tone of the edition is underlined by other portraits – the 'forms of prayer' to mark the 'happy deliverance ... from the most traitorous and bloody intended massacre by gunpowder' (5 November), 'the martyrdom of the blessed King Charles I [30 January], the end of the Great Rebellion and the Restoration of the King and Royal Family' (29 May) and 'the first day of August, being the day on which His Majesty [George I] began his Happy Reign' were adorned with the appropriate regal images. Elizabeth Tudor heads up the Thirty-Nine Articles.

*Reproduced by permission of Sotheby's*

## PLATE 6

# Public baptism, inserted in a copy of the 1662 edition of the Book of Common Prayer, published in Cambridge by J. Field in 1662 and now in Cambridge University Library

The ceremony marked the formal introduction of the infant to the Church of England and to the parish to which he belonged. The baby's mother rarely attended the ceremony which normally took place within a few days of birth while she, by custom, was still confined to the house.

Demographers use baptisms as proxy for births in their studies of the history of population. This is a crude rule of thumb since a variable minority of babies went unbaptised, some baptisms went unrecorded in the parish registers, some registers were poorly kept and others have been lost. Nevertheless calculations based on the intervals between the baptisms of siblings confirm the evidence of letters, diaries and guides as to conduct: the richest women, who hired wetnurses for their infants, had more babies than contemporaries who nursed their own children.

*Reproduced by permission of the Syndics of Cambridge University Library*

The Publick Baptism of Infants.

Mark . 10 . 14 . 16 .
Jesus said unto them , suffer the Little Children to
come unto mee, and forbid them not : etc .
And he took them up in his Armes, put his hands
upon them, and blessed them .

# PLATE 7

## Stoneware statuette of Lydia Dwight (1667–74), made at her father's pottery in Fulham

Lydia was the younger daughter of John Dwight and Lydia, his wife, and the only one of their six children, born between 1662 and 1671, to die in childhood. The companion piece to this image of Lydia on her deathbed shows her resurrected, standing upright, loosely robed in her shroud, with a skull at her feet.

John Dwight was the son of a Gloucestershire yeoman. As a young man, like Robert Hooke, author of *Micrographia*, he worked in Robert Boyle's laboratory in Oxford. In or around 1672 he set up a pottery in Fulham to produce stoneware, a new type of ceramic for which he held a royal patent.

*Reproduced by permission of the Victoria and Albert Museum*

---

## PLATE 8

---

# A tear dropt from the hearse of the Reverend Dr Benjamin Calamy

Benjamin Calamy (born 1642) belonged to a prominent clergy family. Unlike his father and elder brother, who left the Anglican ministry to become Presbyterians, Benjamin Calamy remained within the Church of England.

The skulls, bones, picks and shovels, which decorate the border reinforce the slogan on the banner which issues from the mouth of Death, who presides, robed and crowned like a ruler of this world, at the head of the broadsheet: I overcome and conquer.

*Reproduced by permission of Sotheby's*

# A
# TEAR DROPT
### FROM THE
# HEARSE

Of the Reverend

## Dr. Benjamin Calamy;

LATE

Minister of St. *Lawrence Jury London*, Who departed this Life on *Sunday* the 3d of *January*, 168⅘

*Quis matrem in funere Nati Here vetat?*

AS when some Tempest rages in the Air,
And against all the Wood proclaims a War,
The Humble *Shrubs* are scarce concern'd at all,
Only the *Oaks* and mighty *Cedars* Fall;
Those are a Prize to Beggerly and Low,
But these become the Greatness of the Foe.
Those remain Safe, because Defenceless quite,
But against these doth their own Greatness Fight.

*Dust*, thus it is in the Assaults of Fate,
The Common Herd is seldome Brave or Great;
They by the Foe do Unregarded ly,
And Live so long till they wou'd chose to Die.
But where you see a large and spacious Mind,
Where Worth and Virtue are with Learning join'd;
Where Noble Thoughts do with like Deeds conspire,
And the whole Man is Perfect and Intire;
There you may see the Malice of our Fate,
And what Misfortunes doth on Virtue wait,
Whilst those that never could deserve to Die,
But might have Challeng'd Immortality,
Meet still the soonest with their Destiny.
These are the Noblest, and the greatest Prey,
And Fate by this, goes a compendious way;
For the Wounds us, whilst she doth those Men Slay.
Thus he Great *BEN* with all his Learning Dies,
Too Early, and too Dear a SACRIFICE.
He whose great mind was with all useful Knowledge fraught,
That Nature ever gave, or Art has Taught;
He and his Worth are Wither'd, cold, and Dead,
And the Treasures of his Mind are Fled:
Nothing has scap'd the fierce and angry Flame,
But his great Memory and Immortal Name.
Nought such a Loss can equal or befit
Less than his powerful Eloquence and Wit;
Some small remains of those with us abide,
But all the rest the envious Dark doth hide.
Some single Sheets indeed the Press imparts,
The rest are writ upon the Hearers Hearts:
His Charming Periods are past and gone,
And in his Peoples Lives must now be shown.
Pity such Words in transient sounds should Die,
Or in a Study unregarded ly;
Pity each falling Line had not been Writ
In Charactors as lasting as his Wit;
That the next Age by him might learn to make
Those Rules, by which they from that Place should speak.
The *Gospel* in such streaming Sense did flow,
When the *Apostles* Preach'd to Men Below:

The Current sometimes troubled was, I own,
Which by his seeming Lisping oft was shown;
But 'twas the Torrent of his Eloquence,
The strife betwixt his crowding Words and Sense;
Still with such hidden Influence he could dive,
And to his Hearers Brest himself derive:
So gently touch each Fault and Fester'd Part,
Yet the charm'd Patient not betray the Smart.
Could such a pleasing Force Evidence show,
Yet still the Sinner unoffended go:
It prov'd his *Sermon* could like *Lightning Pierce*
Quite to the Blade, the Scabbard ne'er the worse:
Which shows thou only, and some happy few,
The true and genuine Art of Preaching knew.
Our Church will own, tho' the receives a Blow,
Yet still a Numerous Race of Youths can show,
Who by thy Doctrine and Example fed,
May come in time our Churches Cause to Head.
And, Oh! If thy Example this can do,
Why did'st thou not let fall thy Spirit too?
But say Bless'd Shade, so soon why would'st thou go,
And take thy self from mournful Us below:
Tell me did'st thou by a fore-seeing Eye,
See some Black Tempest gathering in our Skie;
Was that the cause?
I rather think the partial Hand of Fate
Did but too ill thy Soul and Body Mate.
If the Soul's Gaol the Body stile we must,
Into the worst of Prisons thine was thrust:
Thou tir'd and a weary to the Grave did'st come,
But leave that Life which was grown Burdensome.
Hold, happy Shade, here must my Number cease,
No more I will presume to vex thy Peace;
Besides I see thy Predecessors stand,
To meet and joy thee to the promis'd Land.
Go happy Saint, and there injoy that Rest,
Which here on Earth is still deni'd the Best.
All we can do, is to Adorn thy *HEARSE*
And hang it round with this poor Mortal *VERSE*.

This may be Printed, R. L. S.

*LONDON*,

Printed by *George Croom*, at the *Blue-Ball* in
*Thames-street*, near *Baynard's-Castle*. 1685.

260

PLATE 9

# Monument to Lady Deane, St Giles', Great Maplestead, Essex

Lady Deane, in her shroud, is shown reaching up to receive her heavenly crown. The monument was erected by her son, who lies at her feet. It is one of a series showing the subject in a shroud, all dating from the 1630s – the best known is John Donne's in St Paul's Cathedral. Lady Deane's epitaph reads:

> Her shape was rare, her beauty exquisite
> Her wytt acurate, her judgment singular
> Her entertaynment hearty, her conversation lovely
> Her heart merciful, her hand helpful
> Her courses modest, her discourses wise
> Her charity heavenly, her amity constant
> Her practice holy, her religion pure
> Her vows lawful, her meditations divine
> Her faith unfayngd, her hope stable
> Her prayers devout, her devotions diurnal [daily]
> Her days short, her life everlasting.

*Photograph: Jonathan Griffiths*

# PLATES 10 and 11

# The Fettiplace monuments, St Mary's Church, Swinbrook, Oxfordshire

These two-tiered monuments commemorate six generations of the Fettiplace family: the first Sir Edmund, knight (died 1613), his father William (died 1562) and his grandfather Alexander (died 1504); the second Sir Edmund (died 1686) and his father Sir John (died 1672), who were both baronets, and Edmund's great-uncle John (died 1658), the son and heir of the Sir Edmund Fettiplace who died in 1613. The effigies are stratified in proper archaeological style, the youngest occupying the top layer.

The later monument lists the five sons and five daughters Sir John left behind him when he died in 1672: Edmund, his heir, John (over whose head an ominous death's head has been incised), Charles, Lorenzo and George, Anne, Arabella, Diana, Maria and Sophia. On the south wall of St Mary's there is a much less elaborate monument which reads:

> This stone was placed here in remembrance of George and Sophia Fettiplace, the elder (Son and Daughter of Sir John Fettiplace Bart., deceased, who died before George and Sophia Fettiplace in the opposite monument mentioned were born) by their loving sister and godmother Anne Pytts.

*Photograph: Jonathan Griffiths*

# PLATE 12

# Gravestone dedicated to the memory of 'R. W.', dated 1696, in the churchyard of St Mary's, Swinbrook, Oxfordshire

In seventeenth-century England burial and commemoration inside a church was a token of wealth and/or high rank. Modest in comparison with the monument to the successive heads of the Fettiplace family, this gravestone nevertheless marks the burial of an individual with the means to leave a substantial memorial. Most of the community went to unmarked graves.

*Photograph: Jonathan Griffiths*

# PLATE 13

# Jacob Rueff, *The Expert Midwife or an excellent and most necessary treatise of the generation and birth of man*, first English edition, 1637

The thirty-six woodcut illustrations depict normal and malformed embryos – the seventeenth-century writer called them, bluntly, 'monstrosities' – and obstetrical instruments.

The learned Englishman's world extended beyond the Channel. The European community of theologians and natural scientists were bound together by their common language – Latin. (The linguistic community survived into the nineteenth century – in June 1844 Joseph Romilly (born 1791), a Fellow of Trinity College, Cambridge, 'wrote a long Latin letter to a German Professor' about a fourth-century manuscript in the college library.)

*Reproduced by permission of Sotheby's*

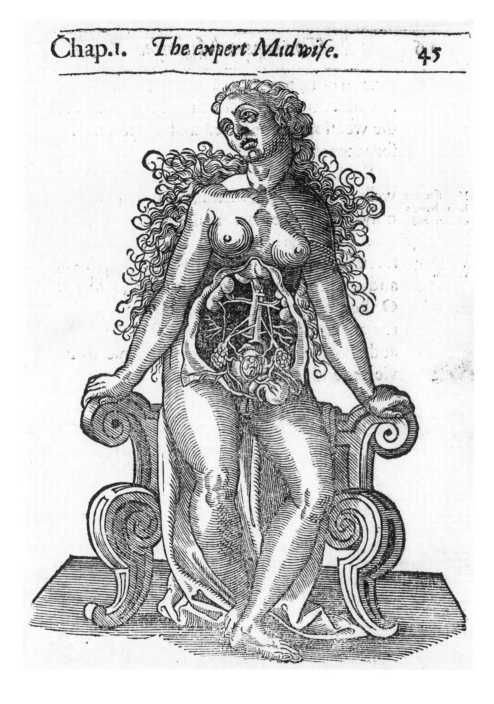

## PLATE 14

# Unknown boy in a baby-walker, Strangers' Hall, Norwich

Until boys were 'breeched', they wore long skirts very much like their sisters'. The subject's gender might be stated with more confidence if he were surrounded by boys' toys; the unflinching response to the lively little dog may be intended as an indication of masculine strength.

While children were often classified as less than fully human, crawling on all fours like an animal was something to be discouraged. The object in the child's hand is multi-purpose: a rattle; something for the teething baby to bite on; a coral talisman to protect the child from harm. The beads round the child's neck are also coral.

*Reproduced by permission of Norfolk Museums Service, Castle Museum, Norwich*

# PLATES 15 and 16

# A set of squares designed to teach the alphabet, 1743–4

The set consists of twenty-four slips of paper 50 by 60 mm, mounted on thin card; the text is printed in red. In line with the conventions of the time, iI and vV were omitted.

The publisher advertised the cards with this rhyme:

> This well-invented *game*'s designed
> To strike the *eye* and form the *mind*
> And he most doubtless aims aright
> Who joins *instructions* with *delight*.

Although the advertising copy reproduced here mentions John Locke, Newbery's set of rhyming cards, which were produced in the middle of the eighteenth century, were in fact a mass-produced version of the hand-made games which parents had been using to teach their children to read for at least a century. The 'nursery library', which Jane Johnson (born 1708), the wife of a well-to-do clergyman, made for her daughter Barbara (born 1738) and Barbara's younger brothers, includes alphabet cards. Much of Jane Johnson's work is now in the Lilly Library of the University of Indiana in the United States.

In Newbery's set 'eE was an egg and became a bird', while, naturally, 'fF was a fool and could not read a word'. 'xX', which always presents alphabet-makers with their greatest challenge, 'was Xanthippe, that scold of a wife', who, according to Abel Boyer's *Wise and Ingenious Companion*, threw a full chamberpot at 'poor Socrates'' head.

*Reproduced by permission of Christie's*

# DIRECTIONS

For Playing with

## A SET OF SQUARES,

Newly invented for the

## USE of CHILDREN.

By which alone, or with very litttle Affift-
ance, they may learn to fpell, read, write,
make Figures, and caft up any common
Sum in Arithmetic, before they are old
enough to be fent to School; and that
by way of Amufement and Diverfion.
The Whole fo contriv'd as to yield as much
Entertainment as any of their Play-games.

Upon the Plan of Mr *LOCKE.*

The Seventh Edition.

*Train up a Child in the Way he fhall go, and
when he is old he will not depart from it.* Sol.

London: Printed for J. Newbery, at the
Bible and Sun, in St. Paul's Church-
Yard; and B. Collins, in Salifbury.

---

# PLATE 17

---

# Cut-paper landscape, 1707

The maker, Anna Maria Garthwaite (born 1690), was the daughter of a country parson. She later became a designer for the silk weavers of Spitalfields – albums of her work survive in the Victoria and Albert Museum. Her cut-paper landscape deserves a good hard look, both as the work of a talented young designer and as a portrait of an English community at the beginning of the eighteenth century.

*Reproduced by permission of Christie's*

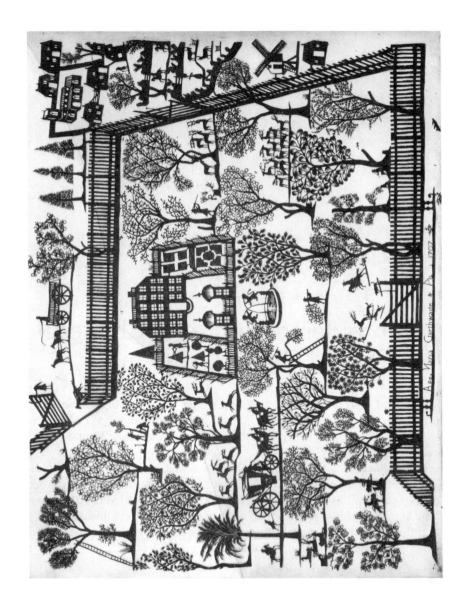

## PLATE 18

# Embroidered portrait of Charles II and Queen Catherine

The date of this embroidered picture is suggested by the biggest and most important figure. He is, unmistakably, King Charles II, who was restored to the throne in 1660; he married his Queen, Catherine of Braganza, two years later.

Work like this was a pastime for women and, probably especially, for girls in well-off households who were exempted, at least partially, from the drudgery of endless plain sewing. Paper patterns provided needlewomen who lacked confidence in their ability to draw with the outlines of the fruit and flowers, birds, beasts, butterflies and beetles in which they delighted – the use of templates helps to account for oddities of scale.

*Reproduced by courtesy of Jonathan Horne Antiques Ltd*

## PLATE 19

# Figures of a schoolgirl and a schoolboy, Burrough Green School, Cambridgeshire

Pevsner described these figures as 'the usual rather inept little statues of a girl and a boy' (Nikolaus Pevsner, *The Buildings of England: Cambridgeshire*, London, 1970). Those more interested in life than in art may be more forcibly struck by the presence of the girl. Until the advent of machine sewing in the second half of the nineteenth century, the needle, not the pen was the characteristic instrument of female handwork. At the school attached to the Children's Hospital at Great Yarmouth, which cared for the orphaned and destitute sons and daughters of respectable households, a system of payment by results applied. Abraham Bayly, the master appointed in 1696, was

> allowed for teaching every child . . . twenty shillings when it can read well in the Bible, twenty shillings more when it can write well, twenty shillings when it can cypher [count] well to the rule of three inclusive and twenty shillings when each girl can sew plain work well.

The children who achieved these skills were given smaller cash rewards. 'None of the girls reached the stage of writing. Their highest achievement was to sew well and to read in the Testament or Bible, but few left the workhouse with fluency in reading' (David Cressy, *Literacy and the Social Order: Reading and Writing in Tudor and Stuart England*, Cambridge, 1980, pp. 30, 24).

The school, built in the first years of the eighteenth century, was Samuel Richardson's legacy to the parish. Thanks primarily to the bequests of former rectors, Burrough Green was rich in educational charities. In Charles I's reign Dr Anthony Cage set up a fund to pay a poor woman to teach reading; Thomas Watson (born 1637), who was deprived of the bishopric of St David's for his determined opposition to the succession of William and Mary and died excommunicate, gave money to support the school. Samuel Knight (born 1675) endowed a charity which gave Bibles to school leavers.

*Photograph: Jonathan Griffiths*

# PLATE 20

# The view of the charity children in the Strand

Published by George Vertue (born 1684), this illustration shows half of a two-sheet panorama.

This day of national rejoicing celebrated the Peace of Utrecht which followed the Duke of Marlborough's string of victories against the French – the first of them, Blenheim (1704) was commemorated in the Duke's new palace at Woodstock. Defeats and other public catastrophes – epidemics, for example, were occasions for officially sponsored demonstrations of repentance.

Notice that the charity boys (the girls mentioned in the legend are hard to spot) are respectfully holding their caps in front of them. The hat-wearing habit was all-but-universal and taking off your headgear was a mark of respect to your betters. Thomas Ellwood (born 1639), the son of a country gentleman who became a Quaker, recalled how his father furiously snatched hat after hat off his head until he 'was forced to go bareheaded wherever I had occasion to go, within doors and without' – he became ill – 'and was laid up as a kind of prisoner for the rest of the winter'.

By the beginning of the eighteenth century much of London had been rebuilt in fire-resistant brick and stone. (The Strand was spared the Great Fire which devastated London within the area bounded by the Tower to the east and Chancery Lane to the west in 1666.)

*Reproduced by permission of Christie's*

The View of the CHARITY-CHILDREN in the STRAND, upon the VII of July, MDCCXIII being the day appointed by her late Majesty Queen ANNE for a Publick Thanksgiving for the Peace, when both Houses of Parliament made a Solemn procession to the Cathedral of St PAUL. By the care & provision of the Truſtees of the ſeveral Charity-Schools in & about LONDON & WESTMINSTER near IV thouſand CHARITY CHILDREN Boys & Girls being new cloathed were placed upon a Machine extended in length 620 feet, which had in breadth eight ranges of ſeats one above another: During the whole proceſſion which laſted near three Hours, they ſung & repeated the Hymns which were prepared upon the proper occaſion.
The like View of the CHARITY CHILDREN was preſented to his Majeſty King GEORGE, on the ſouth ſide of St PAUL'S, when he made his Publick Entry into the City of LONDON, upon the XX of September, MDCCXIV. ———

---
PLATE 21
---

# William Freind of Westminster School

William Freind (born 1715) was the son of Robert Freind, headmaster of Westminster School from 1711 until 1733. Freind's social and pedagogical talents helped to make Westminster popular with aristocratic parents; in March 1733 *The Gentleman's Magazine* carried a verse tribute on his retirement which characterised the Old Boys of his term as 'senators/refined with all the arts of Greece and Rome' and listed a handful outstanding for their birth and political eminence.

The headmaster's son is represented as a model of youthful virtue, the social superior but moral equivalent of William Hogarth's creation Francis Goodchild, the industrious apprentice whose diligence brought him wealth and status – he married his master's daughter and became Lord Mayor of London.

*Reproduced by permission of Sotheby's*

# PLATE 22

# The Gate of Honour, Gonville and Caius College, Cambridge

John Caius (1510–73) was Master and second founder of the college which Edmund Gonville endowed in 1348. A physician to the royal family, Caius had studied at the University of Padua in Italy. He was among the first Englishmen to sponsor the new classical taste in architecture.

Caius designed three gates to symbolise the ideal condition of a student at different stages in his career: at entry, during his residence as an undergraduate and at graduation. They were, respectively, the Gate of Humility (1565), the Gate of Virtue (1565–7) and the Gate of Honour (1573–5) which has been aptly described as 'miniature triumphal arch'. It has been heavily restored.

*Photograph: Jonathan Griffiths*

---

PLATE 23

---

# 'Bibliotheca Pepysiana, 1724', housed in the New Building, Magdalene College, Cambridge

The Pepysian Library is an example of a misleadingly dated building. '1724' refers to the year in which the Pepysian Library was transferred to the New Building at Magdalene, where the donor, Samuel Pepys (born 1633), had been an undergraduate in the 1650s.

Although the building records do not survive, all the indications are that the New Building was designed and erected in the late seventeenth century. Pepys was among the old students who contributed to the cost. He mentioned the New Building as a possible home for his collection of books and bookcases in his will of 1703, the year of his death.

*Photograph: Jonathan Griffiths*

---

## PLATE 24

---

# Jeremiah Rich's shorthand version
# of the New Testament

Jeremiah Rich (died ?1660) promoted the system of shorthand – 'semography or a short and swift writing, being the easiest, exactest and speediest method' – invented by his uncle, William Cartwright.

As its printing history suggests, Jeremiah Rich's tiny, 68 by 40 mm, volume was a popular work. For some purchasers, it was a badge of piety, a novelty, an aid to showing off. But it seems likely that the familiarity of the text made this little volume an ideal vehicle for learning shorthand – a tool which enabled the user to make a verbatim record of meetings or sermons and to protect memoranda from the prying eyes of the uninitiated.

*Reproduced by permission of Sotheby's*

IEREMIAH RICH

LONDON
Printed for Wᵐ Marshall
at ij Bible in newgate
treet & Jnᵒ Marshall at
y Bible in gracechurch
treete neere Cornehill

Fame & y Picture speak yet both are but
Shadows unto y Authors could the Cut
Coppy his Art this would be truly high
To have y Picture speak his Quality. DI

# Plate 25

# Arithmetical cards, 1710

This set of playing cards serves as yet another example of my proposition that, in the seventeenth century, contrary to the assumptions made by most people in our own day, some parents, some teachers and some publishers acted on a belief that learning is easier when it is fun. Of course, others strongly disapproved of cards because of their association with gambling.

In the seventeenth century arithmetical calculations were complicated by two factors: the unfamiliarity of Arabic numerals, which were slowly displacing the Roman, and the use of an elaborate system of weights and measures. Metric place values (10 is ten times as big as 1, 100 is ten times as big as 10, and so on) made computation easier. But the metrication of weights and measures was three centuries away: four quarts made a gallon; 63 gallons a hogshead and four hogsheads a tun.

*Reproduced by permission of Sotheby's*

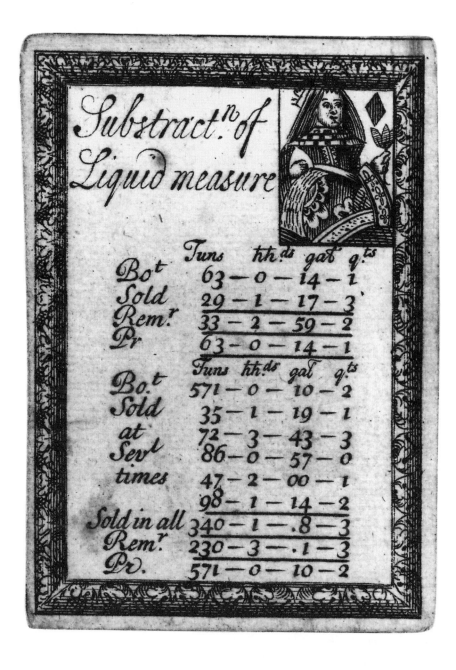

## Substract.ⁿ of Liquid measure

|        | Tuns | hh.ds | gal | q.ts |
|--------|------|-------|-----|------|
| Bo.t   | 63   | 0     | 14  | 1    |
| Sold   | 29   | 1     | 17  | 3    |
| Rem.r  | 33   | 2     | 59  | 2    |
| Pr.    | 63   | 0     | 14  | 1    |

|             | Tuns | hh.ds | gal | q.ts |
|-------------|------|-------|-----|------|
| Bo.t        | 571  | 0     | 10  | 2    |
| Sold        | 35   | 1     | 19  | 1    |
| at          | 72   | 3     | 43  | 3    |
| Sev.l       | 86   | 0     | 57  | 0    |
| times       | 47   | 2     | 00  | 1    |
|             | 98   | 1     | 14  | 2    |
| Sold in all | 340  | 1     | .8  | 3    |
| Rem.r       | 230  | 3     | .1  | 3    |
| Pr.         | 571  | 0     | 10  | 2    |

---
# PLATE 26
---

# *The Complete English Gentlewoman* (1631) by Richard Brathwait

Richard Brathwait (born circa 1588), who spent time at the both the universities of his day – Oxford and Cambridge – was a prolific writer.

Although our gentlewoman is portrayed as the descendant of armigerous families – families, that is, qualified to display coats of arms – one of the messages, conveyed in the nine images, is that the essential qualities of a gentlewoman are displayed, as much, if not more, in her conduct and clothing. Discretion, modesty, constancy and godliness are her hallmarks.

*Reproduced by permission of Christie's*

## PLATE 27

# *The Complete English Gentleman* (1630) by Richard Brathwait

The English gentleman has his feet on the ground but his hopes fixed on heaven. Having steeled himself in youth against the lures of vain pleasure, he survives into tranquil old age. His life is more public and more obviously eventful than that of his female counterpart. A formal education in the seven liberal arts has prepared him for employment – not necessarily paid employment – which demanded intellectual training. Hunting with horse and hound is a characteristically gentlemanly pursuit which provided an excellent training for men who were likely to find themselves serving as mounted officers in time of war.

*Reproduced by permission of Christie's*

---
## PLATE 28
---

# 'The Little Man'

This little wooden figure used to preside over the poor box in the Abbey Church at St Albans. Neither the model nor the maker is known. He stands for the ordinary but locally important person, the farmer, craftsman or shopkeeper who took his turn as an officer in the parish where he lived, serving as churchwarden, constable or overseer of the poor, the sort of person who, before the introduction of commercial photography, was rarely honoured with a portrait – commercial photography reached Cambridge in 1844.

*Photograph: David Kelsall*

PLATE 29

# Robert Hooke, *Micrographia or some physiological descriptions of minute bodies made by magnifying glasses with observation and inquiries thereupon*, published by the Royal Society in 1665

Natural scientists looked to Sir Francis Bacon (born 1561) as their inspiration. He, in his own words, set out to conduct an 'inquisition of nature' which would 'sink the foundations of the sciences deeper and firmer, and ... begin the inquiry nearer the source than men have done heretofore'. Bacon saw himself as a 'trumpeter, not a combatant' in this campaign, which would be waged by succeeding generations.

Sir Thomas Browne (born 1605) was a dedicated observer of the natural world. He was a field naturalist who compiled notes on the birds of Norfolk, his adopted county, among them the coots which were to be found

> in very great flocks upon the broad waters. Upon the appearance of a kite or buzzard I have seen them unite from all parts of the shore in strange numbers ... if the kite stoops near them they will fling up [and] spread such a flash of water up with their wings that they will endanger the kite, and so keep him again and again in open opposition; and an handsome provision they make about their nests against the same bird of prey by bending and twining the rushes and reeds so about them that they cannot stoop at their young ones or the dam while she sitteth.

Browne also kept animals in and around his house:

> two frogs coupled we put in a cistern of water at the first promising days of spring; wherein they continued just about twenty days, nor did they separate although in divers days the water froze over them, at length the female died, the male notwithstanding maintaining a hard complexure at least three days after. In the cistern more spawn was found than both their bodies weighed, beside some part remaining in the body of the female, whereof some hanging out discovered manifestly that passage which at other times is very obscure, some remaining in the body more black, stiff and clammy.

The microscope opened a window on a hitherto invisible world. It is possible that some of the engravings based on Hooke's drawings are by Sir Christopher Wren.

*Reproduced by permission of Christie's*

---

## PLATE 30

---

# Sir Thomas Browne and his wife Dorothy, attributed to Joan Carlile

Thomas Browne (born 1605) was the son of a London mercer. He was educated at Winchester College and at the University of Oxford and at medical schools on the Continent – at Montpellier, Padua and Leiden. In 1637,
probably attracted by the presence in the city and county of men he had
known as tutors and fellow students at Oxford, he settled in Norwich. His
patients included members of the county's best-known families – the Bacons,
Pastons and Windhams – as well as very poor men and women like Elizabeth
Mitchell, the Yarmouth centenarian who depended on a parish pension.

Browne married into a landed Norfolk family in 1641. He and his wife
had twelve children, only four of whom survived them. A friend described
their marriage as perfectly harmonious: Dorothy was 'a lady of such sym-
metrical proportion to her witty husband, both in the graces of her mind
and body that they seemed to come together by a kind of natural magnet-
ism'.

*Reproduced by permission of the National Portrait Gallery*

300

---

# PLATE 31

---

# 'Old Parr', published by
# J. Caulfield, 1797

Thomas Parr's celebrity rested on his claim to extreme longevity – 1483 to 1635. As a prodigy of nature, he was represented by a portrait in the collection of rarities made by John Tradescant (born 1608) which, later in the seventeenth century, formed the nucleus of the Ashmolean Museum in Oxford. Printed portraits were a cheaper substitute for portrait medals. Samuel Pepys left his early and important collection of printed portraits to Magdalene College, Cambridge, with the rest of his library. He organised his collection as follows:

> royal family/sovereign princes foreign/noblemen, great ministers/ambassadors/gentlemen, virtuosi [collectors and others with a cultivated taste in arts and sciences], men of letters, merchants/ladies and virtuosae [female virtuosi] seamen, soldiers, churchmen/lawyers/physicians, chiurgeons [surgeons], chymists [scientists], poets, comedians [actors], musicians/painters, [en]gravers, statuaries [sculptors], architects/trades, arts, mechanics, exempts as not comprehended in any of the preceding classes

– the category to which old Parr would have been assigned.

James Granger (born 1724), whose *Bibliographical History of England from Egbert the Great* [died 839] *to the Revolution* [of 1688] was responsible for the late eighteenth-century craze for collecting printed portraits, divided his subjects into twelve classes, the last of which consisted of 'persons of both sexes, chiefly of the lowest order of the people, remarkable only from one circumstance in their lives; namely such as lived to a great age, deformed persons, convicts etc.'.

*Photograph: Jonathan Griffiths*

Publifhed by J. Caulfield, Decr. 1, 1797.

*Thomas* *Parr,*

*The Old Man* *of Shropshire?*

---
PLATE 32
---

# Monument to Thomas Greene
## St Nicholas' Chapel
## St Ann's Street, King's Lynn, Norfolk

Thomas Greene began his working life as a tallow chandler's apprentice in King's Lynn. He became one of the richest men in the borough: in 1663 he lived in a house in Lath (now Nelson) Street with at least eleven rooms. Greene was mayor three times – he was in his third term of office when he died in the summer of 1675. He and his wife Susannah, who commissioned this effigy as 'a monument to love and grief', had a large family. Only three – all daughters – survived. Elizabeth had married Thomas Thetford, like his father-in-law, an alderman of Lynn; Susannah was the wife of a clergyman, William Falkner; Alice's husband, an alderman of Boston in Lincolnshire, was granted the freedom of Lynn in the 1660s, when Greene was mayor for the second time.

# INDEX

This is primarily an index of topics, but it also collates scattered information on people and places. People are indexed if they are authors or well known, or are mentioned more than once; placenames are indexed by pre-1974 county, apart from London, Edinburgh and country houses. Page numbers in italic type indicate illustrations and their captions.